FISSURES IN THE ROCK

New England in the Seventeenth Century

REVISITING NEW ENGLAND:
THE NEW REGIONALISM

Richard Archer, *Fissures in the Rock: New England in the Seventeenth Century*

Nancy L. Gallagher, *Breeding Better Vermonters: The Eugenics Project in Vermont*

Sidney V. James, *The Colonial Metamorphoses in Rhode Island: A Study of Institutions in Change*

Diana Muir, *Reflections in Bullough's Pond: Economy and Ecosystem in New England*

FISSURES IN THE ROCK

New England in the Seventeenth Century

RICHARD ARCHER

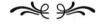

University of New Hampshire

Published by University Press of New England

HANOVER AND LONDON

University of New Hampshire
Published by University Press of New England, Hanover, NH 03755
© 2001 by Richard Archer
Printed in 5 4 3 2 1

CIP data appear at the back of the book

To Ginny

CONTENTS

CONTENTS

ACKNOWLEDGMENTS

The work for this book began roughly two decades ago. At times the delays and diversions were frustrating; in retrospect, however, they appear fortuitous. The last thirty-five years have been a rich period for the study of early New England, and this study, as demonstrated by its notes and bibliography, has benefited from all that has preceded it. As is true of most human endeavors, this book is collaborative, even when I know many of my collaborators only by their published words. I truly am grateful for their insights and methodologies.

Many friends, colleagues, fellow historians, and family members have helped me even more directly. I am forever indebted to Mort Borden, who inspired me to be a historian and who taught me that both synthesis and original research are valuable. John Demos, Joe Fairbanks, Mike McGiffert, and Bob Middlekauff read part or all of an early draft, and I learned much from their suggestions (though I'm sure not so much as they would have liked). Bob Marks valiantly slogged through several drafts and tactfully encouraged me to keep going. Others answered questions, listened patiently, offered advice, and did their best to look attentive as I elaborated on some issue or another. My thanks to Charles Adams, Don Archer, Barbara and Terry Douglass, Gene Fingerhut, Bill Geiger, John Haeger, Anne Kiley, Bob and Roberta MacDonald, Steve Mayo, Gary Nash, Joe Price, Norm and Emily Rosenberg, Anthony Scorcia, Don Simons, Lori Slater, Daniel Scott Smith, Hal Sweet, Mark Taylor, Dennis Thavenet, Laurel Ulrich, and Greg Woirol.

Throughout this long process, I have had continual help from people at Whittier College. Assistance with interlibrary loans has been essential, and I am particularly grateful to Ann Topjon and Tammy Galaviz as well as to all the librarians and staff at the Bonnie Bell Wardman Library for their support and good humor. From helping me to change database programs to solving all types of glitches, Robert Olsabeck of the Computer Center has been indispensable. Financial support for research trips to New England came from the Whittier College Faculty Research Fund and from the Haynes Foundation, and I appreciate their assistance.

People at the University Press of New England have been generous with their help, and I am fortunate to be working with them. I especially thank Ellen Wicklum and her mysterious sidekick, Margaret Brown, for always useful and often funny advice.

My parents, Corwin and Clara Belle Archer, nurtured a love of books, ideas, and diverse peoples, and there has been no end to their contributions to my life. Julie and Steve were children when this project began and now are wonderful adults. They shared in everything from data entry to a three-week trip exploring seventeenth-century New England houses and enriched every day. And Ginny has made it all worthwhile. She has listened to each sentence and each version as I read them to her across our study and has offered important suggestions along the way. She has offered encouragement, energy, and meaning. She has collaborated in everything that matters.

R. A.

FISSURES IN THE ROCK

New England in the Seventeenth Century

Saco

Watertown • • Cambridge
Boston • • Charlestown
Roxbury •
Dorchester •

New Hampshire

Connecticut River

Merrimack River

Portsmouth •
Exeter •
Hampton •
Haverhill • Salisbury
Rowley • Newbury
Andover • Ipswich
Billerica Gloucester
Groton • Chelmsford Salem
Concord • Marblehead
Sudbury • Lynn
Marlborough • Boston Massachusetts
Dedham • Bay
Hingham •
Braintree • Scituate
Duxbury • Marshfield
Plymouth •

Massachusetts Bay

Deerfield •
Hatfield •
Hadley •
Northampton •

Springfield •

Plymouth

Cape Cod
Bay

Eastham

Sandwich •
Barnstable •

Housatonic River

New York

Rhode Island

Providence •
Warwick •
Portsmouth •
Newport •

Windsor •
Hartford •
Farmington •
Wethersfield •
Middletown •

Connecticut

Narragansett
Bay

Martha's
Vineyard

Nantucket

Stonington •
New London •

Westerly •

Hudson River

New Haven

New Haven • Guilford •
Saybrook •
Milford •

Block
Island

Atlantic Ocean

Long Island

**Seventeenth-Century
New England**

~ 1 ~

INTRODUCTION

New England in the seventeenth century could be a mysterious place, much to George Walton's consternation. Beginning on 11 June 1682, Walton of Portsmouth in the province of New Hampshire experienced "showers of stones . . . thrown by an invisible hand" upon his house. Outside, the gate was off its hinges, and stones struck people when they ventured from the house. Glass windows shattered, and it appeared that the stones "came not from *without,* but from *within.*" When Walton traveled by boat to a farm he owned, stones pummeled him there as well. On the way back, the "*anchor* leap'd overboard several times and stopt the boat." Other inexplicable events—a cheese out of its press and crumbled on the floor; heaps of hay found in trees— occurred. And then they stopped. Although the author of the tale, the Reverend Cotton Mather, hinted that Walton's being a Quaker might have been connected with these "wonders of the invisible world," Walton suspected that they resulted from witchcraft performed by a woman unhappy with a land transaction.[1]

George Walton was not immune to controversy, but ordinarily disagreements led to court, not to "preternatural occurrences." He had been one of the approximately twenty thousand people who had migrated from England to New England in the 1630s and was among the group who had organized town government in Exeter in 1639. Later, he lived in Dover and then Portsmouth. Throughout his life, he engaged in business deals, many of which resulted in lawsuits. In the forty-year period between 1642 and 1682, he participated in twenty-six suits—seventeen as a plaintiff and nine as a defendant. Contracts might not be fulfilled; profits from a fishing voyage might not have been disbursed equitably; land boundaries might be disputed. He won some and lost others, and more than half were settled out of court.[2]

Civil suits only indicate part of the story. All told, Walton appeared in New Hampshire court records on fifty-nine separate occasions. Several testified to his respectability. He was appointed to a grand jury twice and once each to a jury of trials and a jury of inquest. He recorded land purchases. He served as an administrator of estates. He repeatedly had his license to run a tavern renewed, and he won the right to run a ferry. Other citations refer to personal tragedies. In 1657, one of Walton's young children—he and his wife, Alice, had at least five children—fell into an unfenced well and drowned. The subsequent investigation found the death to be accidental. In 1660 an unwed Indian servant of his was fined forty shillings and court costs for having a baby. The court may have been alarmed by an "immoral" act, but as usual focused more on the issue of the baby's maintenance. The servant had to pay Walton more than three times her fine for expenses following the delivery. Although Walton was not the father, he apparently continued to provide for the child, for the boy was bound to Walton until he reached the age of twenty-four.[3]

Lawsuits, civic responsibilities, personal tragedies—all of these fell within the "acceptable" range of seventeenth-century New England life. Nonetheless, there were other signs that pointed to Walton's marginality. He frequently was charged with violating the law. Fines for charging too much for beer, for delivering too much wine to a group of men, for customers being drunk were among the hazards of running an ordinary and selling alcohol. Even fines for swearing and for shipping boards on the sabbath were not unusual. But Walton's transgressions did not end there. In the same year his child drowned, he was fined for stirring up a servant against a master. If he had any sense of irony—which is unlikely—he must have smiled grimly in 1672 when authorities ordered him to release a servant whom he had kept beyond the terms of the indenture. The event that proved a dividing line in his life was his and his wife's conviction in 1664 as Quakers.[4]

Although they were not banished from Portsmouth, they were treated differently thereafter. A fine for not attending the established church was a mere annoyance and, for whatever reason, was imposed only once. Lawsuits were a different matter. Eight of the nine times Walton was a defendant occurred after his conviction for being a Quaker, while eleven of the seventeen times he was a plaintiff took place before 1664. After 1666 he didn't win one of the ten remaining suits; he lost four and settled others out of court. In 1674, he was charged with stealing a cloak. There is no evidence that his financial circumstances drove him to such a desperate act. To the contrary, he continued to manage his property and participate in trade successfully. Considering that the records do not indicate he was brought to trial or found guilty, it is likely that the charge grew from a misunderstanding that prior to 1664 would have been resolved short of criminal prosecution.[5]

When he died in 1686, he was more than seventy years old. He had weathered encounters with the "invisible world," lawsuits, business deals and shenanigans, births and deaths, the flaunting of religious practice and the acceptance of Quakerism, marriage, criminal charges, jury duty, acceptance and rejection, and nearly fifty New Hampshire winters. George Walton was not your typical New Englander in the seventeenth century. But then again, who was?

Not everyone was a Puritan, and English, and male, and a minister or a magistrate. In fact, few combined all those characteristics. Skeptics, lukewarm believers, Baptists, Anglicans, Quakers, Jews, shamans, practitioners of magic, and members of various sects dwelled in New England along with separatists and nonseparatists, congregationalists and presbyterians—collectively called Puritans. Massachusett, Irish, Dutch, Pequot, Narragansett, Welsh, Wampanoag, French, Abenaki, Scots, west Africans, and Nipmuck were among the various people who lived side-by-side with English, who themselves displayed regional differences. The English had long been divided by a common language and uncommon ways. Of course, there were women as well as men. For every minister or magistrate, there were hundreds of farmers, carpenters, clothmakers, sailors, traders, blacksmiths, coopers, fishermen, shoemakers, childrearers, ordinary keepers, hunters, servants, food preparers, land speculators, midwives, and merchants. There were children and the elderly, young adults and middle-aged, husbands and wives, parents and offspring. There were town dwellers and villagers. There were poor and transient as well as well-to-do and stable. There were charlatans and saints, murderers and healers, the ambitious and lazy, the kind and cruel. The builders of the Bay Colony and of all New England were a diverse people.

*　*　*

Despite undying references to Puritan New England—as if it were a homogeneous culture—historians now are well aware of the diversity among that region's people. The rich literature on seventeenth-century New England during the last thirty years repeatedly has pointed to differences. No longer is the tale of ministers and magistrates (which itself is multilayered) accepted as the entire story. Those various studies have demonstrated the complexity of early New England beliefs, behavior, economics, family life, towns, encounters between peoples, and more, but they have not provided a comprehensive and coherent examination of the whole.

I hope this volume will fill that void. Combining synthesis and original research, I analyze the parts in order to comprehend the totality.

Throughout I am guided by the question: Despite their diversity, were the people of New England in the seventeenth century members of the same culture? Were there common beliefs, values, behaviors, social structures, and institutions that transcended their differences? Did women experience the world in ways similar to men? Native Americans similar to Europeans? Subjects similar to magistrates? Servants similar to masters? George Walton similar to Cotton Mather?

In the process of constructing a history of seventeenth-century New England, I incorporate the broad range of lives and try to understand whether they fit together and, if so, how. To find whether they were pieces of the same puzzle, parts of the same elephant, is the task ahead. The elite were a part of the New England past, and a history without them would be incomplete—but that is true for everyone else. The political history of power is as essential as the intellectual history of religious beliefs, the social history of the family as important as the economic history of systems of exchange, the ethnic history of encounters as critical as the environmental history of the land. My goal is to provide a comprehensive history that includes and integrates all of these approaches. If along the way I tell a few good stories, so much the better.

~ 2 ~

RELATIONS BETWEEN
COLONISTS AND NATIVE
AMERICANS

Death had haunted the Wampanoag village of Sowams for half a dozen years, when in March 1623, their sachem, Massasoit, took ill. Europeans unwittingly had carried smallpox, influenza, measles, chicken pox, and other diseases to North American shores, and the result was decimation of peoples left unprotected by thousands of years of isolation from Old World inhabitants. There was little immunity to the full onslaught of European contagions. Following contact with traders, fishermen, and sailors, as many as 90 percent of the native population of southeastern New England may have died during those few years. Not a soul remained at the village of Patuxet, when English colonists landed in 1620 and renamed the site Plymouth, nor were there any inhabited villages for nine or ten miles from the coast. In 1621, four years after the first and most devastating outbreak, visitors to Sowams reported that the living still had been unable to bury all the dead, and they witnessed the "sad spectacle" of skulls and bones littering the ground. But Massasoit was experiencing a less exotic, yet no less threatening, assault. He was constipated and dehydrated, he was unable to eat or drink, he had lost his sight, and he and several other villagers were dying.[1]

Massasoit probably was between twenty-five and thirty-five years old at the time. In *Mourt's Relation,* based on the journals of William Bradford and Edward Winslow, he is described in March 1621, as "a very lusty man, in his best years." This from Bradford who then was thirty-one and Winslow who was twenty-five. The epidemics created dislocations that most likely had thrust Massasoit into a leadership position earlier than normal, for the deadly diseases were most disrespectful of the very young and the elderly. Among Algonquian people of the New England region, sachems—men and women alike—inherited their positions. Whether Massasoit had inherited his power or whether he had seized the opportunity presented by unparalleled mortality is not evident. What is known is that Massasoit had consolidated his authority south of Massachusetts Bay from Cape Cod to Narragansett Bay, including the islands of Nantucket and Martha's Vineyard, and that other sachems of the area supported him. Now was the time to unite remnants of peoples whose family, political, economic, and cultural patterns had been severely torn, particularly with the challenge of the Narragansett to the west and the presence of the English to the east.[2]

Had the invasion of deadly viruses and bacteria not preceded the planting of Plymouth, it is unlikely that Massasoit and other Wampanoag would have tolerated English colonization; as of December 1620, however, they were in no position to dispute the existence of their new neighbors. Instead they developed a strategy to balance the English against the Narragansett, who were numerous, powerful, threatening, and thus far unexposed to epidemics. Within three months, they established a treaty, an alliance with the English. For their part, the Wampanoag agreed not to harm the colonists, not to steal tools, and not to take bows and arrows into the English settlement. There also was a provision (later to create a nearly fatal rift) that offenders would be sent to the other side for punishment. The colonists at Plymouth understood this to apply to the Wampanoag exclusively while Massasoit and his people believed it to be reciprocal. The heart of the treaty, however, was the pledge that each would come to the other's aid should anyone "unjustly war" against them.[3] This agreement would last for more than fifty years.

The treaty was equally advantageous to the English. They too had unusually young leadership (William Bradford who would be governor of Plymouth for most of its first forty years was thirty-one when he initially took office). For that matter, the filter of migration during the first big wave from 1620 to 1642 sifted a population much different in age structure from that of England. Roughly 90 percent of the emigrants were forty years old or younger, and the vast majority were less than thirty. Although not attacked by epidemic as were the Wampanoag, the passengers of the *Mayflower* struggled with exposure to the elements and inadequate food supplies—having arrived at the beginning of winter, they had limited opportunity to construct shelter and no time to plant crops. Within six months, nearly half of the 102 migrants, including John Carver, the first governor, were dead.[4] As it was, they were fortunate to have found cornfields already carved and burned from the forest, fields abandoned by their previous, and now dead, owners. The concerns of New England's

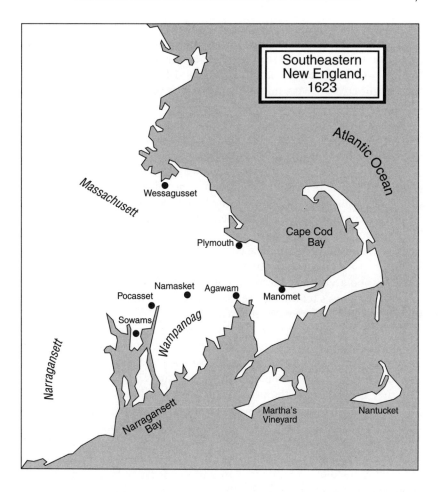

newest residents matched the Wampanoag sense of disruption and insecurity. With a tenuous grip on New England's coastal shore, the English
needed the alliance even more than did the Wampanoag.

Still, neither group fully accepted the other. This was an arrangement
forged by necessity. Each defined humanity by its own traditions. Each
perceived the other as alien. Each distrusted the other: We are The People. To the extent you differ from us, the less human you are. They each
would try to change the other: To become one of us, you must be born
again—you must look like us, you must speak like us, you must believe
like us, you must have a name bestowed by us.

Such attitudes were not unusual for people who had lived in relative
cultural isolation. The Wampanoag dwelled close to Narragansett,

Massachusett, and Cape Cod peoples, and they may have had occasional contact with Nipmuck, Pequot, and Abenaki, but all of these people were Algonquian. They were variations of the same basic theme.[5] The English settlers were a different matter. Occasional European traders or fishermen might create havoc, might introduce new technologies, might induce changes of behavior through such practices as the fur trade, might kidnap, might transmit disease, but they were not permanent residents. They were curiosities, they were bearers of useful goods, and as long as they were transients they could be controlled.

Some of the English colonists previously had resided in Leyden, Holland, and had experienced living among people somewhat, but not entirely, different from themselves. The Dutch were Protestants, they lived in permanent homes, and their appearance and apparel were familiar. Yet they spoke Dutch. They were not English. The differences were enough that the English in Holland feared their children would lose their cultural heritage. So for that and other reasons they moved to what they perceived to be a virgin wilderness, empty land. They soon discovered, in Francis Jennings's telling phrase, that instead the land was widowed and the widow had no intention of leaving.[6]

Neither Wampanoag nor English were cultural relativists. They defined their worlds by what was familiar, by what was traditional. And now they were neighbors. While Massasoit lived, the relationship was cordial. Despite occasional misunderstandings, peace was maintained and they became more than strangers, though still less than friends. But should Massasoit die, what would become of their alliance? In part to assess the situation, in part to hold a conference with some Dutch whose ship temporarily was stuck nearby the Wampanoag village, and in part to follow the Indian custom of visiting the dying, Governor Bradford sent Edward Winslow, accompanied by Hobbamock, a Wampanoag guide who had assisted and lived with the Plymouth colonists, and John Hamden, a curious, London visitor.[7]

Winslow, who frequently represented Plymouth on important missions, was a good choice. From the start, he had been a member of the colony's leadership, and clearly he and Bradford shared similar anxieties and similar hopes for their fledgling settlement. He spoke Dutch and was one of the colonists who had lived in Leyden. Equally valuable, he had visited Massasoit at Sowams on an earlier occasion. Reflecting on the previous trip, Winslow might have had second thoughts. The journey would be arduous, but hardly daunting. It would take two days to reach the village (Sowams, near what is now Bristol, Rhode Island, is roughly forty miles from Plymouth). With most of the underbrush having been regularly burned, the forests proved a minor obstacle, and native hospitality would be offered along the way. Yet, perhaps, the hospitality was Winslow's concern. The last time Massasoit had shared what food was available, but, with many people to be fed, rations were meager; and the alien environment had prevented sleep: "what with bad lodging, the savages' barbarous singing (for they use to sing themselves asleep,) lice and fleas within doors, and mosquitoes without, we could hardly sleep all the time of our being there." With his business concluded and despite Massasoit's wish that he remain longer, Winslow had fled the village after two days (more accurately, two nights) under the pretext that they "desired to keep the Sabbath at home."[8]

Better prepared than before and more accustomed to Wampanoag ways, Winslow and his companions set off to pay their respects to the dying sachem. After an uneventful first day, they spent the night at the village of Namasket. On the following day, shortly after noon, they met a group of Indians who told them that Massasoit had died and been buried and that the Dutch ship would be gone before they would arrive. Hobbamock advised them to return to Plymouth immediately, but Winslow considered it politic to meet with some of the other local sachems. Nearby was the village of Pocasset where Corbitant, the sachem most likely to succeed Massasoit, lived. Winslow knew that such a meeting could lead to a confrontation: Corbitant a year and a half earlier had acted hostilely toward Plymouth in general and Hobbamock in particular; nonetheless, Winslow also knew that it was essential he establish good relations as soon as possible.[9] When they arrived at Pocasset, they learned that Corbitant was at Sowams. Both to alert Corbitant of their presence at his village and to know for certain whether Massasoit had died, they sent a messenger to Sowams. Shortly before sunset, the messenger returned and told them that Massasoit still lived, though his death was imminent. So off they sped.

Winslow had experienced culture shock during his first visit, and upon his arrival the strange and alarming world appeared again. It was late at night when they approached the house where Massasoit was lying. This was not a small, summer hut, such as the one where Winslow had spent his two fitful nights, but rather a large, winter building, perhaps fifty or sixty feet in diameter, sheltering many people. The outside of the house was a series of poles pulled into a dome and covered by tightly woven mats. In the middle of the roof was an opening to allow light to enter during the day and smoke to leave from the fire below, day and night. The astute observer William Wood considered such dwellings "warmer than our English houses," but so smoky that people would "lie all along under the smoke" rather than stand upright. When Winslow opened the flap, he must have been startled by the light of the fire, the unreality of a smoke-filled room with its softened lines and altered shapes, the mass of powwows working their charms and making "such a hellish noise" as they attempted to restore Massasoit's health, so closely bunched that Winslow had difficulty moving through their midst, and the ultimate sight of a figure on a plank being rubbed by "six or eight" women trying to keep him warm. Massasoit, unable to see, inquired who had come and being told that it was Winslow spoke: "*Matta neen wonckanet namen, Winsnow*! that is to say, 'O Winslow, I shall never see thee again.'"[10]

Winslow replied that Governor Bradford was concerned about his illness and had sent "such things for him as he thought most likely to do him good." He then offered the sachem "a confection of many comfortable conserves." With some difficulty, Massasoit dissolved a small amount in his mouth and swallowed the juice, his first nourishment in two days. Winslow noticed that Massasoit's mouth was "furred" and his tongue swollen, and he immediately began cleansing his mouth and scraping his tongue. Taking more confection and drinking some water, Massasoit showed improvement. Winslow continued to minister to him, and by the following day there was "no doubt of his recovery." The next day after, Massasoit had so awakened his appetite that he gorged himself and suffered a relapse. But again Winslow nursed him to health. Before returning to Plymouth, Winslow similarly helped others in the village. After four days, he parted from a grateful Massasoit.

On the way home, Hobbamock told Winslow of a disturbing conversation he had had with the recovered Massasoit on the previous day. Apparently, the Massachusett who lived north of Plymouth colony in the area of Massachusetts Bay were plotting to kill all the English at a trading post at Wessagusset (present-day Weymouth, Massachusetts), and, in anticipation of Plymouth retaliation, all the colonists there as well. They already had won the support of Cape Cod Indians as well as the peoples of Agawam (now part of Wareham, Massachusetts) and Martha's Vineyard but had been unsuccessful in enlisting Massasoit and his people. The Wampanoag sachem advised a peremptory strike killing the Massachusett. That would nip the plot in the bud.

Winslow certainly had plenty of evidence that the men at Wessagusset were a disruptive lot, and it should not have surprised him that they had angered their Massachusett neighbors. Even Thomas Weston, the devious merchant responsible for their settlement, referred to them as "rude fellows," and he hoped (at least he so wrote to William Bradford) "to reclaim them from that profaneness that may scandalize the voyage, but by degrees to draw them to God, etc." Robert Cushman, the Plymouth Colony agent in England, feared "these people will hardly deal so well with the savages as they should," and he suggested that people at Plymouth communicate to the local Indians that the Weston people were a distinct group over whom they had no control and for whom they should take no blame. In short, they were a group of men who came to New England with motives ranging from making a quick profit and a quick return to escaping difficulties in England. Few, if any, were seeking a permanent home, as were the Plymouth colonists. They were the equivalent of gold prospectors—get in, make a killing, and get out—and to that extent were more typical of English colonists in the early seventeenth century than were the Plymouth people. Although the motives of those who migrated in 1620 were much more complex than the seeking of a place to practice their religion and to rear their children (for example, some of that *Mayflower* group came as unattached, single men with no pronounced religious leanings), they were the unusual ones. Many came in family groups, and most wished to create homes for themselves and their posterity. It was in their self-interest to establish bonds with their neighbors.[11]

From the beginning it was clear that neighborly relations were unimportant to the Weston crew. Fifty or sixty of them had arrived at Plymouth early in summer 1622, poorly provisioned and ready to reinforce the Puritan notion of idleness being akin to deviltry. The bulk of them took advantage of Plymouth hospitality, while a few of their number scouted the coast for an advantageous site for a trading post. By the time they left for Wessagusset in August, they thoroughly had irritated their hosts. They had stolen green corn ("it being then eatable and pleasant to taste"), a precious commodity for surviving the winter; they had gossiped; and they had had the audacity to revile their benefactors. No sooner were they settled at Wessagusset than they angered the nearby Massachusett by stealing their corn. Despite Indian complaints, authorities at Plymouth claimed they had no control over the Weston colony.[12]

By February 1623, the situation was desperate at the trading post. Food was nearly depleted, men were starving, and the pillaging of corn continued unabated. Some began to sell their clothes for food, one person allegedly was so weak that while gathering shellfish "he stuck fast in the mud and was found dead in the place," and some became servants of the native people. Trying to restore goodwill, they even hanged one of the corn thieves. Eventually, the Massachusett, both exasperated by the behavior of the English and low on provisions themselves, refused to lend, trade, or sell corn. John Sanders, the overseer at Wessagusset, sent a messenger to Plymouth describing their circumstances and notifying them of his intent to take corn by force.[13]

The Plymouth leadership quickly responded. To pillage the Indians' store of corn would be wrong; it would violate God's law and English law, and it would "breed a distaste in the salvages against our persons and professions," let alone prompt retaliatory violence. Conditions at Plymouth were hardly better, maybe worse, and yet they were making do. At the very least, this portion of their reply was hypocritical, for some of the Plymouth settlers, including Bradford, had been guilty of stealing corn and desecrating graves along Cape Cod during their first month in New England, and they had justified their actions by claims of extreme necessity. But there were other considerations, they argued. The corn would soon run out, and with the Massachusett their enemy they would have to venture farther away to acquire food. Perhaps most important, it was unlikely in their weakened condition they would be successful, and even then they should expect punishment from British authorities. Whether to soften the impact of their message or to exhibit Christian charity, they sent some corn to accompany their words.[14]

Reflecting on the turbulence at Wessagusset, Winslow immediately notified Bradford and others of Massasoit's warning. Arriving at Plymouth at the same time as Winslow, Wassapinewat, brother of the Massachusett sachem, Obtakiest, unveiled the same plot. With this information, Governor Bradford was predisposed to wage war on the Massachusett; fortuitously the annual meeting of Plymouth's General Court was about to occur. This was the appropriate forum to discuss with the "body of the company" what should be done.[15] It must have been during these deliberations that Miles Standish, the military leader of the colony, recalled his experiences at the village of Manomet (now Sandwich, Massachusetts) earlier in the month.

Standish was not a member of the congregation that had left Holland for New England. He was a military man who had been recruited to join the venture because of his experience. He knew violence. He knew force. He knew when to act and when to bide his time. During the last few weeks he had been biding his time, for incidents at Manomet had angered him. Sailing to the village to pick up previously purchased corn and hoping to buy more, he immediately had been surprised by his cool reception. At other villages, he had received hospitality, and Bradford had been well entertained at Manomet when he earlier had negotiated the purchase. What had changed? The answer came at the home of Canacum, the local sachem, when two Massachusett men entered. Wituwamat, the foremost of the two, who later was described by Winslow (reflecting Standish's impression, to be sure) as "a notable insulting villain," presented a gift to Canacum, a dagger acquired from someone of the Weston colony. What followed was a long, "audacious" speech. Although Standish could not understand the words, he took the matter to be menacing to English colonists and insulting to himself. Canacum received the message sympathetically and, from Standish's perspective, was much friendlier to Wituwamat than to the English captain. Standish didn't sleep that night, as he guarded the corn and prepared for attack. Much to his relief, no incidents occurred and he sailed back to Plymouth in the morning.[16]

In retrospect, Wituwamat's speech now made sense. He was trying to enlist Canacum in the plot to exterminate the Weston colony and the people at Plymouth. The pieces were fitting together—Massasoit, Wassapin-ewat, and Wituwamat. The Massachusett were planning a re-creation of the 1622 massacre at Virginia. Such an assault had been much on the colonists' minds, ever since they had learned the previous May of the gruesome details. The Plymouth colony increased their security with warders by day and watchers by night, and after ten months' work they finally completed a fort with cannon.[17] Just in time, it seemed, for the period of treachery was upon them.

Surprisingly, the General Court hesitated. Massasoit, Wassapinewat, and Wituwamat (or Standish's impression) were but three voices. Their own daily conversations with other Indians were different. They were not prepared to make a bloody judgment. Like many deliberative bodies, they passed the buck. The "Governor, his Assistant, and the Captain, should take such to themselves as they thought most meet, and conclude thereof." Together (although Standish seems to have taken the lead) the three concocted a plan where the captain and a sufficient group of men would sail to Wessagusset. There, they would inform the Weston group of the situation and would make their own assessment of what should be done. No matter what, Wituwamat's head was to be brought back as "a warning and terror to all of that disposition."[18] Perhaps they also recognized and hoped that the murder and decapitation would produce so much hostility that the Weston colony would have to be abandoned.

Almost anticlimactically, a confused, lost, and weary Phineas Pratt entered the stage. For two days since he had sneaked out of Wessagusset, he had been trying to elude pursuers (or so he thought) and to find Plymouth. Not able to take a compass but navigating by the stars at night and the sun during the day, he had wandered south. He too told of a conspiracy. The men at Wessagusset were so desperate that they had scattered in search of sustenance. In their weakened state, they were easy prey for their insulting and vengeful neighbors. The Massachusett were ready to attack as soon as they completed the construction of canoes and the snow had melted—in other words, soon.[19] Pratt's tale provides the last piece of evidence of a conspiracy to kill all the English at Wessagusset and Plymouth. But should we, like the General Court, hesitate before drawing that conclusion? Was there such a broad plot? Who should be believed?

The first warning came from Massasoit. Let's begin with him. He had told Winslow of the impending assault. But here is the first problem. Massasoit never told Winslow directly. The word came from Hobbamock. Why would he use an intermediary? For that question, there are ready answers. Winslow was not fluent in the Indian language, and Hobbamock, his guide and interpreter, was a Wampanoag. It would have been possible for Massasoit to speak more privately, perhaps secretly, with Hobbamock than with Winslow, and he would not have wanted the Massachusett or other people to know of his role. Granting that there was legitimate reason for conveying the information through an intermediary, did Hobbamock accurately or faithfully convey a message? For that matter, was there a message from Massasoit?

This was not the first time Hobbamock, who had lived among the colonists since at least August 1621, had described the Massachusett as conspirators. The previous year he had claimed that the Massachusett and the Narragansett had allied and together might pose a threat to Plymouth. Nearly in the same breath, he had implicated his rival Squanto as a confederate in the plot. Such an accusation would have been met with some skepticism, for Squanto had served the colonists faithfully, or so it seemed. Squanto from the village of Patuxet had been captured in 1614 and taken to Europe. There he had learned English and after many adventures had worked his way back, only to find all his people had died. The colonists apparently had become his surrogate people, and he had translated for them and advised them in many helpful ways. Aware of the jealousy between Hobbamock and Squanto, yet desperate to trade for food, the colonists had disregarded the warning and a party of them including Miles Standish sailed off to barter with the Massachusett with the two competitors in tow. Before their ship had sailed from sight, a member of Squanto's "family" with blood dripping from his face rushed into the settlement. According to Squanto's kin, the Narragansett and the Wampanoag, including Massasoit, had gathered at Namasket, from where he had fled, and they were ready to attack as soon as Standish was gone. Cannon were fired, and the ship returned. After investigation, they found the story to be a fabrication and that Squanto had been playing a risky game of lies and distortions for some time. His goals had been to convince Indians that he could manipulate the English as he wished and to discredit Massasoit so as to advance himself. The colonists were furious, but because of his value to them, they protected him until his death from disease in November. Massasoit also was angry, and he demanded that Squanto be turned over to him to be executed. Squanto's luck held out for the remaining months of his life, but relations between Massasoit and Plymouth had soured until Winslow's mission to the dying sachem.[20]

What we learn from all this is that colonists could be pawns in Indian games as easily as the reverse. Indians were not passive victims waiting to be used. They could manipulate for their own personal advancement as well as for the well-being of their people. In this case, it seems unlikely that Hobbamock, who had a genuine affection for Massasoit and who was a Wampanoag, would have lied in a way that could prove damaging to his sachem.[21] Whether Massasoit had more on his mind than gratitude is entirely possible. It was one thing to divulge a plot, but quite another to suggest the Massachusett leaders should be killed. Massasoit may have taken the information that some Massachusett wanted to kill some or all of Weston's colony and enlarged it into a broader conspiracy. With the Massachusett leadership out of the way, he could have extended his and his people's power.

Wassapinewat's testimony is even more puzzling. Why would he reveal an alleged plot implicating his brother and his people? Winslow explained he "had formerly smarted for partaking with Conbatant [Corbitant], and fearing the like again, to purge himself, revealed the same thing." This apparently refers to an incident in August 1621, when Corbitant had captured Squanto. The colonists had gone to Corbitant's village with guns blazing and had freed Squanto. In the process, they had wounded a few villagers (at least one man and one woman, both of whom went to Plymouth to have their injuries treated), had frightened others, and had implanted the understanding that they would retaliate when provoked.[22] Although Winslow never indicated apart from the quoted line how Wassapinewat was involved, it is plausible that Wassapinewat, after August 1621, upon hearing any plans for actions against the English might have attempted to dissociate himself. It is also possible that when Winslow wrote "revealed the same thing" it wasn't the same thing. Wassapinewat may have told of a plot against all the colonists in Wessagusset and Plymouth or he may have discussed a more minor proposal that didn't include himself, his brother, or most of his people. He might have said that some Massachusett were planning to kill some of Weston's colony.

The Miles Standish evidence is less convincing still. Standish could not understand what Wituwamat was saying in his speech at Canacum's village. At the time, it seems he viewed the threat as focused on himself and his men, but no more. It was only weeks later, after he had heard from Winslow and Wassapinewat, that he surmised he had been witness to a larger plan. It is possible that the volatile Standish, angered by Wituwamat's insulting manner but temporarily in no position to retaliate, enlarged the story to justify an assault on Wituwamat's head.

And last we have the frightened Phineas Pratt. Pratt's story is highly suspect in many of its details. He wrote his "Decliration of the Afaires of the Einglish People [That First] Inhabited New England" in 1662, nearly forty years after the event, as part of a petition to the General Court of Massachusetts asking for land. Even though he plagiarized portions of the "Decliration" from Winslow's *Good Newes From New England* (printed in 1624), critical parts of the two accounts don't fully coincide. Both commented on the weakened condition of the Weston colony, their bad relations with the Massachusett, and Pratt's journey to Plymouth. But where Pratt described his motivation for traveling to Plymouth as the desire to warn the old colony settlers of the threat to all English in the area (the reason the Massachusett were waiting for the snow to melt, according to Pratt, was so that they could kill all the English colonists on the same day), Winslow indicated an anxious Pratt, who fearing violence at Wessagusset, rushed to Plymouth for his own safety. There is no mention at all of a direct threat to Plymouth. Bradford's more abbreviated description supports Winslow.[23]

One last piece of information should be added to this analysis. The Massachusett had suffered from a recent epidemic that had killed half their number.[24] Considering their weakened state, it is unlikely that they would have ventured a massive, perhaps suicidal, attack, even had other Indians joined them. More specific retribution aimed at the corn thieves, whose actions were a mortal threat, is far more plausible.

Where does this leave us? The Massachusett were angry at the behavior of the Weston colonists, and the ongoing thievery imperiled their well being. Some of their young men were quite vocal in their outrage and had discussed the situation with sachems of other villages. They resented the inability of the English, at Wessagusset and at Plymouth, to control their own people. They were contemptuous of how low some colonists would stoop, yet wary of the English capacity for violence. In their own weakened state, they were examining strategies of how to respond to the colonists. They may have fantasized about massacring all the people at Wessagusset and Plymouth or at least driving them out of New England. They most likely were prepared to kill the corn thieves, but it is unlikely that there was a conspiracy to murder every colonist.[25]

Standish saw it differently, and as usual he was ready to act. Yet when he arrived at Wessagusset, all seemed peaceful. Not a drop of blood in sight. Perhaps the area was *too* silent; in fact, there was no sign of life. When he and his men approached the colony's ship, they "found neither man, or so much as a dog therein." This was suspicious indeed. After firing a musket, they finally spotted the master of the ship and others "on the shore gathering ground-nuts, and getting other food." The scene and the situation were quite different from what Pratt had described, and

Standish was incredulous that they had left the ship unoccupied and carried no weapons. To which they responded, "they feared not the Indians, but lived and suffered them to lodge with them, not having sword or gun, or needing the same." In fact, the Weston colonists were scattered throughout the area, and three of them were living in the Massachusett village at the very moment.[26]

Standish asserted he hoped their assessment was accurate and went to meet with the colony's leaders. He told them of the danger they faced, apparently much to their surprise, and of the purpose of his trip. Should they wish, they would be welcome at Plymouth "till they could be better provided" or they could go elsewhere. In the short term, however, secrecy should be maintained and no one should leave until Standish had completed his mission and the outlying settlers had returned to the plantation.

And then the deadly game commenced. As Winslow, who is the only source for these events, reported, Massachusett men and Miles Standish and his party began to size each other up. One Massachusett man, bearing furs to trade, visited Standish, who suspected that the occasion was more for gaining information than for bartering goods. The English captain later claimed that he "saw by his eyes that he was angry in his heart," an indication that the native people understood the colonists' intent. Other visits followed, turning the smoldering coals into an intense fire. Pecksuot, a key advisor of the sachem, met with Hobbamock who had accompanied Standish.[27] He indicated that he was well aware of Standish's murderous intent but that neither he nor his people were afraid, and then he threw down the gauntlet: "let him begin when he dare, he shall not take us at unawares." Others brandished knives where Pecksuot had brandished words. In Standish's presence, they sharpened their blades while making "many other insulting gestures and speeches." Wituwamat taunted further. Bragging that he had killed French and English before, he suggested that his knife soon would enter English flesh again. Pecksuot, upon return, foolishly challenged Standish's manhood. The taller of the two, he said that while he was not a sachem, he was "a man of great strength and courage," and that conversely Standish was "a great captain, yet he was but a little man." Proud men. Bold words.

No less proud and no doubt boiling with rage, the short Englishman once again bided his time. His revenge would come the following day. Pecksuot, Wituwamat, and two other Massachusett men somehow were enticed into one of the English houses where Standish and his men waited. Whether the Massachusett believed that the English from Plymouth were as weak as their Wessagusset countrymen, whether they interpreted Standish's silence as fear, or whether they believed themselves impervious to harm, we shall never know. Immediately the door was fastened tight, and the carnage began. Standish grabbed the knife dangling from Pecksuot's neck and repeatedly stabbed him until he was dead. Others killed Wituwamat and another man. According to Winslow's account, "it is incredible how many wounds these two pineses received before they died, not making any fearful noise, but catching at their weapons and striving to the last."[28] The fourth Massachusett, a young man of eighteen, was hanged. It is fascinating to speculate on why Standish spent his fury on Pecksuot rather than on Wituwamat, the ostensible target of the mission. Was it simply a matter of proximity and opportunity? Or could Pecksuot's jibes about Standish's height have sealed his fate?

The bloodshed then spread beyond the trading house. Three more Massachusett men were killed, but another escaped and informed Obtakiest, the Massachusett sachem. Shortly thereafter, a skirmish occurred, and in the midst of flying shot and arrows Obtakiest drew back his bow aimed in the direction of Miles Standish. Before he could release the arrow, Standish and another Englishman fired at him, breaking his arm. The wounded Obtakiest and his fellow Massachusett, no match for English weapons, then took cover in a nearby swamp. The combatants exchanged words, and the belligerent captain "dared the sachim to come out and fight like a man, showing how base and woman-like he was in tonguing it as he did."[29] Standish, perhaps revealing more of his feelings than he intended, no longer had to remain silent.

With all goals accomplished, the Plymouth contingent arranged for the safe departure of Weston's men and headed home—quite literally; for they brought Wituwamat's head with them and placed it on their fort as a warning. One visitor in a letter sent back to England the following September noted the grisly trophy, still in place six months later.[30]

The episode didn't end just yet. Although one of the Weston group who was residing with the Massachusett escaped, two others were killed in retaliation. Still in hiding, Obtakiest through an intermediary apologized for their deaths; not long after, peace returned to the beleaguered Massachusett. Cape Cod Indians, who had been implicated, rushed from their villages in terror, fearful that similar violence would be directed toward them. In swamps and "other desert places" they contracted diseases and many died, including the sachems, Canacum, Aspinet, and Iyanough. Dislocation and disruption continued.

The news of this affair appalled even some of the colonists' English supporters. John Robinson, their former minister, wrote from Leyden: "O how happy a thing had it been that you had converted some before you killed any!" Edward Winslow wrote his *Good Newes From New England* partially in response to such criticism, and it is almost exclusively from that source that we know of these events at all (and this was the best face that could be put on them!). William Bradford glossed over the entire episode. All we learn from him is that Standish "cut off some few of the chief conspirators."[31]

* * *

And so it went through the seventeenth century—mercy and murder, kindness and violence, communication and manipulation, action and reaction, respect and distrust. It is too simple to look for good guys and bad guys or for violators and victims. It was far more complicated than that.

At one level, all inhabitants of New England, Indian and English alike, had common goals: they wanted to survive and prosper, to practice their beliefs, and to continue the manner of living to which they were accustomed. If only it were so simple. The problem was that while there were similarities in their beliefs (all believed that the world was governed by supernatural forces) and manner of living (they resided in villages and, among people south of the Saco River, the bulk of their diets came from agricultural production) there were significant differences as well.

No area of difference had greater consequence than land: its ownership and its use.[32] It is inaccurate to say that New England Indians had no sense of land ownership, but that sense was not European. Central to understanding the Indian views are the concepts of sovereignty and usufruct. An Indian village or confederation had a distinct idea of possessing a particular territory that should not be infringed by other people without their consent. The Wampanoag held sovereignty over one part of New England, for example, the Narragansett over another, and so on. Within the Wampanoag territory, there could be individual or family ownership of a particular piece of land. As long as the land was being used (generally meaning being farmed), it belonged to that individual or family. When those family members migrated to winter territory, leaving their agricultural land, they did not relinquish its use for the following spring when they returned; it still was reserved for them. Nevertheless, other members of the village could hunt on that land and could gather "wild" food, such as groundnuts and berries. When the individual or family no longer farmed that land (this generally occurred every few years, as the soil lost its fertility), it returned to the community. It was not theirs to sell, trade, or bequeath. Having left one plot, they simply would begin farming other "unused" land within the territory. In such a way, all land within a people's sovereignty was used: for hunting, fishing, sleeping, burying the dead, raising crops, gathering food and firewood, playing, practicing religion. Individual property was temporarily owned by whoever farmed it, but it reverted to the community when it no longer was used for agricultural purposes. Sachems could sell or trade their people's land, but in doing so they were acting for the community. Even so, at least until they understood English ways, they were selling or trading the use of the land, not its sovereignty. In their minds, they still could hunt and gather food, even farm if the land was not being cultivated. They sold or traded the rights to do the same; they did not sell its ownership.

English settlers also held a concept of sovereignty. They recognized the control and the power of a monarch as legitimate. They supported the rule of a colony over its territory and of a town over its land. The town supervised the use of common land for grazing animals, gathering firewood, building meetinghouses, and holding militia drills, and it or designated proprietors distributed property. When individual English acquired property, they owned it whether they used it or not. Their land had fixed boundaries that were recorded. Although they might have to obtain permission to transfer a deed, they still had the right to sell or trade their land. In short, individual property was a commodity, just the same as a manufactured product. Here was a key area of conflict. When a sachem sold land, in his mind he was selling only the right to use it and that right was not absolutely exclusive. When an Englishman purchased land, in his mind he was acquiring a commodity for his exclusive and perpetual control.

Land use also produced irreconcilable differences. New England Indians were mobile. In general, they had summer bases where land was good for agriculture and winter bases where hunting was prevalent. From time to time they would move these bases as the fertility of the soil declined or as the amount of game decreased. Twice a year they set fires to clear underbrush, which made farming, hunting, and traveling easier. They altered the landscape to fit their needs; but partially because of a population density compatible with their way of living and partially because of their values and attitude toward the natural world, they were able to sustain themselves. The English were more permanent in their residences. They cleared land for farming, and they lived on that land year-round. Using manure and fish for fertilizer and rotating crops and land, they tried to keep the same land in production as constantly as possible. When they sold their land and moved, in their subsequent location they cut back the forest for new fields while the old land continued to be farmed by the new owner. Over time, the New England landscape changed, as deforestation occurred. The cleared land and cultivated fields reminded colonists of their former homes on the other side of the Atlantic (and, of course, that was the idea), but it proved disastrous for flora and fauna and ultimately for the original human population. Some species died out, while others became depleted. In either case, food sources for native peoples diminished. By contrast, English settlers felt less threatened by the decline of game; they were used to raising animals for food as well as for labor. Mutton and pork for the table and oxen and horses for the field fit English agricultural practices, but the domestication of animals with the resulting need for additional forage and space contributed to the decline of the wild.[33]

Had the English population remained at the level of Plymouth and Wessagusset in 1623, a few hundred souls at most, these differences in land ownership and land use would have been minor annoyances. But the increase in population produced by migration (during the period known as the Great Migration from 1630 to 1642, approximately 20,000 English people came to New England) and the unusually high birthrate of this healthy and long-living group produced pressures with profound effects. Parents of growing families wanted land for future generations. With the rapidly increasing population combined with the English lust for land (land speculation being almost synonymous with English colonization), there was no way that the cultures of native peoples would remain unaltered.[34]

The task, then, of the original inhabitants was to devise strategies for keeping their cultures as intact as possible and advancing their interests for the future. It was impossible to foretell with certainty whether there would be conflict or harmony any more than whether there would be famine or plenty. There might be signs, both natural and supernatural, but no one knew for sure. They did know that English and Indians lived in near proximity, but it was unclear whether either would prevail. In the short run, at least, the relationship could prove beneficial. Just as the English needed the Wampanoag and the Wampanoag needed the English, there was reciprocity between peoples in other parts of New England. Indian and English would be active agents in their intertwined futures.[35] Individual strategy and behavior was as varied as the individual people, but group strategies and behavior formed patterns that may be summarized as follows: negotiate, accommodate, acculturate, retaliate, and exterminate.

The treaty in 1621 between Massasoit for the Wampanoag and John Carver for the Plymouth colonists is a model of negotiation between equals. Each side maintained its autonomy, each side benefited, and each side recognized the value of the other. The critical element was the degree of equality. As long as neither side could dictate terms, peaceful resolution not only was possible but lasting. It also helped when leaders who desperately needed the assistance of the others at the time of an agreement lived long and remembered. By the 1660s, after the deaths of Bradford, Winslow, and Massasoit, and with the balance of power shifted toward the English, the colonists began to dictate terms to the Wampanoag, and their relationship deteriorated. Elsewhere in New England, colonies sometimes acted upon principle and sometimes flaunted power. Rhode Island, often influenced by Roger Williams of Providence Plantations, generally negotiated rather than dictated, particularly when it came to the acquisition of land. Massachusetts Bay, the most populous and the dominant of the English colonies in New England, also was the most bellicose and, under the impression that it knew what was best for all concerned, coerced agreements and alliances whenever it could. For their part, New England Indians would negotiate when they could and accommodate when they had to. With no pan-Indian alliance, each people spoke for themselves and for their own particular self-interest. The Narragansett, a people weakened by epidemic in the 1630s, even went so far as to ally with Massachusetts Bay in an attack against the Pequot, a neighboring competitor.

The process of acculturation began at first contact, well in advance of colonization. At first, it was subtle (except for disease, almost benign) and it worked in both directions. The English and other Europeans brought goods, such as metal implements and cloth, that Indians would alter to conform to traditional practice—but nevertheless would modify what had been. A metal object, for example, might be turned into an arrowhead or an ornament. In return, indigenous people offered furs that, with modification, would change European ornamentation. Over time and especially after colonization, acculturation by trade and example became increasingly effective. Firearms and alcohol irretrievably changed Indian ways. Maize and squash sustained English lives in an unfamiliar landscape. New words and place-names entered the various languages. Skulking ways of warfare gradually modified colonists' military practices, and wampum served as currency. Indian uses of herbs and English medical practices were exchanged, though not always followed.[36]

Although these exchanges and examples had important cultural consequences, they were passive, indirect, and unintentional. The English, however, didn't stop there. As a matter of policy, they actively attempted to change Indians into Englishmen. One of the avowed purposes of establishing colonies in the first place was to convert the native people to Christianity. William Bradford, in his list of reasons for emigrating to New England, attributed "a great hope and inward zeal they had of laying some good foundation, or at least to make some way thereunto, for the propagating and advancing the gospel of the kingdom of Christ in those remote parts of the world." Matthew Cradock, writing for the Massachusetts Bay Company on 16 February 1629 to John Endicott, the leader of early arrivals in Salem, reminded him "not [to] be unmindful of the main end of our Plantation, by endeavouring to bring the Indians to the knowledge of the Gospel." Puritans believed they knew the true religion and had a responsibility to enlighten others. They wished to serve God by bringing his word to the uninitiated and to serve human beings by offering them the possibility of eternal salvation. Such was a cultural imperialism with the best of intentions.[37]

Had they immediately begun their missionary efforts, we might accept their word as they wrote it; but their timing and the nature of their activities betrayed additional, less altruistic, purposes. They not only wanted to save Indian souls by converting them to Christianity; they wished to save their own hides by converting Indians to English ways. An English Indian, who had been "reduced to civilization," was less dangerous than a "heathen savage." Missionary activity did not begin until the mid-1640s, more than twenty years after colonists first landed at Plymouth and more than a decade after the Winthrop fleet had anchored in Boston Bay. By then circumstances had changed. There was renewed need to convince Puritans in England of the authenticity of their claims, and there was increased opportunity to control nearby Indians. Not stopping at preaching the word and teaching ritual, the English missionaries organized converts into "praying towns." The inhabitants of those towns worshiped the English god, wore English clothes, took English names, and remained permanently in place. Recognizing that children were the most malleable subjects, whenever possible the missionaries separated children from parents and placed them in special schools. Nearly equally subversive was the imposition of English law. Whenever there was an English victim of an alleged Indian offense, the colonists demanded that the appropriate sachem deliver the offender for trial in an English court. Sometimes English law would even be extended to incidents between Indians.[38]

Indians were not passive victims in this process. For some, a modified Christianity provided a welcome spiritual experience. For others, their choice was part of a strategy to preserve as much of their traditional culture as possible. Weakened by disease, loss of land, and warfare, they joined praying towns for the protection of the English god and English guns. Accommodation was preferable to extinction. On occasion, English law could be beneficial. During King Philip's War, for example, when English anger and desire for revenge was at a peak, several Indians were acquitted of murder and complicity. They should not have been tried in the first place, for the only evidence against them was their ethnic identity; acquittal, however, was preferable to execution by a band of vigilantes. On less dramatic occasions, English courts might find for Indians against settlers and require restitution. For the most part, Indians resisted or avoided English religion and English law. Writing in 1677, the colonial historian, William Hubbard, asserted that Massasoit "was never in the least Degree any Ways well-afected to the Religion of the English, but would in his last Treaty with his Neighbours at *Plimouth,* when they were with him about purchasing some Land at *Swanzy,* have had them engaged never to attempt to draw away any of his People from their old Pagan Superstition, and devilith Idolatry to the Christian Religion." Massasoit, like others, was aware of the connection between religion and cultural autonomy, and he was as concerned about the danger of alien beliefs as of the threat of hostile bullets.[39]

Indian attempts in New England to acculturate the English were rare, if not nonexistent. To be sure, there were occasional colonists, lured by the less restrictive Indian environment, who ran away to native villages. Roger Williams wrote of a William Baker of Plymouth who lived among the Pequot and Mohegan. He dressed in the Indian manner, cut his hair in Indian fashion, and "after many whoredomes, is there maried." Whether Williams, well known for his sympathy toward Indians, was more concerned that Baker might join with his hosts in attacking English towns or that Baker had "turned Indian" is unclear, but he was much relieved when Baker was captured, brought to Hartford, and whipped. Unlike the Iroquois, the Indians of New England apparently did not take English prisoners to replenish the population of their villages. When they did capture English, such as Mary Rowlandson, their purpose was ransom or, for unluckier souls, revenge.[40]

If no other strategy was working, there was always retaliation. An eye for an eye, a tooth for a tooth. As we saw earlier, the colonists might "retaliate" to prevent a threat from developing, and to their eyes conspiracies were abundant. A peremptory action not only stopped possible attacks before they began, it also served as a notice that even the discussion of violence toward the English could result in bloodshed. There were alternatives, however, to Standish's approach. English authorities often summoned "plotting" sachems, interrogated them, and on occasion demanded that they as well as their people disarm. Among the Indians, retaliation more typically was an individual or small group act than the response of a village or a confederation. Stray English animals eating or trampling Indian crops might be slaughtered, English goods might be stolen, English houses and barns might be set on fire, and English people might be killed.[41]

Prior to the imperial conflicts between France and England that began in the last decade of the seventeenth century, there were only two examples of wide-scale warfare in New England between the long-term residents and the new arrivals. Though misnamed, they are known as the Pequot War and King Philip's War. The Pequot War in 1637 was waged by Massachusetts Bay against the Pequot to secure control of the land in the region of the Connecticut River in what is now Connecticut. There had been disputes with the Dutch and with Plymouth Colony over the area, rich as a center for the fur trade and for fertile soil. Quite simply, Massachusetts Bay authorities viewed the Pequot, who held sovereignty over the territory, as unreliable allies and obstacles to English interests. Under the guise of retaliation for the murders of some unscrupulous English traders, Massachusetts Bay forces joined with Narragansett in what became a war of extermination. There were atrocities committed by all involved (the worst being the massacre of an entire fortressed, Pequot village of no less than five hundred people); in the end, after death and the enslavement of captured people, only a scattered remnant of Pequot remained.[42]

The result of the Pequot War—conquest of people and acquisition of land by force—created conditions that ultimately exploded in King Philip's War. Metacom (Philip was his English name) was the son of Massasoit, and he had been sachem since his brother's death in 1662. By June 1675, when the war began, Metacom had witnessed constant diminishment of his people's land and frequent humiliation. The survival of the Wampanoag as well as other New England peoples as autonomous and viable cultures was in jeopardy. There were discussions of strategies with Indians throughout New England, and war against the English may have been one of the options debated. Still, there is little evidence of a pan-Indian conspiracy for what transpired from June 1675 to fall 1676. Precipitating events involved some young Wampanoag men, English retaliation, and eventually Metacom himself. In succeeding months, Narragansett, Nipmuck, and Abenaki (generally after direct English provocation) reluctantly entered the fray. By the time the blood had dried, a higher percentage of a population—English and Indian together—had died than in any other American war.[43] Again, death haunted the Wampanoag village of Sowams and the rest of New England. Economic, social, and cultural chaos prevailed.

The options for the cultural survival of the native peoples of New England were greatly reduced. They could resume warfare as did the Abenaki with their French allies. Or they could try to become invisible to English eyes. That was the course chosen by most New England Indians for the next three hundred years.

*   *   *

Native peoples and English colonists lived in separate worlds, even when they were neighbors. Differences of language, religion, family structure, government, work, gender roles, agricultural practices, land ownership, and architecture bred distrust among these cultural absolutists. Tragically, their very propinquity disconnected them. Just as travel and awareness of people unlike ourselves illuminates who we are, so did the proximity of Indians constantly remind English colonists of their own individual and collective identities. New Englanders in the seventeenth century sometimes exploited one another, sometimes treated each other harshly and disdainfully; they fought and disagreed, but at heart they knew they had a common heritage. There was a connection between John Winthrop and Roger Williams that was not true of Edward Winslow and Massasoit. At their best, the settlers recognized their common humanity with Native Americans; nonetheless, "savage" as a reference to Indians was part of almost every colonist's vocabulary.

Had diseases not decimated the original inhabitants of New England, had English migration been more gradual, had power been more evenly distributed, had interdependence lasted longer, perhaps the wary cooperation of the early years might have developed into more comprehensive cultural exchanges and some form of bicultural society. Praying towns and "white Indians" might have been forerunners rather than anomalies. But it wasn't to be. King Philip's War destroyed any lingering possibility. The Miles Standishes prevailed over the Edward Winslows. The severed head proved more portentous than the gently scraped tongue.

~ 3 ~

"ALL THINGS ARE TURNED UPSIDE DOWN AMONG US"

Religion, Power, and Order

He could not have known it at the time; but when John Winthrop rose to speak before the Boston church on the last Sunday of October 1636, he was about to precipitate a controversy that would rage throughout Massachusetts Bay for the next year and a half and would lead to the exile of nearly a hundred people. On the previous Sunday, members of the congregation had proposed that John Wheelwright should join John Wilson and John Cotton as their third minister, and it was clear that nearly everyone supported the nomination. Unlike the Salem church, where a majority was sufficient for approval, the Boston church required unanimous consent, whether for admitting new members, passing policy, or selecting a new minister. Near full accord would not be sufficient to move the proposal forward. At most, only a few members had reservations about Wheelwright and they might remain silent, but it only took one member with courage, principles, arrogance, or insensitivity to veto.[1]

As Winthrop faced his fellow Boston residents and church members, he must have been aware of their hostility when he told them he opposed the proposal. He argued that they didn't need a third minister. Surely John Wilson, who had been their minister from the beginning in 1630, and John Cotton, the preeminent minister in the Bay, could fulfill all the congregation's religious needs. The church, Winthrop continued, would risk its present well-being by choosing a person "whose spirit they knew not, and one who seemed to dissent in judgment." Despite attempts at reconciliation by Henry Vane (the governor of the colony), Cotton, and Wheelwright himself, Winthrop, while acknowledging Wheelwright's "godliness and abilities," refused to consent to the appointment. A disappointed and frustrated congregation then chose an equally dismayed and disheartened Wheelwright to minister to members at Mount Wollaston (then under Boston's jurisdiction; now Braintree).

Disputes within congregations were nothing new to Massachusetts Bay, and Winthrop when governor had helped resolve conflicts on a number of occasions before. Resentments and bad feelings may have persisted, but they generally remained below the surface and within individual congregations. But this was different. Rather than submerging or disappearing, the conflict grew until all the ministers and magistrates of the colony and many of the citizens were involved. The seeds of the problem were among the cargoes of the ships that transported the emigrants to New England.

When John Winthrop left England in 1630, he quite naturally brought the concept of a hierarchical society with him, and he intended to institute it upon his arrival in Massachusetts Bay. As he understood it, a stratified society not only was England's way, but God's way. "God almightie in his most holy and wide providence," he lectured his fellow passengers aboard the *Arbella,* "hath soe disposed of the Condition of mankinde, as in all time some must be rich some poore, some highe and eminent in power and dignitie; others meane and in subieccion."[2] The unequal distribution of wealth and power was the natural and proper condition of human affairs.

Winthrop's views of social order were held by ordinary people as well as by the elite. The issue before the passengers of the Winthrop fleet and the entire first generation of New England immigrants was not whether they should transplant inequality, deference, and rank, but rather what forms those values should take. The task of instituting hierarchical values was made more difficult by changing circumstances and was challenged by the New England experience. The range of wealth and privilege of the voyagers to New England did not match the extremes of the English society they had known. The youthfulness of the emigrants—only slightly more than 10 percent were as old as forty—reduced the possibilities of gray eminence. Even some of the beliefs coming from Reformed Protestantism were at odds with their wishes for hierarchy. If the authority of popes, priests, archbishops, and bishops could be questioned and if salvation was a matter between God and the individual, any hierarchical arrangement potentially was suspect. Changing circumstances and beliefs confronted traditional behavior and values.[3]

Along with his hierarchical values, Governor Winthrop transported the charter of the Massachusetts Bay Company, and he led the General Court in transforming the organization of a joint-stock company with religious purpose into the government of a colony. The governor, deputy governor, and assistants (in business parlance: the chairman, vice chairman, and board) became magistrates with executive, judicial, and legislative powers. According to the charter, freemen (the name for stockholders) were to elect officers and to participate as a legislature at four meetings a year. Because the number of freemen was small, because he wanted to broaden support of the government, and because he wished to connect government and religion, Winthrop persuaded the court to declare that any male church member could be a freeman. Although the court enlarged the number of freemen, it reduced their power by limiting their role in government to electing assistants, who in turn selected the governor and deputy governor. It expanded citizenship but consolidated authority. Winthrop was able to make these changes almost unilaterally, because he possessed the charter and did not allow others to read it.

Over time, pressures made the government more representative of the people. Less than two years after Winthrop's innovations, residents of Watertown refused to pay a tax providing for the construction of fortifications at Newtown (in 1638, it became Cambridge) because they had no voice in the decision. To eliminate the discontent, Winthrop and the other magistrates agreed that representatives of each town (called deputies) should participate in deliberations on taxation, but that was to be the extent of the deputies' involvement in government. By the annual court of election in May 1634, there were demands that deputies should participate in all legislative decisions, and there were calls from the general populace and even from fellow magistrates to make the charter public. With little choice Winthrop reluctantly revealed the document and the alterations he had made. In the tumult that followed, the court agreed that deputies should be involved in the revision and creation of all laws as well as in issues of taxation. Winthrop was rebuked, and although elected as an assistant, for the first time he did not win reelection as governor.[4] This was not the political or social order he had envisioned.

Little did he know at the time that his world was to become more topsy-turvy, and he would have been surprised in 1634 to learn that a source of much of the disruption was the Puritan minister John Cotton. Although he was so outspoken as to have been harassed from his pulpit in Boston, Lincolnshire, and forced to escape English shores, Cotton was a "meek and cautious man." Here was the paradox of his personality. He was a leading theologian and a charismatic preacher, yet he disliked controversy and sought reconciliation. In political matters, time and again he sided with the elite. Before the 1634 election when Winthrop was elected an assistant but removed as governor, Cotton preached "that a magistrate ought not to be turned into the condition of a private man without just cause." In September 1634, he supported the authority and veto power of the magistrates and in the process delineated the rights and proper place of magistrates, people, and ministry: "the strength of the magistracy to be their authority; of the people, their liberty; and of the ministry, their purity." When the town of Boston chose not to have any of its elite members appointed to the committee for distributing land in December of that same year, Cotton sided with the privileged and convinced the population to hold a second election. And yet his theology based on an all-powerful God and disdainful of human agency for salvation could be interpreted as an attack on human authority.[5]

Cotton arrived in Massachusetts Bay on 4 September 1633, and the following month was installed as teacher of the Boston church. He joined John Wilson, who was pastor of the church. Although there was a theoretical separation of responsibilities (the pastor oversaw church discipline and presided at services and sacraments while the teacher explained doctrine, provided instructional sermons, and counseled the flock), their actual efforts overlapped considerably. They worked well together, and Cotton's presence brought immediate success as evidenced by the rapid growth of the congregation. On 5 December 1633, Winthrop noted in his journal: "It pleased the Lord to give special testimony of his presence in the church of Boston, after Mr. Cotton was called to office there. More were converted and added to that church, than to all the other churches in the bay." After elaborating on Cotton's accomplishments, Winthrop, as if in afterthought not wanting to slight Wilson, penned: "Also, the Lord pleased greatly to bless the practice of discipline, wherin he gave the pastor, Mr. Wilson, a singular gift, to the great benefit of the church." To Wilson's credit, there appears to have been little rivalry—at least at first. When each of the ministers of the colony received a heifer as a gift, the longer-established Wilson gave his to Cotton; and when he returned to England in 1635 for nearly a full year, he left confident in the compatibility of their religious views.[6]

Although their theology was not absolutely identical—that would be true for all the New England ministers—their differences within the sweep of European doctrine were small indeed. Christianity as it was believed and practiced in New England was in part a manifestation of Reformed Protestantism in Europe and in part an outgrowth of the historical circumstances and culture of England and New England in the sixteenth and seventeenth centuries. Its influences came primarily from Protestant theologians throughout Europe and secondarily from Christian theology throughout the centuries, Judaism, and folk religion, yet its particular nature grew from English structures, controversies, events, and issues, as well as from the relative freedom to innovate on New England soil. Its theology may have been broadly European, but its application was aimed at English institutions and practices. As the historian Stephen

Foster reminds us, Puritanism was a movement, not a fixed set of principles.[7] But then the questions arise: What was it a movement for? What were its goals? What did it hope to accomplish?

Puritans wanted to alter human behavior to more closely follow God's law—in particular, the Ten Commandments. They were concerned with individual behavior and the moral behavior of nations. The king's closing of Parliament in 1629 helped prompt the migration of many disillusioned souls to New England; they believed that their one accessible institution for national change had been destroyed. Puritans also desired to reform religious rituals and structures so as to return to original practices as described in Scripture. They searched the Bible for evidence of the nature of the early church, and they attempted to implement their findings in their own churches. Only those who despaired of the possibility of changing the Church of England separated from it; most hoped to reform from within. Last, Puritans focused on individual, spiritual conditions, particularly salvation. They examined themselves to uncover whether they were destined to be saved, to be joined with God. In the process, they combed Scripture for guides to their religious status, and they elaborated a covenant theology.

By the early seventeenth century, Reformed Protestant theologians, particularly Puritans, concluded that God had made a series of agreements with human beings. In the first, the *covenant of works,* God had contracted with Adam. All Adam had to do to ensure eternal life for himself and his descendants was to obey God's law. His failure to do so resulted in the damnation of all humankind. If justice were to prevail, there would be no exceptions; but God in his mercy offered a testament, the *covenant of grace,* that would save a preordained few. God's gift was salvation for those who had faith in Christ.[8]

Within this broad outline, John Cotton and his fellow New England clergymen agreed. Moreover, they concurred that salvation was entirely the work of God. Human beings were incapable of earning election. Nothing people could do would influence their ultimate destiny. They each learned of their election individually through a conversion experience (called justification), and once saved, always saved. Just as people could not receive salvation as a reward, they could not lose it as a punishment. A person's behavior, whether before or after justification, had no impact on his or her eternal condition. What mattered was the spiritual union, out of which grew faith and most likely goodness (sanctification). At the very least, goodness did not produce election, but rather election could produce good behavior. To argue that humans had any causal role in their own salvation was to support the lost and now discredited covenant of works—the heresy of Arminianism.

Disagreement between the vast majority of New England clergy and Cotton and a few other ministers centered on human agency, and even then it might have been more a matter of emphasis than of substance. For one, most ministers preached that sanctification might be apparent before awareness of justification. This could be a fine line; while they didn't propose that good works without a conversion experience indicated salvation, they argued that godly behavior—even without a person being conscious of having received God's grace—could mean that the person in fact was one of the elect. Second, they argued that people had to seek faith actively before they would be justified. Human will was essential to the conversion experience and was part of the order God had established. Reading Scripture, listening to sermons, and introspection all prepared people for acquiring faith, but no human activity obligated God to offer salvation. Last, they explained that conversion was a dynamic process, not a once-and-forever event. People acquired faith and had a spiritual union, only to doubt and then acquire faith and union again, and so on. None of these theological points necessarily broke from Cotton's essential views. Although he held that preparation was unnecessary for justification, he never claimed it was unimportant; and although he reasoned that sanctification might not follow conversion, he thought it unlikely that a member of the elect would not try to obey God's law.[9]

In their sermons during the early years, the New England clergy may have emphasized—even exaggerated beyond their own beliefs—human behavior partly as a way to strengthen civil order. Traditions and institutions were not so well established as in England, and the ministers may have wanted to build a secure foundation for the fledgling colony. Cotton (a person who supported authority, Scripture, and a moral order) upon arriving in New England may have been startled by what he heard and in his sermons may have attempted to counterbalance their views, thus creating the impression of serious disagreement. Whatever the motivation of the New England ministers, members of the Boston congregation, and eventually of some other congregations as well, perceived that this was a cosmic conflict and that the souls of New Englanders were in peril.

Among John Cotton's strongest supporters was Anne Hutchinson. A former resident of Alford, Lincolnshire, she frequently had traveled the twenty miles to England's Boston to hear Cotton preach. To her mind, he spoke the truth and was an inspiration. When he was driven from England, she was distraught; and the following year she and her family— William, a well-to-do merchant, eleven of their fifteen children (three had died before the voyage, and one more was born in New England)— moved to be near him. They settled in New England's Boston, where

William continued to prosper, and Anne and William soon became members of the town's church.[10]

Women often met together on days following a Sunday sermon or a Thursday lecture to discuss what had been said and for friendship. At first, Hutchinson had kept her distance from the meetings; responding, however, to negative reactions to her absence, she began to hold discussions in her own home. She commenced each gathering by summarizing what had been preached and typically added comments of her own. In the discussions that ensued, she became a dominant force—much as had Cotton in the meetinghouse—and attendees began to direct questions to her. Her brilliance and personality attracted enthusiastic followers, and soon fifty, sixty, perhaps as many as eighty people at a time assembled at her home. These meetings proved so popular that a second meeting was held each week, this time with men present. Such conventicles long had been welcome in Puritan circles, particularly when they supported Puritan ministers and concentrated on their understanding of Scripture. But by spring 1636, something appeared to be askew. The meetings of a substantial number of members of the largest congregation in Massachusetts Bay at Mistress Hutchinson's home were becoming altogether too influential, and there were rumors that they were undermining the authority of the colony's clergy.[11]

Attending church meetings served a social as well as a religious purpose, and it was not unusual for people to visit churches other than their own, especially for Thursday lectures. They not only became acquainted with other colonists, but they also heard different perspectives on the Gospel and they made comparisons. A scholarly, ministerial nuance might be interpreted as a theological chasm or even a heresy by inquisitive, but less-educated laity. A clerical exaggeration, ambiguity, or poorly constructed phrase might be taken as a sign of the preacher's spiritual disrepair. And any real differences between clergy might be viewed as evidence of God's displeasure with New England. Members of the Boston congregation, those attending meetings at Anne Hutchinson's home, began to question whether some ministers—perhaps all but John Cotton—by emphasizing sanctification were preaching a covenant of works and whether those ministers actually had the "Seale of the Spirit."[12] Did they deserve the respect and authority they were accorded? Had they been truly saved? Were they doing the devil's work in their midst?

While John Wilson had been in England during most of 1635, such suspicions were directed at clergy outside of Boston; but after a year of listening only to John Cotton within the walls of the Boston meetinghouse, members began to wonder about the credibility of their other minister, when upon his return he sounded like all the others. A division within the Boston church was developing, with Cotton (seemingly unaware), Hutchinson, and the vast majority of the congregation on one side and Wilson and a scant few, including Winthrop, on the other.[13]

The splintering of the Boston church and the criticism of New England clergy would have been unpleasant to Massachusetts Bay authorities and worthy of addressing, but hardly threatening, had that turmoil been the only challenge. But the religious disharmony combined with the political disruption, aggravated by events in the spring of 1636, alerted many magistrates and ministers alike to the necessity of defending and fortifying their places in the hierarchy.

The train of events began in May, when for the third year in a row freemen did not elect John Winthrop as governor. Although they selected him as deputy governor, they chose Henry Vane for the most powerful position. Vane was the son of the comptroller of the king's household, charming, and bright, but he had resided in Massachusetts Bay for little more than half a year and he was only twenty-three years old. A member of the Boston church, he frequently attended meetings at Anne Hutchinson's home, and during his two years' residence in New England he lived at John Cotton's home.[14] There could be little doubt where the new governor's allegiance rested.

Cotton's political influence, which had been considerable since his arrival in New England, began to match his religious prominence. When there was the question of flying the king's colors on their fort, the magistrates sought Cotton's advice. As part of a committee of ministers and magistrates charged with drafting a body of laws for the colony, Cotton was the one who created the document.[15]

Although Cotton's growing political and religious stature must have pleased all but a few of the Boston congregation, it alarmed a number of his colleagues. Perhaps Cotton had become too powerful, for now his voice reached well beyond the Boston meetinghouse. Whenever people's beliefs or behavior were suspect, the preferred approach was for a few church officers to speak privately with them. Only after their failure to change the person would a more public meeting occur. A letter from Thomas Shepard to Cotton may have been the beginning of such a process; it is clear that he was writing not just for himself, but for "diverse of our members, whose harts are much endeared to you." Shepard, recently ordained at Newtown, delicately but pointedly posed six questions concerning Cotton's theology. His underlying concern was whether Cotton was unintentionally preaching a message that might lead to *familism*—a heresy as New England Puritans understood it that freed people who believed themselves saved from following church ordinances and obeying

God's law; in short, an excuse for licentiousness. He wanted to know Cotton's views on whether faith nullified the need for moral behavior, whether the Spirit is revealed in ways other than Scripture, and whether a person can be justified without being sanctified. Obliquely, he warned Cotton to look for heretics "(though I know none nor judge any)" who might harm his congregation and ministry.[16]

No fool, Cotton was well aware of the letter's concern and message, and he cordially but cautiously responded. He downplayed differences between himself and others and attributed them largely to misunderstandings. He denied that he had ever suggested that moral behavior was unimportant or that the Spirit was revealed other than through Scripture. Yet he made it clear that the conversion experience was the only sure sign of salvation. Sanctification was the consequence of justification, but moral behavior alone was no indicator of God's grace: "I would not wish christians to build the signes of theire Adoption upon [any] sanctification, But such as floweth from faith in christ jesus." Bristling from Shepard's reference to familism, he countered that neither he nor any member of the Boston church harbored such views. Not wishing to close on a contentious point, he thanked Shepard "for this pretious fruite of your unfeigned brotherly love" and sent salutations to the rest who had urged Shepard's letter.[17]

The second "visit" of an elder came in the form of a written exchange with Peter Bulkeley on the relationship of faith and salvation. Bulkeley argued that human agency, in this case an active faith, was critical in joining the soul with Christ. Humans did not receive grace without effort; the act of receiving complements God's act of giving. Cotton would have none of the argument. Salvation is entirely God's work for undeserving people. There is nothing a sinful human can do that will cause a conversion experience. As Cotton explained: "In this union the soule Receyveth Christ, as an empty vessell receyveth oyle: but this receyving is not active, but passive." Despite what appears to be a significant disagreement, their actual differences were smaller than their words would lead us to believe. Bulkeley did not contend that active faith caused justification or that God was obligated to reward human efforts. God had ordered stages toward salvation, and active faith was one of the steps indicating a person was on the right path. Cotton, for his part, believed that a person should participate in church services, should read and contemplate Scripture, and should pray but that none of those activities would cause salvation. Both supported the conduct of moral and spiritual lives, both believed that God alone selected the elect, and both believed the covenant of grace had replaced the covenant of works. Yet in the contentious New England air, their differences were magnified.[18]

Cotton may have had the best of the arguments in these early skir-
mishes, but he was being warned that there were consequences to his and
the Boston congregation's words. Vane might be governor, Cotton might
be the most prominent of the ministers, and the Boston congregation
might be confident, perhaps arrogant, in their light, but all human activity was temporal; all humans could be reduced in pride and power. Cotton had heard the warning. He did not capitulate, but he was on guard.
Other members of his congregation may not have been aware of the
threat. Their time would come, and soon.

The first test of will came with the propounding of John Wheelwright
as the Boston church's third minister on 23 October 1636. Wheelwright,
the "silenced" minister of the village of Bilsby, Lincolnshire, and a
brother-in-law of Anne Hutchinson, had arrived with his family the previous spring. He shared the theological views of his fellow Lincolnshire
emigrants and of nearly all of the Boston congregation. Human behavior
had no influence on God's free offering of grace. What mattered was the
joining with the Holy Spirit, to whom humans—sinners all—could make
no claims. He would be a brother to John Cotton and an offense to John
Wilson. If Wilson should leave, so much the better.

Before the congregation met on the following Sunday to confirm
Wheelwright, the ministers of the colony who were in Boston for the
meeting of the General Court conferred to discuss the dangerous views
that were being attributed to members of the Boston congregation: "1.
That the person of the Holy Ghost dwells in a justified person. 2. That no
sanctification can help to evidence to us our justification." Were their suspicions accurate, they would have to warn the church of the perils it
faced. Cotton and Wheelwright, of course, were present, and this was the
opportunity for conveying to them the displeasure of their colleagues.
Anne Hutchinson also had been invited to the meeting, apparently to ob-
serve and be warned rather than to participate. In the discussion that ensued, the beleaguered Cotton and Wheelwright tried to defuse the attack
by minimizing their differences. The ministers seemed satisfied. They had
eldered their wayward brothers. They had succeeded in bringing Cotton
and Wheelwright to acknowledge that sanctification could be a sign of
God's grace.[19] Just as important, they had sent a message to Cotton's
flock. Even their esteemed teacher could be taken to task.

Nevertheless, on 30 October, the Boston church defiantly sought to
confirm Wheelwright as one of their ministers. The New England clergy
might be imposing, but what could they do? Congregations were autonomous, and the selection of a minister was an internal decision. Only
Winthrop's refusal blocked Wheelwright's appointment.[20] And now we
can better understand what he thought was at stake when he stood alone

in the Boston meetinghouse. The issue was not whether a third minister was extravagant and unnecessary, nor whether Wheelwright was qualified. When Winthrop defied the will of the congregation, he was defending the besieged hierarchy. In his own way, he was standing for the authority of magistrates over subjects and of clergy over laity.

The confrontation, despite the words of angry neighbors, energized Winthrop. Soon, he was engaged in debate with Henry Vane. According to Winthrop's account, Vane, Hutchinson, and others held that the Holy Ghost not only dwelled within a justified person but also formed a "personal union." The implication of such a belief, known as the heresy of *antinomianism,* was that the actions of a saved person were not the person's own but rather the work of God. If that were the case, such acts were beyond the judgment of mere mortals. How could a magistrate, for example, find God's behavior unlawful? Winthrop couldn't point to any evidence of immoral or illegal acts, but to his mind the potential was there. The outcome of the battle of words, again according to Winthrop's account, was agreement that the Holy Ghost and God are the same and that God lives in a person without deifying that person.[21]

By December, Winthrop and his allies began a three-pronged attack, aimed at Vane, Cotton, and Hutchinson. Vane was finding that the heady experience of governing had lost its joy. When the December General Court convened, he surprised everyone by announcing that affairs in England required his return and that he was resigning as governor. When one of the assistants lamented his leaving, he "brake forth into tears" and confessed he was reacting to "these differences and dissensions, which he saw amongst us, and the scandalous imputations brought upon himself, as if he should be the cause of all." The court decided to accept his resignation, to adjourn for four days, and then two days later to hold an election for governor and deputy governor (should Winthrop, the current deputy governor, become governor). Before the election occurred, members of the Boston church persuaded Vane to retain his office; and so he did for the next five stormy months.[22]

The main purpose of the court session had been for the ministers to join with the magistrates and the deputies in discussing the religious disputes within and between the congregations and to find a way to resolve them. Already in Boston and with time available before the court would resume, the ministers met with Cotton at his home to pressure him once again to modify his opinions. In the course of their conversation, their attention turned to the center of lay dissension—Anne Hutchinson—and they summoned her to their meeting. Showing little restraint, the ministers questioned her about rumors that she and other members of the Boston church had said that all the ordained clergy of New England preached a covenant of works and had not undergone genuine conversion experiences and that only John Cotton preached the covenant of grace. At first, she was wary and spoke little. Whenever possible, Cotton, fearful of both his associates' wrath and his parishioner's tongue, interjected remarks, attempting to reduce the perceived differences between himself and his colleagues. Hutchinson, although she became increasingly outspoken and less intimidated, apparently never quite confirmed the rumors, despite distinctions she made between Cotton and the others.[23] Although not fully victorious, the ministers gradually were reasserting their authority and building their confidence. But their work was not yet done.

When the court returned to session, no one doubted that power had shifted. In response to some petulant remarks by Governor Vane, Hugh Peter, speaking for his fellow minister and no longer deferring to the young magistrate's authority, criticized him extensively. As if orchestrated, John Wilson then gave "a very sad speech of the condition of our churches." Earlier in the day, Cotton had delivered a sermon with his familiar theme that sanctification without prior justification was merely good work, not a sign of God's grace. Although that was common doctrine, few would miss that he was subtly suggesting that his Bay colleagues were preaching otherwise. Barely trying to disguise his anger at his congregation and his co-minister, Wilson attributed the problems and the "inevitable danger of separation" to the "new opinions risen up amongst us." He left little room for doubt about what or whose opinions these were. On that disharmonious note, the court ended its session.[24]

Wilson's speech fueled the flames of discontent within his own congregation. What had been a flanking maneuver in the attempt to add Wheelwright to the Boston ministry now became a full frontal assault. In the past, Cotton had removed himself from the fray, but now he became a participant. Perhaps the demand that he answer the sixteen questions of the Bay ministers coming at the same time that Wilson implicated him as a source of the religious turmoil pushed him to uncharacteristic action. Whatever the cause, he joined with others of the congregation in admonishing Wilson privately. Wilson defended himself by saying that the court had called for candid views; and when pressed further, he disingenuously claimed that his remarks were no more aimed at the Boston church and its members than at any of the other churches. Unsatisfied, the church "called him to answer publicly" on 31 December. Bitter charges flew, and only a few accepted Wilson's explanations. With the congregation prepared to censure Wilson, Cotton intervened and reminded the seething crowd that unanimity was necessary for such drastic action. Although Cotton gave Wilson a "grave exhortation" in front of the entire congregation, he was not willing to humiliate his fellow minister further. When a battered Wilson preached in a conciliatory fashion on the following day, even the mercurial Henry Vane congratulated him. Others were less forgiving. For most of the next year, a strange malady plagued the Boston congregation. When Wilson conducted services, church members (mostly women) suddenly found the need to rise, turn their backs, and leave the meetinghouse.[25]

Although drawn into the Wilson affair, Cotton knew he must devote most of his energy to responding to the sixteen questions. The ministers of the Bay, like water slowly dripping on a stone, persisted in their pressure. Before his standing would be worn away, he needed to reestablish his religious authority. He would modify his views where appropriate, obfuscate where necessary, and accommodate where possible, but he had not moved to New England to be silenced once again. Drawing on his years of scholarship, he would bulwark his theological principles with countless scriptural citations, and with God's help peace would return.

In their sixteen questions, the ministers expanded the six questions of Shepard's earlier letter, but they continued to stress the central theme of human agency and salvation. As Cotton interpreted the queries, his clerical opponents in Question Thirteen, on the relationship of justification and sanctification demonstrated the "greatest Agitation and Exception" to his views, and it was there he devoted the greatest attention. For all but Thirteen, he wrote no more than a short paragraph each. He staked out no new positions, but simply elaborated his well-worn theological opinions. For Question Thirteen in seven carefully worded propositions, he again argued that moral behavior without a prior conversion experience signified nothing about a person's eternal state and that to preach otherwise was to support the covenant of works.[26] Again, he implied that others were not speaking so precisely as they should by placing undue focus on human efforts.

Predictably, the Bay clergy were not satisfied with Cotton's answers, and they mustered a reply. They were wary of being associated with the covenant of works, yet they were not about to abandon a place for human activity in the cosmic drama. Although they fortified their beliefs with scriptural citations, their underlying argument was the potential consequences of Cotton's theology. If human beings had no role in acquiring faith, if godly acts did not represent a saved soul, if a person were forever saved regardless of future behavior, what was in store for Massachusetts Bay? They feared "much hypocrisie and delusion in the Churches," "a Plain forsaking of the Scriptures," and an opening to temptation and sin. Left unsaid was the concern for their own authority and their place in the hierarchy.[27]

Bruised but not defeated, Cotton had the last word in this round—in fact, thousands of words. In his rejoinder, he expanded his earlier responses and bulwarked his position with even more substantial scriptural and theological references. To compensate for what he took to be minority opinions, he used frequent citations to establish his orthodoxy.

It is He that openeth the eyes of our Understanding Ephesians 1.17.18. It is he that openeth all the mysteries of grace and of Christs kingdom to us, 1 Corinthians 2.10. It is he that openeth the Scriptures John 14.26. and 16.13. and declareth to us all the works of God in us, and about us. 1 Corinthians 2.12. 1 John 3.24. Yea Calvin is so clear in this point, That he professeth the Scriptures themselves cannot find faith to acknowledg them to be the word of God till they be sealed and confirmed to the hearts of men by the inward testimony of the Spirit Instit. 1.1. Cap. 7.§.4.[28]

God was all-powerful. Neither human works nor even Scripture had spiritual significance without God's prior intervention. Few, if any, of the clergy in Massachusetts Bay disagreed with those propositions, but context altered all. Cotton questioned whether his fellow ministers were not giving too much credit to preparation and obeying God's law, while they suspected that he might be flirting with familism. In that light, these were challenging words.

Cotton forcefully presented his views, but he was weary of the conflict. Respect, authority, power—these were welcome, and he steadfastly would stand by his principles. And yet: his fellow clergymen might be mistaken in their emphasis, but they still were men of God. His Boston congregation might be correct in their beliefs, but they might be less zealous in their expression. Now was the time to end the contention.

His first opportunity came in a fast-day sermon on 19 January 1637. The General Court had called for a day when the entire colony would seek an end to the "dissensions in our churches," and he would do his part. Before the Boston congregation, he called for the restoration of harmony.[29] At the conclusion of his remarks, he was succeeded at the pulpit by Wheelwright who could reinforce Cotton's plea for goodwill and peace. That was not to be Wheelwright's way.

Still smarting from attacks by Winthrop and the Bay clergy and lacking Cotton's subtlety, he lashed out. Taking sides almost immediately, Wheelwright explained that "the only cause of the fasting of true beleevers is the absence of Christ." People in the congregation could quickly deduce that either this fast was inappropriate and had been called by people who were not "true beleevers" or that Christ was absent. Before long, Wheelwright made clear that Christ was still present, but to keep him they must "prepare for a spirituall combate." They must fight for the Gospel, and the Gospel's meaning was clear. Jesus is "our wisdome, our righteousnes, our sanctification and our redemption," and "neither before our conversion nor after, we are able to put forth one act of true saving spirituall wisdome, but we must have it put forth from the Lord Jesus Christ, with whom we are made one." That was the covenant of grace. Those who believed they were saved "because they see some worke of sanctification in them" were misguided. That was the covenant of works. Having laid out the differences between the two covenants, Wheelwright was ready to identify the enemy: "not onely Pagonish, but Antichristian, and those that run under a covenant of works." He acknowledged that doing battle with God's enemy would "cause a combustion in the Church and comon wealth," but keeping Christ was more important. At no point did Wheelwright encourage more than a "spiritual combate," and he requested that "both in private and publike and in all our cariages and conversations, let us have a care to be holy as the Lord is holy." Neither did he identify by name who were God's enemies—but then he didn't have to. Wheelwright was challenging religious authority as he had in England. He was calling for a holy war without bloodshed.[30]

Despite Henry Vane being governor, Bay authorities no longer tolerated such behavior. Now on the offensive, they were ready to reassert their power, to reestablish what they considered proper order. As an omen of what was about to occur, the next General Court in March first censured and fined Stephen Greensmith for saying that all but a few ministers preached a covenant of works. Then onto the main business. Wheelwright was charged with sedition and contempt. Asked whether those who maintained "sanctification as an evidence of justification" were enemies of God, he agreed that was what he had said in his sermon and was what he believed. When the ministers of the colony told the court that Wheelwright's accusation applied to them, he was found guilty. Rejecting the protest of Vane and a few others, the court postponed sentencing Wheelwright until the next meeting, which to be on the safe side would be held in Newtown rather than Boston.[31] Their purpose was to change Wheelwright and to reduce his subversive influence, not to banish him. Perhaps in the interim between court meetings, he would reconsider and rejoin the brotherhood. Then they could rejoice in his redemption and welcome his return.

Wheelwright and his Boston allies apparently did not recognize how serious their troubles were. In less than a year, they had fallen from positions of power and influence to being the subjects of criminal trials. Although numerous, they still were a minority of the colony's population and except for Cotton their voices seldom carried outside of Boston. They were not in a position to irritate the political and religious elite any further, but passions were high and they could not resist a contemptuous gesture. Not even John Cotton could restrain himself from the delicious but dangerous act. When Peter Bulkeley and John Jones were ordained at Concord in

April, neither Vane, nor Cotton, nor Wheelwright, nor the two ruling elders, nor the "rest of that church, which were of any note" attended the ceremony. They were not willing to honor "legal preachers."[32]

It was a futile, if not petty, display, and only the most naive of the Boston congregation failed to realize by the election at the May General Court that the early order had returned. Governor Vane attempted to present a petition with seventy-four signatures protesting Wheelwright's conviction, but he was easily rebuffed. The election went forward, and Winthrop could feel vindicated. After three years, he returned to the governor's office. No other member of the Boston congregation was elected as a magistrate. Henry Vane, William Coddington, and Richard Dummer, to use Winthrop's phrase, "were left quite out." Angry words were exchanged, and fights erupted, but soon the tumult ended as people began to understand the consequences of the political restoration. With their leaders out of power and themselves under attack, the defeated opposition resorted to one of their last weapons—contemptuous inaction. Upon Winthrop's election, the sergeants, all members of the Boston church, "laid down their halberds" and refused to accompany him to Sunday services, as had been the tradition with previous governors.[33] The proud governor would not forget the slight.

The new government quickly displayed its power. The court told a belligerent Wheelwright that his sentencing was deferred to the next court meeting and suggested that if he would reconsider his statements it would reconsider his conviction. More threatening, it ordered that no person would be admitted to Massachusetts Bay for longer than three weeks without a magistrate's approval. That would prevent more insurgents of the Boston type from taking residence. John Cotton was so discouraged that he began to investigate moving to New Haven.[34]

Aware that he had the power to crush the opposition, Winthrop applied the alien act in July. A group of people, including a brother of Hutchinson and friends of Wheelwright, arrived from England with the intention of settling in Massachusetts Bay. Winthrop, concerned that they would bolster the dissidents, admitted them for a trial period of four months. Any resident hosting the newcomers for a more lengthy stay without a magistrate's permission would be subject to penalty. In this way, the behavior of suspected residents and newcomers alike could be monitored. Out of power, the Boston congregation could only respond with "hot speeches" and threats of leaving the colony.[35] Henry Vane had had enough. With his supporters firing rifles and cannon in farewell, the young former governor departed for England on 3 August. Proving that pettiness, at least, could be shared by all, Winthrop didn't see him off.[36]

Political and religious authorities surely celebrated Vane's removal, but Cotton's departure would be a different matter. Should he leave, supporters in England might question the wisdom of their leadership. They needed to recover Cotton's goodwill while still moderating his potentially subversive views. If they could also win back Wheelwright, so much the better. Wilson met with Cotton and Wheelwright and told them that his remarks the previous December were not directed at them but at others. He had pleaded the same point earlier in the Boston meetinghouse, but this time Cotton and Wheelwright were more forgiving. They too were prepared for reconciliation. Before the Boston congregation, Cotton went so far as to defend and pardon his co-minister. Other ministers met with their estranged colleagues, and all agreed that a synod should be held to investigate and condemn suspected heresies in the land. Although they almost agreed in the identification of eighty-two errors, there were five issues, later reduced to three (Cotton adamantly held that faith is acquired at union with Christ, that sanctification cannot be the primary evidence of justification, and that justification is freely given by Christ and is not the consequence of human efforts to acquire faith), that seemingly divided them. Those could be resolved at the synod.[37]

When the synod began on 30 August, Cotton and Wheelwright soon found themselves caught between competing forces. On the one side, the ministers, clearly in charge, pressed for unanimous condemnation of the eighty-two heresies and for agreement on all unresolved issues. On the other side, representatives of the Boston congregation, belligerent to all but their two favorite ministers and clearly outsiders, expected their loyalty to be returned and their beliefs to be supported. As the deliberations proceeded, Cotton conveniently found for "the first time of my discerning a real and broad difference, between the judgments of our Brethren (who leaned to Mistris *Hutchinson*) and my self." Pulling them aside, he told them of his concern and scolded them for not having discussed "these Bastardly Opinions" openly before the congregation prior to their being selected as representatives. Cotton feared that his and the congregation's reputation would be tarnished.[38]

Perhaps hurt by their leader's rebuke and perhaps sullen because of his seeming abandonment of them, some of the Boston contingent withdrew from the synod and the others thereafter remained silent. For his part, Cotton reiterated his well-known beliefs, often in the face of heated opposition, but ultimately he and the other ministers worked out wording ambiguous enough that all could agree. Not quite defeated but certainly compromised, the embattled Cotton removed his objections to the three issues. He also supported a series of resolutions intended to defuse the Boston congregation and their like: women could meet in small groups but not in large assemblies; lay members were to ask questions in church only with the approval of church elders and they were forbidden to challenge religious authorities; a person could be censured although absent; and church members with a differing opinion, "which was not fundamental," should continue to participate in all services. It had taken a year and a half, but now the Bay clergy could reclaim their eminent colleague. John Wheelwright, however, remained outside the fold. He had attempted to find a common understanding, but he could compromise no further, even when it meant jeopardizing his mortal self.[39] From then on, as far as the ministers were concerned, he was on his own.

Heedlessly, Wheelwright continued to preach the distinction between the covenant of works and the covenant of grace so as to stigmatize most Bay clergy: Hutchinson continued to hold meetings as before, and members of the Boston congregation continued to leave the meetinghouse when Wilson conducted services. The magistrates, led by Winthrop, in full fury and unrestrained power chose to end the disruption. In their minds, they had offered an olive branch, and it had been rejected.[40] At the General Court, beginning on 2 November, they unleashed their force.

The court decided to begin with the signers of the March petition in support of Wheelwright. Immediately conspicuous was William Aspinwall, one of Boston's deputies. When he refused to disavow the petition, he was dismissed as deputy. One of the other Boston deputies, John Coggeshall, rose in protest. Although he had not signed the petition, he agreed with it and therefore he should be dismissed as well. The court obliged him. The last of the Boston deputies, William Coddington, seeing the futility of Coggeshall's remarks, went to the heart of the matter and moved that the court reverse its judgment against Wheelwright. Recognizing that their approach was not changing behavior, the magistrates summoned Wheelwright to appear before them.[41]

They gave him one last chance to recant, but Wheelwright stood firm. He retorted that "hee had committed no sedition nor contempt, hee had delivered nothing but the truth of Christ, and for the application of his doctrin it was by others, and not by him, &c." The problem, according to the magistrates, was not so much his doctrine as the impact on the people of his implying that most of the ministers preached a covenant of works and were therefore "enemies to Christ." Before he had expressed his subversive opinions, there had been peace in the land, but now "all things are turned upside down among us." The grounds for church admission were reversed. Wives were disagreeing with husbands "till the weaker give place to the stronger." Ministers were being rebuked. There were civil disturbances at all levels. The distribution of land and tax rates were being challenged. The turmoil had gone so far that even sergeants refused to attend the governor. Despite efforts to convince him of his errors, he had remained intransigent. With light fading, the court postponed sentence until the following day.[42]

Still defiant, Wheelwright arrived late. When asked why sentence should not be imposed, he stated that "no sedition or contempt [had been] proved against him," and he challenged the court to offer evidence that he had called magistrates and ministers "enemies to Christ." Except for a few deputies who spoke in his behalf, the court was unmoved. They disfranchised Wheelwright and, when he declined to leave voluntarily, banished him. He countered that he would appeal to the king, and he refused to provide security "for his quiet departure." After spending a night in the custody of the marshall, the next morning he withdrew his appeal and posted bond. If he would agree not to preach, he could stay in the colony until the end of winter. When he didn't accede, the court ordered him to leave within fourteen days.[43]

With Wheelwright out of the way, the magistrates called John Coggeshall to account for his earlier outburst. Seeing what the magistrates might do, Coggeshall pulled back. Although he still defended Wheelwright, he explained that overwork had made him irritable. Impressed with his submissiveness, the court ("though a great part of the Court did encline to a motion for his banishment") stopped at his disfranchisement. William Aspinwall must not have been paying attention. The court had intended only to disfranchise him as well, but he continued so unbending and contemptuous that he was banished.[44]

The way was cleared for Anne Hutchinson, who now was required to appear before the court. The magistrates apparently planned only to humble her, to reduce her pride, to break her spirit—not to remove her from the colony. She was to be made an example to the others, and her fall would reassert the authority of clergy over laity, magistrates over subjects, and men over women. The order that had been turned upside down would be restored. As her trial would prove, she was not a willing victim; like Wheelwright and Aspinwall, she would not play the role expected of her.

Winthrop, as governor, presided, and he initiated the interrogation. He accused her of being among "those that have troubled the peace of the commonwealth and the churches here." She had promoted opinions that were the source of the turmoil, she was a friend and ally of the men who had just been censured, she had undermined the churches and the ministers of the colony, and she had conducted meetings with women after the court had declared them "not tolerable nor comely in the sight of God nor fitting for your sex." Her choices, the governor warned, were to repent and return to the fold or to maintain her "erroneous way" and be banished. Pointedly, Winthrop asked her whether she supported Wheelwright's fast-day sermon and the petition.[45]

Rather than answer her interrogator's question, Hutchinson demanded to know what law she had broken. This was not in Winthrop's script. She was supposed to be submissive before authority and to answer inquiries directly and meekly, and he was supposed to be in charge, not on the defensive against her insolent attack. After a few weak responses, the flustered Winthrop finally charged her with breaking the Fifth Commandment, by not honoring her parents—by extension, the magistrates and ministers. Hutchinson denied it, and after a short flurry of exchanges, Winthrop in exasperation exclaimed: "We do not mean to discourse with those of your sex but only this; you do adhere unto them and do endeavour to set forward this faction and so you do dishonour us." Changing the subject, the governor challenged by what right she held her weekly meetings. Hutchinson retorted that such meetings had been in practice before she arrived in Massachusetts Bay and that hers broke no laws. More exchanges followed, and it became clear that Winthrop was overmatched. At one point he resorted to the claim that families were being neglected, because women were spending too much time in meetings. Even his fellow magistrates realized such exaggerations weakened their case. To relieve the struggling governor, they interjected questions and remarks and attempted to break the accused's defenses.

They shifted to what they hoped was a more successful topic. Hadn't Mrs. Hutchinson disparaged the ministers by saying that they "preached a covenant of works, and only Mr. Cotton a covenant of grace"? Here she was on less firm ground, and she had to choose her words carefully. She never said they "preached nothing but a covenant of works." Just because one preaches a covenant of grace more clearly than the others does not mean that the others preach a covenant of works. She may have said that some were "not able ministers of the new testament," but statements made in private are different from public testimony. Seeing an opening, the Reverend Hugh Peter requested permission to speak. Recognizing the impropriety of divulging remarks made in a private conference, Peter rationalized that the good of the colony overruled his desire to protect confidences. He then revealed the conference the ministers had had with Hutchinson at Cotton's home the previous December. According to Peter, she had said that Cotton preached a covenant of grace and the others a covenant of works, that they were not able ministers of the New Testament, and that they had not "the seal of the spirit." Hutchinson denied Peter's testimony. Other ministers spoke out in support of Peter's account, and she argued in return that they were inaccurate. At that impasse, the trial ended for the day.

Winthrop opened the court the following morning with a review of the charges and the evidence the ministers provided. Hutchinson countered that the clergy spoke out of self-interest, and she requested that they testify under oath. This was a serious matter, for an oath would require the ministers to speak more precisely than they were willing or, perhaps, were able. They wanted to silence her voice, to remove her influence—yet could they be sure what she had said? There could be no doubt of her hostility, but she was clever. Had she spoken the exact words they had attributed to her? The ensuing debate began to raise doubts not only in the minds of spectators but also of some of the assistants.

Short of forcing the ministers to take oaths, Hutchinson was allowed to present her own witnesses, John Coggeshall, Thomas Leverett, and John Cotton. Coggeshall, who already had suffered before the court, quickly was intimidated into silence, but Leverett, ruling elder of the Boston church, was bolder. He remembered at the December conference that Hutchinson had said Cotton's colleagues "did not preach a covenant of grace so clearly as [he]." Everyone present realized what a different cast that put on the ministers' recollections. To claim that the ministers preached a covenant of works was seditious in the context of Wheelwright's sermon, but to compare who was clearer on the covenant of grace (regardless of hidden messages) was a matter of judgment, not subversion.

The cautious Cotton began with a disclaimer that not expecting to be called as a witness he had not refreshed his memory, and he warily trod between the two camps. As Cotton recalled, he was uncomfortable with the comparisons Hutchinson had made. She had told the ministers, "You preach of the seal of the spirit upon a work and he upon free grace without a work or without respect to a work, he preaches the seal of the spirit upon free grace and you upon a work." Cotton remarked that his associates were not offended at the time; some even had their concerns removed, but soon afterward some remarked that "they were less satisfied than before." Gaining courage, he concluded, "I must say that I did not find her saying they were under a covenant of works, nor that she said they did preach a covenant of works." Under examination by the magistrates and fellow ministers, Cotton defended his parishioner. When asked by the deputy governor, Thomas Dudley, whether Hutchinson had said the clergy "were not able ministers of the new testament," Cotton simply replied: "I do not remember it." Point by point, Cotton had undermined the ministers' version of the conference. Without evidence, was it possible that the case against Mrs. Hutchinson would disintegrate? Might she be exonerated?

Who knows what was going through Anne Hutchinson's mind at the time? For whatever reason—exhaustion, exhilaration, relief, vindication—she decided to unburden herself. Earlier she had experienced a period of confusion, but God had led her to see the truth from a passage in Scripture. Since then she had understood "those which did not teach the new covenant had the spirit of antichrist, and upon this he [God] did discover the ministry unto me and ever since." Although she might be derogating New England's own, she carefully avoided direct confrontation. Struck by the possibility of an opening, Increase Nowell inquired how she knew it was God who guided her. The now-confident Hutchinson shot back: "How did Abraham know that it was God that bid him offer his son, being a breach of the sixth commandment?" Thomas Dudley coaxed, "By an immediate voice." And Hutchinson triumphantly uttered, "So to me by an immediate revelation." There, she had said it, as all around her knew. "How! an immediate revelation," shouted Dudley, as his blood quickened. She was wandering onto dangerous ground, but there was no stopping her. She gave additional examples of how God had revealed himself to her; but still within the bounds of orthodoxy, she showed how each revelation had come through the vehicle of Scripture. And then, she unleashed her outrage at the proceedings with a malediction and a warning: "if you go on in this course you begin you will bring a curse upon you and your posterity, and the mouth of the Lord hath spoken it."

This outburst was no longer acceptable revelation. She had crossed the divide between understanding God's way as revealed through Scripture and the claim that God was foretelling concrete, human events. The magistrates pressed her to confirm what they thought they had heard, and much to their delight she complied, telling them she expected to be saved from them by a miracle. Cotton tried to save her by distinguishing between types of revelations—miracles that occur outside natural phenomena and without scriptural guidance and insights into the future provided by Scripture and God's providence. Cuing Hutchinson to a way out of her self-imposed trap, he asked her which type she meant. Although she responded, "By a providence of God I say I expect to be delivered from some calamity that shall come to me," it was too late.[46]

The magistrates finally had caught her, and despite the objections of two of their number (both members of the Boston church) they were not about to let her escape. For procedural reasons, two of the ministers took the oath and seconded Peter's version of the December conference. All that was left was the formality of the magistrates' vote. Found "unfit for our society," Anne Hutchinson was banished. She was to remain in custody as a prisoner at the home of Joseph Weld in Roxbury "till the court shall send you away."

With the exhausting trials of Wheelwright and Hutchinson concluded, the court adjourned for a week. Upon its return, it set out to finish dismantling its opposition. Winthrop got his revenge when two of the Boston sergeants, William Balston and Edward Hutchinson, were disfranchised and fined. Thomas Marshall, "the Ferry-man," was disfranchised and deprived of his position. William Dinely, disfranchised. William Dyer, disfranchised. Richard Gridley, "an honest poore man, but very apt to meddle in publick affaires," disfranchised. Captain John Underhill was disfranchised and removed from his military office. It was no coincidence that three of this group were military officers. The magistrates were taking no chances that an armed uprising would occur. Taking additional precautions, they transferred the colony's powder and weapons from Boston to Newtown and Charlestown, safely across the Charles, and they ordered all who had signed the Wheelwright petition to turn in their arms. Rather than relinquish their weapons and fearing further reprisals, nearly fifty men asked to have their names removed from the petition or claimed that they had not signed the petition in the first place.[47] At least for the time, the original order reigned triumphant.

But their work wasn't quite done. Two or three members of the Roxbury church, who had signed the petition and refused to recant their views, were excommunicated.[48] The Boston church, intimidated, defenseless, and now severely divided, provided the setting and the occasion for the final event—the church trial of Anne Hutchinson.

Ordinarily, church proceedings, such as the admission of new members and the censuring of old, followed a congregational model. The congregation, led by its elders, conducted the meeting and decided what should be done. In this case, ministers from throughout the colony provided their weighty presence. The purpose of such church trials was not to punish the offender but to restore her or his vision of God's truth. Repentance and return rather than retribution was the goal.[49]

During the period of Hutchinson's imprisonment, various ministers had visited her. Perhaps they had meant to counsel her, but at her trial they testified of new heresies she was advocating. Not only did she hold to her opinion of immediate revelation, but now she asserted that souls were mortal, that sanctification was no evidence of justification under any circumstances, that justified people were not required to follow the law (the Antinomian heresy), and other related errors. Hutchinson rebuked the ministers for revealing private conversations and defended her views. By the end of the day, there was a call for the vote of the congregation. When two members, Edward Hutchinson and Thomas Savage (Hutchinson's son and son-in-law), disagreed that she should be censured, they were admonished and thereby removed from the proceedings. Unanimity was achieved.

John Cotton gave the formal admonition. Working his way back into the good graces of his fellow ministers, he thanked them for their assistance, and he warned the congregation, particularly its women members, to return to orthodoxy. They should not be seduced by Hutchinson, "for you see she is but a Woman and many unsound and dayngerous principles are held by her." Although Cotton praised her for the good she had done, he rebuked her for the dangerous consequences of her erroneous beliefs. Before he could impose the censure, Hutchinson requested that she might comment. Shaken and emotionally spent, she pleaded: "All that I would say is this that *I did not hould any of thease Thinges before my Imprisonment.*" Sorry that he had not discerned and curtailed this drift into heresy, Cotton completed the admonition. Her old nemesis, John Wilson, then required her to return the next Thursday for further inquiry and the opportunity to renounce her opinions.[50]

A week apparently brought about significant change. Gone was the defiant Hutchinson; instead a defeated and submissive person entered the Boston meetinghouse. When presented with a list of new and previously charged heresies, she recanted. Reading from a paper (possibly suggested by Cotton), she renounced views she had defended the previous week, one by one.[51] The ministers were skeptical. These changes were too good to be true, and she had been reading rather than speaking extemporaneously. Why should they believe her now? To allay all concerns, Cotton asked her to clarify what she used to believe and what she currently believed. No longer willing to play the game, Hutchinson answered, "My Judgment is not altered though my Expression alters."

With that admission, there was little Cotton could do for her, and he gave up trying. Her views remained the same, and all could see her repentance was a ruse. She had lied, and her excommunication from the church was inevitable. Before John Wilson could cast her out, Hugh Peter, addressing Hutchinson, disclosed why she and her party posed such a threat: "I would commend this to your Consideration that you have stept out of your place, *you have rather bine a Husband than a Wife and a preacher than a Hearer, and a Magistrate than a Subject.* And soe you have thought to carry all Thinges in Church and Commonwealth, as you would and have not bine humbled for this." With that message lingering, Hutchinson was excommunicated. Soon after, she and her family, and others adamant in their beliefs, left for Rhode Island.

Neither Cotton, nor Wheelwright, nor Hutchinson, nor any of the others had posed a danger to the survival of Massachusetts Bay. They were not robbing or murdering or jeopardizing the charter. They did not mount the barricades, nor is there any evidence they intended to—despite precautions taken by the magistrates. What they threatened was the authority of the standing order, the hierarchy. As Hugh Peter indicated, people were not staying in their place. They were upsetting the proper order of the government, the church, and the family. Their religious beliefs irritated the ministry, but their lack of deference and respect for their betters and their direct challenge to the legitimacy of the clergy were what prompted the reaction. Pressure was placed on Cotton so that he would moderate views that were instigating insolence. Wheelwright was banished because of his assault on ministerial authority, not because of his doctrine. Hutchinson was banished and excommunicated, because she did not accept her place as a church member or as a woman and she was encouraging others to act similarly.

The termination of the Antinomian controversy reestablished the early political leadership and established a religious orthodoxy in Massachusetts Bay, but that orthodoxy should not be viewed as *the* belief system of New Englanders in general. There simply were too many exceptions, and Puritanism as a form of Reformed Protestantism held the seeds of its own subversion. The belief in salvation being individual and being dependent exclusively on God's grace, intentionally or not, challenged all authority but God's, and the insistence on the individual's role in reading Scripture as a way of understanding God's will bred proliferation of sects and diversity rather than unity. Winthrop and others may have stopped the flood of Antinomians, but they were unable to prevent the fragmentation that was inherent in their own beliefs.[52] They won the battle but ultimately lost the war.

Immediately after 1638, people who held beliefs in conflict with the Bay Colony's orthodoxy had the choice of keeping their views private or moving to more tolerant areas, such as Rhode Island and northern New England. Otherwise they faced prosecution and possibly—as happened to Quakers in the late 1650s—whipping or execution. Even so, a variety of spiritists, millenarians, Baptists, and Quakers made their presence known. Particularly irritating and embarrassing to orthodox Puritans was the breaking away of such prominent individuals as Charles Chauncey, president of Harvard College, and William Pynchon, magistrate and near ruler of western Massachusetts. Such dissenters remained a minority of the New England population, much smaller in number than Puritan church members (who themselves were a minority), but they helped shape the religious culture of the region.[53]

As the century progressed, the orthodox leadership reluctantly but continually allowed greater public religious diversity. After 1664 when New Haven colony was absorbed by Connecticut and Massachusetts Bay enlarged its criteria for freemanship, nowhere in New England was church membership required for active citizenship. In 1665 the first Baptist church in Massachusetts Bay was established in Charlestown. By the end of the century, new charters issued by the British Crown provided for religious toleration, and royally appointed governors

worshiped as Anglicans. For a short period of time, the congregation of
the Puritan South Church had to share its meetinghouse space with Anglican communicants.[54]

* * *

Even among members of Puritan churches, there was not complete agreement, and tension between clergy and laity over their respective power
became more typical than not. The church at Wenham was but one example of such strain. When the town of Wenham separated from Salem,
it soon grew large enough to justify having its own church, which was
gathered in 1644. Approval of the church and its core members as well as
the ordination of their minister, John Fiske, was achieved without difficulty. The first substantial issue to determine was the admission of new
members. Following the lead of most of the other Massachusetts Bay
congregations, they decided on limiting membership to "visible saints."[55]

When people sought admission, they initially met with a screening
committee composed of the minister and a layperson. With no personal
animosity directed toward Fiske, the Wenham congregation agreed that
"it would be neither safe, comfortable, or honorable" for the pastor to
select prospective members by himself. Esdras Read, the church deacon,
was elected by vote to represent the congregation. In later years, the
growing church designated two of their number to join Fiske in the
screening. The committee expected the candidate to have sinned and
doubted (descriptions of lives free from temptation, indiscretions, and
bad decisions would be viewed suspiciously), to have repented genuinely,
and to be living a moral life. The person should hold orthodox religious
opinions. Most important, the person must be able to relate a conversion
experience. Good behavior and orthodoxy might be sufficient for presbyterians, but congregationalists required detailed testimony of a person's
receiving God's grace. If there were any problems (a conflict with a neighbor, an unclear expression of faith), the committee would work privately
with the candidate and attempt to overcome them. In these cases, post-
ponement was a certainty, rejection a possibility. If all was satisfactory,
the committee propounded the person to the congregation for membership. The minister could prevent a person's being propounded, as could
the lay members of the committee, but no person could become a member without the congregation's consent. No one claimed that the pastor
was just another church member, yet few were willing to acquiesce in the
minister making decisions unilaterally.[56]

After the committee recommended the candidate to the congregation,
individual members had the opportunity to object. Private concerns, almost always connected with personal conflict or questionable behavior,

were brought to the committee's attention, and, if possible, were worked out privately. Church members as a body discussed issues of public knowledge. Perhaps the person had a reputation of excessive drinking or had given birth only five months after being married. Had the person repented and changed? If so, all was well.

The next stage was for the person on a Sunday afternoon after lecture to relate before the congregation his or her spiritual development. For the faint of heart, this was a daunting prospect, and the minister would read a timid person's testimony. For others, this was that rare moment when, within the context of their spiritual pilgrimage, they could express their religious views in front of an assembly of their friends and neighbors inside the meetinghouse. There might be other occasions for men, such as a debate over church policy or during a church trial, but for women the conversion narrative was the only opportunity to speak publicly in the meetinghouse. Some congregations had the minister read for all of their prospective women members. The Wenham congregation deliberated on whether women would be allowed to speak for themselves. Someone objected that Scripture forbade women's preaching, for "such a speaking argues power." Another pointed out that women were not to ask questions in public but rather to refrain until in the privacy of their own homes they could ask their husbands. In response, a member of the congregation acknowledged that questions were also a form of power, but defended women's voices in the conversion narrative on the basis that they would be judged. Despite issues of power and patriarchy, this argument along with the corollary that the congregation could better evaluate a person speaking for herself decided the issue. Only on these occasions could women speak in the meetinghouse. However, in 1656 the Wenham congregation (after they had moved to Chelmsford and with others formed a new church) reversed the decision; John Fiske thereafter read women's relations. By 1660, some men had their narratives read as well.[57]

The last stage for admission was for the candidate to express orthodox religious doctrine. Should any member of the church require greater clarification, he would pose questions at that time. And then the congregation voted. They never rejected anyone at Wenham or Chelmsford.[58] Although they hoped to admit only people who were among the elect of God, they understood that an occasional hypocrite would join them; it was better to admit a hypocrite who would be placed under church discipline than to turn away a true believer whose presentation was weak.

Simultaneous to deciding the procedure for admitting new members, the Wenham church had to develop a policy for people transferring membership from other churches. Many in their community already had been judged by their peers elsewhere and been found worthy. Now that they had taken residence in Wenham and been dismissed from their previous churches, must they undergo the admission process once again? Letters of dismission and recommendations from their minister and congregation were important, but not enough. Concluding that they must "judge by our own light and not others," the Wenham church applied the requirement of a conversion narrative before the congregation for people who sought to transfer membership as well as for new members. Most of the transfers as well as the original core group came from the Salem church, and they understood and approved each other's ways.[59]

The practices of the Newbury church were different, and they presented problems for people who wished to transfer from that congregation. Their admission requirements did not include a testimony of having received grace; only good behavior and agreeing to abide by the church covenant were needed. Of course, as they would have to testify at Wenham regardless of previous affiliation, that difference hardly mattered. The issue was that the Newbury church flirted with presbyterian ways. The ministers had exclusive authority over admitting members, and the church was more hierarchical than the congregational norm. When the Newbury clergy sent a letter of dismission, for example, they did so in their own names—not as representatives of the congregation—and they addressed their missive to John Fiske alone. The elite approach offended the jealous and independent-minded Wenham lay leaders and apparently Fiske. Rather than turn their resentment into a public quarrel, they decided to act as if no letter had been sent and to inquire discreetly of other churches what they were doing. Ultimately, they interpreted the offending letter as de facto dismission, and the former Newbury members were allowed to participate in Wenham's admission process. When Fiske informed the Newbury church of what had transpired, he carefully addressed the letter to "the reverend and beloved, the elders and brethren of the church at Newbury," and following his signature wrote: "in the name and with the consent of the church."[60] Church governance was a balance of clerical leadership and lay participation and consent. The easiest way for a minister to generate lay hostility was to forget that equation.

* * *

Most of New England—specifically the colonies of Connecticut, Massachusetts Bay, New Haven, and Plymouth—required all residents of towns, whether church members or not, to contribute to the support of their minister and church. Even so, many people chose not to become members. Perhaps they didn't believe that they had received God's grace or they didn't wish to testify and risk rejection by an assembly of friends and neighbors or their beliefs diverged from those of their town's church or they were apathetic or they didn't want to be subject to church discipline. There could be a multitude of obstacles to joining a church. Yet a substantial number of the first generation of English migrants endured the process of investigation, testimony, and congregational voting and emerged as visible saints. For some, the process itself was part of the attraction. Here was the opportunity to speak publicly. And there were rewards of membership. A person could participate and worship within a community of fellow believers and was recognized by the entire town as one of the elect. The sacrament of the Lord's Supper was open only to church members, as was the right to vote in church affairs. There also was one prominent family benefit: members could have their children baptized, and those children through baptism became members, though without the privileges of taking communion or voting. Everyone expected that when the children became adults they in turn would relate their own conversion experiences and thus gain full rights of membership.[61]

By the late 1640s it became clear that such expectations were not being realized. Adult offspring were marrying and having their own children and yet were not taking the final step toward full membership. When they sought to have their own children baptized, they forced New England's Puritan churches to choose between lineage and purity. Ministers such as Richard Mather argued that baptism was not an integral part of salvation and that since there were no scriptural prohibitions children of the baptized children of the elect should be allowed to be baptized. At the very least, the ritual would place the grandchildren of the saints under church discipline and guidance, and their parents would have to renew their commitment to the church covenant. Mather and others must have noted that during the 1650s church membership was lagging. This innovation might resuscitate religious fervor.[62]

Other ministers, such as John Davenport, were not convinced. Even if they would gain more members, the cost would be too high. Their purpose was to match as closely as humanly possible the visible saints and the visible church with the invisible saints and the invisible church. Only God was infallible and only he could differentiate between the saved and the unsaved. Human churches might admit the occasional hypocrite, but they should strive for perfect selection. To Davenport's way of thinking, there were true members (those who had conversion experiences) and there were secondary members (those who were baptized children of true members). Only the elect were entitled to have their children baptized. The purity of the church should not be diluted further.[63]

In 1662 a synod of the ministers and church representatives of Massachusetts Bay took place, and their achievement has since been called the "half-way covenant." The synod recommended that baptized children of the elect, on the condition they owned their church's covenant, be allowed to have their own children baptized. Without a religious conversion, related to a congregation and accepted, neither parent nor child could partake in the Lord's Supper or vote in church matters. They were half-way members, recognized constituents of the religious community but not full participants. The vast majority of New England ministers agreed with the synod. Some already had persuaded their congregations to adopt the practice. With only a handful of exceptions, the remaining clergy set out to introduce the proposal to their churches.[64]

They must have anticipated some objections, similar to those voiced by their skeptical colleagues. Over time, however, all but their most determined brethren had changed their minds. Surely their congregations would do the same, particularly when they understood that the half-way covenant would extend the religious ties of their families another generation. Old family members of the church certainly would welcome bringing their own grandchildren into the fold. As in most human affairs, it was not so simple. Self-interest may be expressed in a variety of ways.

From the time the innovation was first suggested and throughout the 1650s, 1660s, and 1670s, the chief opponents were lay members of the churches. As late as 1672, a decade after the synod, less than half of Massachusetts Bay's churches had adopted the practice, and even those that had, seldom used it. It is understandable that there would have been resistance to change. But why was there such a division between clergy and laity? By 1662, almost all of the ministers supported extended baptism, but well into the 1670s and even later a substantial number of church members opposed its adoption. The half-way covenant enlarged church membership; it reinforced familial self-interest.[65] Why then were lay members so more adamantly resistant to this change than were the ministers?

There is no reason to believe that laity were more committed to the purity of church practice than were their clergy. Their differences, most likely, were more personal than theological. It is possible that a veteran mentality—"if we had to testify about our conversion experience, so should you"—may have been present, for only members who had undergone investigation, testimony, and acceptance could vote. Age may have been closely related. Church members from the first generation of migrants had a stake in the New England way of admission. They were its creators and defenders. As long as they were alive, there were people arguing for what had become traditional practice. Even as their numbers dwindled and their churches adopted the half-way covenant, their presence may have discouraged younger generations from presenting their children for baptism. By way of contrast, in newly established churches and in churches with presbyterian leanings, the half-way covenant was much more readily approved and used than in older churches with strong congregational views.[66] But still, most of these possible explanations could have been applied to clergy. Ministers had a stake in the New England tradition of admission and baptism, they and their families were veterans of the process, those with presbyterian leanings had long supported more open admissions, and younger clergy were more apt to welcome change than were their older colleagues.

A clue to why laity were more opposed to the half-way covenant than were clergy comes from a report of the deputies of the Massachusetts Bay General Court in 1670. They accused the ministers of "declension from the primitive foundation worke, innovation in doctrine & worship, opinion & practise, & invasion of the rights, liberties, & priviledges of churches . . . to the utter devastation of these churches." Most of these charges had a familiar ring. For two decades, ministerial opponents of extended baptism had been warning that such a practice broke from the early Christian church and was an unwarranted innovation. What they hadn't commented on was the "invasion of the rights, liberties, & priviledges of churches."[67]

This was the threat of the half-way covenant to lay power. Although it was a seemingly small change and although full membership still required the relation of a conversion experience and the acceptance of the congregation, the half-way covenant reduced the role of church members in the admission process and proportionately enlarged the role of the clergy. Should a minister convince a congregation to adopt the half-way covenant, other changes might soon follow. People who had not been baptized might be allowed to own the covenant and to have their children baptized. Presbyterian admission practices, such as in Newbury, where only a moral life and declaring support of church doctrine was required for admission and where the ministers were solely in charge of the admission process, might replace congregational ways. Those alterations already could be seen in some of the churches of the Connecticut River valley. Perhaps it wasn't a coincidence that the Chelmsford church adopted the half-way covenant and restricted women's testimony to written form read by the minister before the congregation within the same twelve-month period. The half-way covenant overturned what had become traditional practice but also provided a wedge for increased clerical authority.

The ghost of the unrest of the 1630s could never quite be buried. Following the deputies' report in 1670, the ministers once again used their influence to restore order, and at the next election new deputies replaced those who had challenged the increased power of the clergy. As in 1638, however, this was a temporary victory.[68] Wherever there was congregational autonomy and wherever the radical possibilities of Reformed Protestantism appeared, new ideas, new sects, and disdain for established authority emerged.

* * *

Although Puritans formed the most numerous, influential, and powerful religious sect, "Puritanism" is too restrictive a term for describing the religious beliefs of the general population: paradoxically, it lacks the precision it implies. Those who were members of Puritan churches were a minority of the population, and even among themselves there were splits in doctrine and in intensity of belief. Despite Philip Gura's efforts to combine dissenting sects and the orthodoxy of Massachusetts Bay within the folds of Puritanism, we are better off using a generalization with less baggage and broader applicability. That is not to abandon the importance of Puritanism within New England culture but rather to enlarge our understanding of the breadth of religious beliefs. Better to use a different term, such as Reformed Protestantism, and to identify the common beliefs.[69]

Reformed Protestantism's umbrella sheltered Congregationalists and Presbyterians, as well as Baptists, Quakers, Dutch Reformed, some Anglicans, and members of a variety of small sects. These men and women wanted to restore the structure and rituals of the early Christian church. They wished to remove the intermediaries between God and themselves. Most believed that ministers and Scripture assisted the person to understand God's grace. All agreed that salvation ultimately was a matter exclusively between God and the individual. They were evangelical and, by seeking to convert people to their beliefs, produced conflict. They were moralistic, as they attempted to obey God's law, and reformist as they tried to convince and sometimes coerce others to do the same.

Religious beliefs reinforced hierarchical views. The world was composed of rulers and subjects, leaders and followers, wealthy and poor, clergy and laity, masters and servants, husbands and wives, parents and children, eminent and lowly. That was God's intent. That was God's order. Yet those religious beliefs also were subversive. The Reformed Protestant insistence on salvation being individual, intentionally or not, challenged all authority but God's. It led to sectarian proliferation, questioning of clerical interpretation, attacks on political leadership, and demands for written laws, social mobility, and equal rights. New England in the seventeenth century was caught between those forces. There was a tension between a traditional hierarchy and an emerging individualism.

≈ 4 ≈

THE EMINENT AND THE MEAN

Social Stratification, Status, and Power

At least the meetinghouse built at New Haven in 1640 provided a better setting for holding services than outdoors or in Robert Newman's barn as had been the practice for the first two years of settlement. But even after expending £500 for construction, William Andrews built a structure constantly in need of repair. Perhaps he used lumber that hadn't aged properly or perhaps he was in too big a hurry to complete the job. Whatever the cause, workmen frequently reported back to the town that the shoring of posts and other corrections were desperately needed. In 1657, they cautioned that timbers were so rotten that even with maintenance the meetinghouse would last no more than four to six years longer. Even so, New Haven's first public building stood for another decade before it finally was replaced.[1]

Built for public meetings of all types—not just religious services—the New Haven meetinghouse of 1640 looked little like what we now take to be a quintessential New England church. The largest meetinghouse of its time, it was a squat fifty feet square. It had a hip roof topped by a railed platform for watches and a bell tower. There were drafty casement windows at first; but in 1651 the glass was removed and replaced with tight-fitting boards against cold winters, and the space was left empty for fresh air on hot, humid summer days.[2]

A raised pulpit with stairs, located in front of the wall opposite the entry door, dominated the inside of the building. There were no pews—they would wait for late in the century—but rather hard benches that stuffed the interior. "Long benches" directly in front of the pulpit were divided by the main aisle and surrounded by other aisles, with women to the right and men to the left. Cross benches, again with women to the right and men to the left, were on both sides of the pulpit and perpendicular to the long benches. Various configurations of side and rear benches crowded the remainder of the interior. To accommodate a growing population, a balcony was added in the 1660s.[3]

Most of the adult members of the community were assigned individual seats. In addition, benches were designated for soldiers next to the door, for "scollers" (those attending school), and for "boys and youth," and there were general benches for unassigned adults and girls. Young children sat on the pulpit steps and anywhere else they could find space. Infants and toddlers most likely squirmed on parents' laps. Despite requirements that everyone attend religious services, it is unlikely that the meetinghouse provided room for all townspeople simultaneously assembled. In 1656, some 130 men and 106 women had assigned seats. Six years later following a new seating, those numbers had grown to 132 men and 114 women. Following the construction of the balcony, the 1668 seating listed spaces for 165 men. The seating of women had not been completed when the town records published the list of men, and whenever the seating committee finished its sensitive work it neglected to publicize its decisions in the town records.[4] How much space remained on the limited general benches is not known.

The seating of the population was serious business: it publicly placed people according to their status. An assigned seat fine-tuned the social stratification of the community (in general, the closer the seat to the pulpit, the higher the status of its occupant), but an unassigned seat sent a message as well. The sermons and lectures of John Davenport sparked religious insights and gave hope of salvation and fear of damnation, the rituals of baptism and communion tightened the bonds of family and community and reminded people in the routine of their lives of the cosmic connection between deity and individual, but where one sat incited pride, envy, insecurity, loathing—human qualities against which Davenport railed and in which his flock reveled.

The men composing the seating committee had to be so secure in their status that their judgments would not create irreparable damage to their reputations. Deacons were a part of every committee, and they were joined by current town and colony leaders (generally some combination of magistrates, deputies, and selectmen). In their deliberations, they considered gender, age, wealth, reputation, church membership, the number of years a person had been seated, marital status, public offices held, community service, family connections, education, and on occasion even the preference of the designee.[5]

The committee assigned people to their places as individuals, not as family groups. Here the family was not "a little commonwealth." Husbands sat separate from wives; children (except for the very young) sat apart from their parents. These divisions reinforced the understanding that salvation and damnation came to people as particular souls rather than as members of groups, and in part they reflected traditional hierarchical values. Parents and masters were superior to children and servants. Yet men's and women's seatings mirrored each other. The meetinghouse might be divided by gender, but it was divided equally. Except for the elders and deacons, women had as prominent seats as did men. Men might be considered superior to women in civil and domestic life, but men's and women's souls were equally capable of salvation. Meetinghouse seating physically represented that belief.

The separation of husbands from wives and children from parents was just the beginning. The seating committee recognized titles of respect by designating men as Mr. (roughly 10 percent of the total) or by their whole names. They subdivided women even further, listing them as Mrs., sister, goody, or as somebody's wife (for example, the designation might read "James Russells wife"). The few with the coveted Mr. achieved their status by holding a magistrate's office (Francis Newman served as an assistant and as governor and died in 1660 with an estate of £430), by possessing above average wealth (the town physician and merchant Nicholas Auger had a probated estate of £1638), by being related to one of the town's ministers (John Davenport Jr. and Nathaniel Street fit this category), or by completing a degree at Harvard (John Bower recently had left Cambridge in 1653 for the position of schoolmaster at New Haven; he later moved and became a minister). Women referred to as Mrs. were married to men with such status or were their widows. Three of the four ways of describing women (Mrs., goody, and somebody's wife) depended on the woman's being married, and New Haven's seating committee used *sister* to describe married members of the church. In 1656 with the exception of the daughters of the prominent, but departed, merchant Stephen Goodyear, all seated women were or had been married.[6]

Marriage didn't guarantee seating for women, but the single life assured scrambling for a general seat. Marriage didn't automatically produce the recognition of one's own seat for men either, but single men with respected, dead fathers (especially eldest sons, such as John Clarke) occasionally were assigned seats. Neither Nathan Andrews and his wife Deborah Abbot Andrews nor Samuel Andrews and his wife Elizabeth Peck Andrews were seated in 1662, even though they all had been married the previous year. Their omission must have refuted any cries of favoritism; Nathan and Samuel were sons of the meetinghouse builder and early church member William Andrews, and Elizabeth was the daughter of one of the seating committee members, Deacon William Peck. The chief problem for these newly wedded couples must have been that the meetinghouse had little available unassigned space. The addition of a balcony soon thereafter helped, for both Nathan and Samuel were seated in 1668 and we can assume that their wives were equally fortunate.

One characteristic—church membership—guaranteed all married people, men and women alike, designated seats. Remaining seats were distributed to nonmembers, who constituted approximately half of the seated population. Among those seated in 1656, some 70 of the 130 men and 56 of the 106 women were members. In 1662, some 59 of the 132 men and 78 of the 114 women were members. The seating in 1668 appears to be anomalous, for only 52 of the 165 men held church membership. Yet it probably reflects the dynamic of much of New England, where original members were dying and their children were either slow to join, uninterested, or unqualified. Perhaps the enlarged seating better represented the number of members in relation to nonmembers than on previous occasions. Even allowing for the likelihood that there were unmarried servants and other single people who were unseated church members (although there is no extant evidence), it is unlikely that more than half of New Haven's adult population, at the most, were church members during the seatings of 1656, 1662, and 1668.[7]

Although the combination of church membership and marriage assured being seated, it didn't necessarily secure the best seating. Some nonmembers had better seats than members did. Conversely, some church members without the designation Mr. had more prestigious seats than did nonmembers who held such title. Other convolutions appeared. Church member William Fowler sat a row in front of fellow church member Mr. Thomas Yale, and Mr. Henry Rotherford, who was not a church member in 1656 (although he soon after was admitted), sat ahead of church member Mr. Nicholas Auger. The seating of the New Haven community was a complicated matter.

Apart from the seats of the ministers and deacons (who were above being formally seated, their places being understood) the most prestigious location for men was the first two rows of the long benches. Until New Haven colony merged with Connecticut the first row was exclusively for magistrates, generally the governor and deputy governor alone. In 1662 the second row was infiltrated by relations of John Davenport and Theophilus Eaton (the founding and long-term governor until his death in 1658). By 1668, two prominent merchants joined this select group in proud worship. The first two rows of the cross benches were only slightly less distinguished. Wealthy and long-term merchants (not all of whom were church members) typically occupied these hard and prominent planks. The next rung down belonged to the third and fourth rows of the long benches and the third row of the cross benches. Men with the title Mr. still could be found in this area, but they were packed somewhat more closely together and non–church members could more frequently be found in their midst. The remaining five rows of the long benches and two rows of the cross benches grew increasingly crowded the farther back they were. There, middling church members, long-term residents, and upwardly mobile, middle-aged men rubbed elbows and viewed the backs of the heads of their superiors. There were a few scattered benches—the little seat, the seat before the governor, the seat before Deacon Miles—that were reserved for older church members and perhaps the hard of hearing; while they may have been more respectable than the back half of the long benches, they did not provide support for the more powerful or wealthy members of the community. The rest of the assigned seats hugged the outer walls. Located next to the soldiers' seats or on the stile on both sides of the door, younger, recently married men (many, if not most, of whom were not church members) craned their necks to see their fathers, uncles, more advanced neighbors, and the sites of their longed-for futures. After the balcony was added, its front row was composed of prosperous newcomers and successful, upwardly bound residents. The balcony's back rows offered space for increased numbers of younger men.[8]

As the New Haven seating committee pondered where people should sit, they placed great weight on a person's wealth. As Appendix A demonstrates, the greater the person's wealth, the more likely he would be seated in a prominent location. Comparable wealth established people in comparable positions. Francis Newman (estate of £430) sat in the second row of the long benches while John Benham (legacy of £80) was five rows behind him, and Thomas Lamson (£167) sat next to Edward Parker (died with £124 of land and goods). Among the apparent exceptions to these generalizations were Isaac Allerton—proclaimed Mr.—and Joseph Nash. Allerton (probated estate of only £118) sat on the first of the cross benches while Nash (probated estate of £419) was relegated to the nether world of the fifth row of cross benches. The life cycle of wealth— where a person is relatively poor in early adulthood, accumulates an increasing estate that peaks in late middle age, and following gifts of land and goods to adult children dies with decreased wealth—largely explains the discrepancy. Allerton was among the original passengers on the *Mayflower* in 1620. In the 1620s he served as an assistant, and by 1633 he was the most affluent person in Plymouth, if tax rates can be believed. When he moved to New Haven in 1646, he was probably sixty years old (his first marriage was in 1611), well-to-do, and respected in that town of prominent merchants. Joseph Nash probably was in early middle age at the time of the 1656 seating (his first child was born in 1650), and almost certainly his estate increased substantially afterward, following the death of his father and his move to Hartford, where he died twenty years later in 1678.[9] Despite the differences of their probated wealth, in 1656 Allerton had long been a person of substance while Nash was only early on the path toward respect and prominence. Their relative positions at that seating appear true to the pattern after all.

The economic life cycle not only helps explain the seating of Allerton and Nash; it also highlights the inextricable relationship between wealth and age. A few souls, through the good fortune of birth and marriage, might start adulthood well off, but most New Englanders built their estates in step with accumulated years. Improved seating came with both increased wealth and advancing age. In contrast, youth and a meager estate might not entitle a person to any assigned bench. Nathaniel Turner died in 1662 with only £75, no spouse, and no designated seat. Even Daniel Bradley, who was married but apparently young (he had no children) and with an estate worth only £33 at his death in 1658, had to take whatever general seat he could find.[10]

Yet age and wealth were only two of many variables. John Benham, who was a church member and who died with an estate of £80 sat in the same row with John Thompson, who was not a church member but who had a probated estate assessed at £229. William Judson, a church member as of 1659 and a man with substantial wealth, sat a row behind William Gibbard, who had held membership since 1641, whose wealth was slightly less than Judson's, and whose political power as expressed in elected colonywide office surpassed Judson's. New arrival and Harvard graduate John Bower, who taught at the New Haven school, sat beside the weathered Thomas Kimberly, one of the original New Haven planters. Joseph Tuttle, who was married, had better seating than his unmarried, older brother David did.[11]

In general, women's seating mirrored their husbands' places in the meetinghouse. When Allen Ball sat in the fifth row of the cross benches on the men's side, Dorothy Ball sat in the identical location on the women's side. Mary Barnes rested on a bench in the seventh row of the side seats while her husband Thomas occupied his place in the seventh row on the stile. And so it went. As a result of widows continuing to hold their places, of women not being eligible for political office, and of fewer seats for women than for men, wives frequently were one or two rows farther from the pulpit than were their husbands. Matthew Gilbert as deputy governor prominently perched on the first of the long benches, but the best that Jane Gilbert could do was the third row of the long benches behind the governor's mother, the two ministers' wives, and the widows and wives of more long-term, prestigious citizens. Similarly, as a result of the 1656 seating, Matthew Moulthrop was assigned to the sixth row of the long benches while Jane Moulthrop was placed in the seventh row. Less frequently husbands and wives sat in distinctively different sections of the meetinghouse. Ann Wakefield enjoyed the fifth row of the cross benches, yet John Wakefield was relegated to the sixth row of the stile. Thomas Morris sat in the respectable eighth row of the long benches during the same period that Elizabeth Morris sat in the fourth row of the side seats. These discrepancies were not accidental. Ann Wakefield and Thomas Morris were church members at times their spouses were not.[12]

Between formal seatings, some people moved from New Haven or died and sometimes new benches or balconies were constructed. Open spaces allowed the seating of new designees and the advancement of previously assigned members of the community. Time was a benefactor. Barring excommunication, a person could expect gradually to progress toward the pulpit. Matthew Moulthrop may have sat in the sixth row of the long benches in 1656, but in 1662 he was assigned to the fifth row and in 1668 he moved ahead an additional row. In 1668 his namesake son, twenty-nine years old and married, received his first seating in row eight of the long benches—an excellent location for an initial placement. Like his father, he could anticipate a steady progression forward.

Yet time by itself could move a person only so far forward. There were limits to advancement. The elder Moulthrop most likely had progressed as far as he could. Never a magistrate nor a deacon, John Gibbs was stuck in the third row of the long benches in 1656, 1662, and 1668. Year after year, non–church member Henry Gibbons sat before the little seat. Further back, William Thompson and Christopher Todd were unable to move beyond the fifth row of the long benches. The situation was similar to today's season subscriptions to cultural and athletic events. Within a section, a person receives slightly better seats with each year's new seating, until reaching the front of the section. Personal preference may allow for lateral moves, should space be available, but there is no jumping to a better section without a substantial, additional contribution of hard cash.

In seventeenth-century New Haven, the equivalent of today's cash outlays—in the meetinghouse that would come with the creation of pews—included becoming a member of the church, experiencing unusual financial success, or being elected to an important political or ecclesiastical office. The careers of John Hudson and James Bishop exemplify unusual leaps between sections. Even though Hudson secured a connection with the town's elite by marrying Abigail Turner, daughter of Captain Nathaniel Turner and sister of Mr. Thomas Yale's wife, and despite his once having been referred to as Mr. in the town records, he was listed as plain John Hudson when in 1656 he was seated in the first row on the stile. His wife

Abigail had a comparable seat, but her family background was acknowledged by the designation of Mrs. Nevertheless, that was not a bad location for a young man, and his next seating in 1662 in the fourth row of
the long benches dramatically demonstrated his rapid rise of reputation.
Between the two seatings, the town records began to address him as Mr.
each time he was cited, his wealth grew (in part from his wife's inheritance), and he became an increasingly important merchant. Once established, he advanced at the next seating to the third row, even though he
was not a church member and regardless of his conviction in 1666 for
fraudulently selling bad meat.

James Bishop's progress on the long benches from the seventh row in
1656 to the fourth in 1662 and to the second in 1668 had no comparable, spectacular leap, but he continued past Hudson. The difference was
his church membership and his political activity. A member of the church
by 1648, Bishop was first chosen a selectman (called townsman in New
Haven) in 1653 and a deputy in 1661. His selection as assistant in 1668
gave him the clout to break the third-row barrier. By 1670 town records
called him Mr., and he was elected deputy governor of the colony in 1683
and for many years thereafter.[13]

Bishop and Hudson might have been pleased with their placement,
and Gibb, Gibbons, Thompson, and Todd might have accepted theirs,
but some New Haven residents probably resented their assignments or
exclusion. Little more than a decade later, disorders in the meetinghouse
created by disgruntled people who sat where they wanted rather than
where they were relegated compelled authorities to impose fines, to construct additional benches, and to reseat the community.[14] Despite the un-
happiness of some, New Haven and New England remained socially
stratified throughout the seventeenth century. The stratification of the
meetinghouse reflected a society where people attempted to proclaim
their social position by the display of apparel, where land often was distributed by rank, and where political opportunities were structured by
status.

* * *

Political leadership throughout New England divided into two nearly distinct groups: colonywide leaders and town leaders. Selectmen, town
clerks, and constables infrequently left their towns to participate in colonywide affairs, except as representatives of their towns, and governors,
deputy governors, and assistants seldom began their political careers in
local government. Fewer than 10 percent of any of those colony officeholders ever served as selectman, and fewer still as town clerks or constables (see appendix B). A fortunate person ordinarily began and ended

as a colonywide officeholder. The former member of Parliament, Richard Bellingham of Massachusetts Bay, was that rare individual who was elected as selectman, deputy, assistant, deputy governor, and governor. Church office was not the usual path to political prominence, either; few magistrates ever were elders or deacons.

Less than 2 percent of the male population became governors, deputy governors, or assistants, but that is not to argue that those offices belonged to a closed caste. There were ways to the most powerful political positions in New England. A broad, political route was through the office of deputy. Eight percent of the entire adult, male population at some point served in that office. That was an opportunity open to an unusually wide spectrum of people. As a town representative to the General Court, a deputy gained legislative experience. Should a person prove adept as a legislator and worthy of his constituents' trust, he afterward might be elected as an assistant (10 percent of representatives were), and later and more rarely as a deputy governor or governor. More than 50 percent of all assistants previously had served as deputies, and more than one-third had acted as deputies before gaining the office of governor or deputy governor. Deputies were links between towns and colonial governments, and that office provided people with political ambitions a potential avenue to status and power.[15]

Nearly half of all assistants and a large majority of deputy governors and governors, nevertheless, attained office without the political experience of having been a deputy or a town officer. Other attributes elevated them to power. The recognition necessary to enter political life as a magistrate could result from family connections. John Winthrop Jr., certainly benefited from being the eldest son of an eminent father, but there can be little doubt that he had the talent to attain prominence on his own. That is the difficulty of attributing political success exclusively to family line. A powerful father or grandfather not only put an offspring into contact with other important individuals and brought name recognition to the aspirant to elective office; such a parent or grandparent also helped by providing financial assistance, formal education, and training in the skills of leadership. The son of a leader could be better prepared for leadership than were his competitors. As it was, far more men became magistrates without the benefits of family connection than with those advantages. In this study, there were 155 different surnames for the 203 individuals who were magistrates.

Closely connected to family connections was birth order. Although it probably mattered little to the electorate whether a candidate was firstborn or tenth-born, eldest sons by virtue of inheritance (economic, status, and position within the family and kinship group) had a distinct advantage over younger brothers. Among officeholders whose order of birth is known, slightly more than half to two-thirds of deputies, assistants, deputy governors, and governors were firstborn sons. They also were disproportionately successful at acquiring the town offices of selectman and constable. Second-born sons had a small advantage for colonywide offices, but not for town offices. Those further down the line than second-born were disproportionately less likely to attain office of any type.[16]

Previous high status or governmental experience in England could elevate a person to the New England magistracy. The gentry and lower gentry in the mother country might well expect abundant political opportunity across the ocean. They built their reputations on years of service and on the connections they long had forged. Richard Bellingham, Theophilus Eaton, William Coddington, Israel Stoughton, William Pynchon, John Winthrop, and others brought with them experiences from the manor, local and national government, law, business, and the intrigues of London. Those few titled gentlemen who ventured to New England were assured of deference and position. Sir Richard Saltonstall was an assistant during his entire, brief residence in Massachusetts Bay. And how else do we explain the ascendancy of Sir Henry Vane—inexperienced and twenty-three years old—to the governorship of the Bay colony?

Titles usually resulted from accidents of birth, but individuals had somewhat greater control over accumulation of wealth. Although great wealth was not essential to the officeseeker, financial substance—a firm stake in the society—contributed substantially to the person's chances of election. In general, the more prestigious the office, the greater the wealth needed by the aspiring officeholder (see appendix C). Colony-wide and town officers alike were more affluent than most, but magistrates typically came from the top 20 percent of the population while town officers usually were in the second quartile from the top (see appendix D). Deputies were intermediaries in wealth as well as in political position, although their estates usually were more similar to those of selectmen than of magistrates. What cannot be ignored, however, was the range of wealth. No set of officeholders was uniformly well-to-do. Every major town and colony office, including governor, at various times had occupants whose probated estates placed them in the bottom quartile.[17] Wealth alone was not a sufficient qualification for public trust and position.

Maturity also was an important characteristic of the successful officeseeker (see appendix C). For the seventeenth century as a whole, whether one was a first-time constable or a first-time assistant he most likely was in his mid-forties. Deputy governors and governors when they first entered those offices typically were in their late fifties. Maturity, however, is relative to the age structure of the society. Until 1660, when New England still reflected the youthfulness of its immigrants, many new officeholders were younger than forty and only a minority were as old as fifty. After 1660, when the age structure contained an increased number and percentage of people over fifty, the age when first entering office also increased. For the first half of English occupation of New England in the seventeenth century, there were unusual political opportunities for young men. The last forty years of the century resumed a more familiar pattern.[18]

Church membership, like a number of these variables, is difficult to assess. For lack of comprehensive evidence, it is impossible to discover all who were church members, and acceptance into church fellowship (like above-average wealth) was more likely to be achieved by middle age than in early adulthood. Although church records are far from complete for the seventeenth century, they—along with lists of freemen in Massachusetts Bay between May 1631 and 1664 (the period when church membership made a person eligible for freemanship)—provide a general understanding of the relationship between church membership and political office. No less than 20.7 percent of adult males from all parts of New England were church members, while no less than 47.2 percent of officeholders were church members. In towns that still have at least fragmentary evidence of church membership, between 14.3 percent and 45.7 percent of the male population and between 27.3 percent and 75.5 percent of deputies belonged to the church.

Without exception in all towns surveyed, a higher percentage of deputies than of the general adult, male population were church members. A ratio of two to one, as in Charlestown where 68.1 percent of its deputies and 32.9 percent of its adult males had joined the church, was typical. Was membership important in itself or was it only one of many possible indications of a candidate's likeliness to be a "good ruler"? In Massachusetts Bay, it was a requirement for colonywide office for most of the century (as was true for the life of New Haven colony and for the governor's office in Connecticut). Regardless of legal qualifications, however, elected New England officeholders at both the colony and town level outside of Massachusetts Bay as well as within were more likely to be church members than was the general population.[19]

Church membership was not always essential for office, but it enhanced a person's chances for political election. The two poorest deputies in this study (Thomas Marshall of Boston, who died in 1665 with an estate of £49 and George Allen of Sandwich [Plymouth colony] who died in 1648 worth £64) and the two richest (Hezekiah Usher of Boston, who acquired £14,000 of goods and land by his death in 1676 and John Pynchon of Springfield, who died in 1703 with an estate valued at £8,446) were all church members. By comparison, John Griffin of Simsbury, Connecticut, with probated wealth of £125 was the poorest non–church member who served as a deputy, while Thomas Bishop of Ipswich whose estate of £4,039 at his death in 1671 was the richest. The key here may have been Griffin's residence in Connecticut, where membership was less politically essential than in Massachusetts Bay or New Haven colony. The poorest nonmember in Massachusetts Bay was Robert Clement, who served as deputy for Haverhill from 1647 to 1653 and who died in 1658 with goods and property worth £494, placing him at nearly the median wealth of deputies and well above most other New Englanders. In Clement's case, age and affluence compensated for his lack of church membership.[20]

Although New England ministers greatly influenced political decisions and although they clearly were among the elite members of the various colonies, they did not hold political office. Nonclerical church officers—elders and deacons—on the other hand, did occasionally serve as elected political officials, but far less frequently than their age, wealth, and reputation would suggest. And even then, they concentrated almost entirely on town affairs or on representing their towns. Rarely did they take office as assistants or deputy governors, and none of the elders and deacons identified for this analysis were governors.

If colonywide officials composed the top political strata and town officials the next rank down, freemen (those formally accorded all political rights, including eligibility to vote and hold office) who never held office fell directly below them. In Massachusetts Bay during its first forty years and in New Haven colony throughout its existence, church membership was the only requirement for being designated a freeman. For the life of the Bay colony's original charter, church membership continued to be the prime qualification; after 1664, however, enough property to be taxed at the rate of ten shillings provided an alternative. The criteria for other colonies—separately or in combination—included oaths of fidelity, age, wealth, and "settled" residence. Incomplete records make it impossible to know with certainty how many men were freemen. The current consensus among historians is that a majority of adult males met those qualifications, but that many made no effort to become freemen.[21]

Nonfreemen often voted at the town level, sometimes illegally, as in Massachusetts Bay prior to 1647, and some even may have been selectmen or more rarely deputies.[22] On the political scale, they ranked below freemen, but they still were above the bottom, the absolutely disenfranchised—servants, slaves, women, and children.

* * *

Aboard the *Arbella* in 1630, shortly before landing, John Winthrop called for an orderly hierarchical society—a society where people knew and accepted their appropriate places. Order, harmony, deference, and authority would promote a godly commonwealth. God's plan included social stratification: "some must be rich some poore, some highe and eminent in power and dignitie; others meane and in subieccion."[23] To a certain extent, Winthrop's wishes were fulfilled. New England remained socially stratified throughout the seventeenth century. People's status influenced where they sat in church, who they married, how much land they acquired in town distributions, and which political offices they held, if any.

Yet New England was different from England. The extremes were not so great, particularly at the upper end. There was no nobility and, although New England was not free from poverty, the poor were nowhere so numerous relative to the general population. New England had fewer levels than did the mother country, but its strata still were quite evident. In the meetinghouse, there were no fewer than four distinguishable sections—prominent, assigned seats; middling, assigned seats; outlying assigned seats; and unassigned seats—and they reflected the town social order. Politically, there were colonywide leaders, town leaders, non–officeholding freemen, others eligible for more limited political activity, and the excluded. Economically, there were the affluent top 10 percent (for example, the Reverend John Cotton, Governor Theophilus Eaton, and the merchant Robert Keayne), the prosperous next 20 percent (with such representatives as Benjamin Church, and the Reverend John Fiske), the solid citizens of the seventieth to tenth percentiles (such as the Salem carpenter John Pickering, and William Russell of New Haven), and the bottom 10 percent composed of the poor, servants, and slaves (including Philip Phillips, who died in Boston with an estate of £2, and the fisherman Thomas Randall of Marblehead, who died with £6).[24]

Social stratification in seventeenth-century New England was not a conspiracy from the top. To be sure, those in privileged and powerful positions sought to maintain the standing order, and outsiders regularly attempted to challenge authority and tradition. But support for the various strata and attacks on the social structure and its symbols were far more complicated than haves versus have-nots. When political leaders attempted to curtail ostentatious display of wealth and status, popular outcries thwarted them. Although people were defined by status and although a privileged background gave those so favored a significant edge, the hierarchy was fluid, as demonstrated by the continuing need to reseat congregations. Natural processes alone saw to that. The flux promoted by birth, aging, and death could not be restrained. In comparison to England, New England was far more open. New leaders were more likely to emerge from previously undistinguished families. New wealth was more likely to come to those who once had been servants. New England society was stratified, but not petrified.[25]

~≈ 5 ≈~

LIFE CYCLE, GENDER, AND FAMILY

Wh, her father died, Herodias Long's world changed quickly and forever. Although her brother remained at home, her mother sent her bereaved daughter to London, where at Saint Faith's, the underchapel of Saint Paul's, she married John Hicks on 14 March 1637. Soon thereafter, to her "great griefe," they sailed for New England, settling at Weymouth in Massachusetts Bay. She was only "between thirteene and fourteene years of age" at the time.[1]

Why she married Hicks is unclear. Marriage at such a young age was not unheard of in seventeenth-century England but nevertheless was quite extraordinary. Depending upon class and circumstances, women ordinarily married in their early to mid-twenties, with twenty-three to twenty-six being typical. What is clear is Herodias did not marry for love. As she later described the event, she was "taken by one John Hickes unknowne to any of my friends." Hicks must have been at least a decade older than his bride to have been financially able to provide for the passage of the two of them; and were he typical of the time, he would have been in his mid- to late-twenties.[2] Whether Herodias's mother arranged the match remains a mystery.

Herodias and her husband dwelled in Weymouth for two and a half years before moving to Newport, Rhode Island, in 1640. John Hicks appears to have been a respectable citizen. At Weymouth, he had been granted land, and soon after their arrival at Newport he was admitted as an inhabitant (testifying to his financial stability) and was made a freeman (evidence of his political and economic soundness; however, unlike in Massachusetts Bay, not a sign that he was a member of the church). He served on a jury at least twice between 1641 and 1643, and he and Herodias had two, perhaps three, children. But not all was well.

In early 1645 authorities charged him with beating his wife and bound him for £10 until Herodias could testify. Before the end of the year, John Hicks took the children and became one of the original European settlers at Flushing, Long Island. His wife was left behind, possibly on her own.[3]

Years later, Herodias claimed she had been abandoned and that Hicks not only had departed with their children but also with "most of my estate" that she had received from her mother. With her mother, brother, and friends in England dead and the English Civil War raging, she was unable to return to her homeland. According to her, "being one not brought up to labour, and young," she "knew not what to doe to have something to live, having noe friend; in which straight I was drawne by George Gardiner to consent to him soe fare as I did, for my myntainance." Hicks saw it differently. In a letter from Long Island to his former Newport townsman, John Coggeshall, he accused his wife of "whoredome" and sought a divorce. It is possible that Herodias had had sexual relations with another man, perhaps Gardiner, during their marriage and that Hicks's discovery prompted his violence. It is also the case that adultery was an accepted reason for obtaining a divorce; Hicks may have fabricated the charge to justify his own behavior and to establish a basis for ending his marriage. Ten years later on 1 June 1655, when Hicks wished to remarry, Governor Peter Stuyvesant of New Netherlands issued him a divorce on the grounds that his wife had "broken the bond of marriage." Herodias was not present to argue her side.[4]

Gardiner too was a respectable citizen of Newport. He was a landowner and a freeman. In 1642 he was a constable and senior sergeant for the town, and in 1644 he was an ensign in the militia. At some point, Herodias married George Gardiner in a Quaker manner. A Quaker neighbor, Robert Stanton, whose wife also was a Quaker, later testified that one evening at his and his wife's home Herodias Long and George Gardiner "did say before him and his wife that they did take one the other as man and wife." Such a ceremony was not sufficient to be recognized as legal in the colony of Rhode Island after May 1647. Following that date, a couple with their parents had to publish their intent at two town meetings, had to be wed by the "head officer of the Towne," and had to enter the event in the "Towne clerk's Booke." Regardless of its legality, the union produced offspring every two to three years, six or seven children in all. The birth date of their firstborn, Benoni, provides fuel for speculation. In 1727, Benoni, imprecise and inaccurate about his age as was usual for the time, claimed to be about ninety years old. Were that true, he would have been born the year of his mother's marriage to John Hicks. A more reliable, genealogical source states he was born "about 1644" and his brother Henry "about 1646."[5] Should that be true, as is possible, Benoni's birth preceded the beating of his mother that brought Hicks before the magistrates. At the least, it is possible that Herodias was pregnant with Benoni before Hicks left for Long Island, and it is all but certain she had delivered Benoni, if not several of her other children, before the Quaker ceremony.

Herodias took her Quaker beliefs seriously, and she was among the Quakers who went from Rhode Island to Massachusetts Bay to challenge that colony's anti-Quaker legislation. In June 1658, she "with a babe sucking at her breast" and a girl, Mary Stanton (most likely, a daughter of Robert Stanton and his wife), walked from Newport to Weymouth "to bear witness" of their faith. The Bay laws of 1656 and 1657 made it clear that Quakers who entered their territory would be whipped, and Herodias must have returned to her former town with that knowledge. Her reward was ten stripes of the whip and, perhaps, religious ecstasy. Unlike Mary Dyer and others, she didn't return again and thus was spared additional punishment, including execution. The psychology of martyrdom is complex, and any analysis of Herodias Long Hicks Gardiner offers many possibilities. Did she venture to Massachusetts Bay to convince others of the truth of her beliefs by her willingness to suffer? Was she testing the strength of her faith? Was she confirming her loyalty to her fellow Quakers or seeking their approval? Was this an extreme form of postpartum behavior? Had she abandoned herself to a life of grief and torment? Was she attempting to cleanse her guilt for previous behavior? Any combination of these alternatives is possible; nonetheless, if guilt contributed to her martyrdom, it was not enough of an inhibitor to thwart future involvement in affairs of the heart.[6]

In March 1664, she petitioned the King's Commissioners in Rhode Island for a separation from George Gardiner. By then, they were living in Pettaquamscut (now Kingston), where Gardiner had purchased one thousand acres from the Pettaquamscut Company. In her petition, Herodias reviewed her marital life from the time of her father's death. She described the circumstances of her marriage to John Hicks and her eventual arrangement with Gardiner. As she presented her case, she had agreed to live with Gardiner out of desperation and had remained his captive for nearly twenty years. Repeatedly, she claimed, in exchange for her labor and possessions she had asked him to maintain her in a separate dwelling "or else not to meddle with mee," but he had refused. She had not judged him to be her husband, "never being married to him according to the law of the place." She requested to be allowed to live in the house upon her land and for Gardiner to provide for the maintenance of their youngest child who would live with her, "and that hee may bee restrained from ever meddling with me, or trobleing mee more."[7]

Justice moved slowly, and it was not until May 1665, that the General Court of Rhode Island (the case having been referred by the commissioners to the governor, who in turn presented it to the General Court) rendered a decision. Their chief concern was whether the couple had ever been married. Gardiner acknowledged that "he cannot say that ever hee went on purpose before any magistrate to declare themselves, or to take each other as man and wife, or to have their aprobation as to the premises." At that point, most likely at Gardiner's request, Robert Stanton testified about the ceremony at his home. The court was not satisfied and fined George Gardiner and Herodias Long twenty pounds each, and it commanded them "not to lead soe scandolose a life, lest they feel the extreamest penalty that either is or shall be provided in such cases."[8] In short, they should marry in a proper manner or live apart. They chose to separate.

If we leave the story here, we have a sad tale of a girl compelled to marry too young, a marriage in which she was battered, followed by twenty years of being forced to serve as a concubine. All of that may well have been true, but there is more to be told. First, we should recognize that Herodias was not an entirely reliable witness. Although it is accurate, as she claimed, that she and Gardiner had never been married "according to the law of the place," they had been married in a ceremony in keeping with her faith. There is no evidence that she disputed Robert Stanton's account, and there is proof that for at least one intense time of her life she was a committed Quaker. Whether Gardiner oppressed her may also be questioned. It is possible that she was having an affair with Gardiner while she still was married to John Hicks; Hicks certainly thought so. Perhaps, at first, she felt strong affection for Gardiner and chose to live with him—or, she could have manipulated him to offer an escape from Hicks. If Gardiner was keeping her against her will, surely her neighbors (including the Stantons and fellow Quakers) would have intervened. There were limits even to the tolerance of the residents of Rhode Island. Also she was free enough in 1658 to travel from Newport to Weymouth. Even so, we shouldn't forget that while Herodias may have been physically free, and while there may have been neighbors who would have provided refuge, she had experienced a life that could have left her emotionally dependent and insecure.

What tips the balance toward concluding that she was an active agent as well as a victim is a second petition that reached the Rhode Island Court during the same session that heard the case of Gardiner and Long. Margaret Porter, also a resident of Pettaquamscut, complained that her husband, John Porter, "is destitute of all congugall love towards her, and sutable care for her." He had left her, and she had been "brought to a meere dependence upon her children for her dayley suply, to her very great grieffe of heart." She requested that the court order him to provide for her out of his sizable estate "before hee and it be convayed away." This was a serious matter indeed: they had been married for more than thirty years, and he was a substantial citizen of the colony. They had lived at Roxbury as early as 1633, when he was designated a freeman, and later resided at Boston. Supporters of Wheelwright and Hutchinson, they had moved to Portsmouth, Rhode Island, in 1638 with others of that party, and then to Newport. In 1641, John Porter was an assistant. Sometime after January 1657, they moved to Pettaquamscut where with others of the Pettaquamscut Company (including the prominent Boston merchant and goldsmith, John Hull) they purchased a large section of land from the Indians. Their daughter, Hannah, married one of the other purchasers, Samuel Wilbore, the following year. Porter was a pillar of the community, and he was supposed to act as such. The General Court supported Margaret Porter and declared all of her husband's business transactions since he had deserted her void. Within a month, John Porter made arrangements for Margaret's perpetual care. Soon thereafter, the Porters were divorced, and John Porter married Herodias Long Hicks Gardiner.[9] It is entirely possible that Porter had left his wife about the same time that Herodias first petitioned the court for George Gardiner to stop troubling her. In that petition, she had asked for maintenance for her child, but not for herself—an indication that she had some sort of outside support.

The remainder of Herodias's life must have followed the more typical ebbs and flows of growing old in seventeenth-century New England. Porter, her third and last husband, apparently was devoted to her and her children, for he gave and bequeathed land to all of them. Her first husband, John Hicks, married a widow, Florence Carman, in 1655; when she died, he married another widow, Rachel Starr, in 1662. He attained positions of prominence at Hempstead, New York, and died in 1672. George Gardiner married Lydia Ballou soon after the court settlement, and together they had five children before his death in 1677. Herodias disappeared from the record after January 1671, when she and John Porter conveyed land to her son, William.[10] Perhaps her death, unlike her life, came simply and peacefully.

* * *

Herodias Long's marriage at the age of thirteen was extraordinary both in England and New England, and I have uncovered no records of a marriage of anyone that young during the seventeenth century in those northeastern colonies. Yet age at first marriage on average in New England was significantly younger for girls and women than in the mother country. Slightly under 5 percent of girls and women living in New England by 1650 (either by birth or migration) married before the age of sixteen, and slightly more than 10 percent married before reaching seventeen. By the age of twenty, 50 percent of all these women had married, and 90 percent were married by the age of twenty-five. For the unusual decade of the 1650s, nearly 25 percent of women who married did so aged sixteen or younger.[11]

Their husbands, by contrast, conformed more closely to English and French patterns. During the first decades of settlement the mean age for first marriage of men was between twenty-six and twenty-seven. That average fell to just below twenty-five after 1650. In the following decades of the seventeenth century, the span of age between first-time husbands and wives on average was a little more than four years. At that time, this gap was comparable to European experience; for the entire century, however, New England men and particularly New England women married younger than did their European counterparts.[12]

The unusually young age at first marriage for New England women can in part be explained by the imbalance of the ratio of men and women. Although most people who ventured from England to New England during the Great Migration migrated in families, a substantial number of men—roughly one-third of all adult males—were single, young, and without family connection in their new land; single males outnumbered single females by at least four to one. In addition, among minors unaccompanied by adult family members or kin, boys outnumbered girls by three to one. Many, if not most, of those who migrated without family came as servants, and therefore had to serve out their terms (and for men establish a livelihood) before they could marry. Because the typical-aged marriageable population was disproportionately male, the marriage age for women, and even girls, was unusually low.[13]

This may well explain why so many women were married before the age of twenty, but the marriage of girls—those sixteen and younger—demands greater explanation. Girls typically had their first child more than two years after they had married, with fourteen and fifteen year olds averaging two-and-a-half years, while women who had married at seventeen or older gave birth to a first child, on average, within two years. Some of these girls married mariners who soon shipped out, and they may have avoided pregnancy by abstinence; it is also possible that some of the others were being married off before the onset of menstruation or prior to regular ovulation. This suggests that early marriage of girls was one way of reducing family size and financial pressure.[14]

Other evidence bolsters the contention. For each of the age groups from fourteen to sixteen, a majority of the girls were eldest surviving daughters. Although they were a scant majority for fifteen and sixteen year olds (51.7 and 50.8 respectively), they were at least 55 percent of fourteen year olds; if we include girls who most likely were an only child in New England at the time of their marriage, the percentage rises to 72.7. Many of these girls, a majority of fourteen and sixteen year olds and almost half of fifteen year olds, came from families with seven or more children. Nearly two-thirds of fourteen year olds and slightly less than 60 percent of fifteen year olds married at Boston and its immediate environs or at other New England seaport towns while just over 45 percent of sixteen year olds married at those locations. Although a family could face financial difficulties anywhere in New England, Boston and other seaports attracted families who had little or no land and whose existence often was dependent on maritime activity. A large family, rather than providing cheap labor for the parents (as would be true for farming people) might instead enlarge financial burdens. They would be tempted to marry off their daughters as soon as husbands could be found. Hannah Hough may fit these criteria. She was the eldest daughter of William and Sarah Hough's ten children. William Hough was a deacon of his church and may have been a housewright. His residences—first at Gloucester in Massachusetts Bay where Hannah was born and later at New London in Connecticut where she married—offer the possibility that he also may have been involved in maritime pursuits. Hannah was fifteen when she married John Borden.[15]

Many of these girls shared Herodias Long's fate of dislocation and early marriage following her father's death. More than 20 percent of the fourteen and fifteen year olds married shortly after a father's death, while that was the case for just under 10 percent of the sixteen year olds. Elizabeth Tilley had the double misfortune of both her parents dying shortly after the *Mayflower* anchored off Plymouth in 1620. As a fourteen-year-old orphan, she married the twenty-nine-year-old John Howland in 1621. They remained wed until Howland's death more than fifty years later. In the meantime they had ten children, and he rose to political prominence within the colony. A father's death, of course, did not always induce financial disruption. Elizabeth Sheaffe was fourteen and the eldest daughter of six children when her father died, and she was fifteen when she married the twenty-four-year-old Robert Gibbs. But Jacob Sheaffe was a wealthy merchant whose estate was worth £8,528, and Gibbs came from a well-to-do English family. For all we know, this may have been a marriage based on love and abiding affection, but it also formed an alliance between powerful families across the Atlantic—a perfect arrangement for merchants. The prospect of a family alliance (in this case between ministers) may have contributed to the marriage of the fourteen-year-old

Esther Warham, daughter of the Reverend John Warham of Windsor, to the twenty-two-year-old son of the Reverend Richard Mather of Dorchester, Eleazer Mather.[16]

For some girls, the remarriage of a surviving parent could be as threatening and traumatic as the other parent's death. At a time when as many as one woman in ten died from childbirth, and when surviving spouses typically remarried, Hannah Hollard's plight was not unusual. The eldest daughter of Boston shoemaker Angel Hollard, she was fourteen when in July 1652 she married the cooper William Ballentine. Her mother had died sometime after March 1646, but before Hannah's marriage. Angel Hollard's second wife gave birth to a daughter in December 1653, which indicates that Hannah's father and stepmother had married about the same time as Hannah, perhaps earlier.[17] Hannah may have been deeply smitten with William Ballentine and he may have been charming, but she also may have wished to escape becoming a New England Cinderella.

* * *

The marrying off of young daughters was not the only way financially strapped families reduced the number of mouths to feed. Although the apprenticing of children offered potential job training, it also provided homes for the offspring of poor parents as well as for orphans and abandoned children. Town records from throughout New England during the entire century tell these sad stories.

In 1645 Samuel and Elizabeth Eddy of Plymouth, "having many children, & by reason of many wants lying upon them, so as they are not able to bring them up as they desire," apprenticed their seven-year-old son John until he reached twenty-one. Two years later, they apprenticed John's younger brother Zachery, who by then was seven years old, for the same length of service. William and Mary Baker of Warwick, Rhode Island, placed their six-year-old son William with Thomas Bradley "to bringe up as his owne child" and "to sett him free at twenty one yeares ould"; some years later they also apprenticed their five-year-old son John to Bradley. When they "graunt[ed] & asigne[d] over" their six-year-old daughter Mary to Abiah Carpenter, they received a calf in return. Sarah Rysbie's parents, also of Warwick, left town without her when she was five, and she was apprenticed to Job and Mary Almy, who already had cared for her for two years, until she reached the age of seventeen.

Often, as with Sarah Rysbie, what formally was an apprenticeship was actually the creation of foster or adoptive parents. In some instances, a town would pay the new "parents" for the child's care, while in others the couple were seeking a child of their own. Nathaniel and Lydia Morton of Plymouth appear to have been adoptive parents: they expressed "a desire to have a child of the said William Harlow," the two-and-a-half year-old Nathaniel. The Plymouth Court, nevertheless, stipulated that the boy be freed when he reached twenty-one.

The one-year-old child of Frances Tree of Dorchester was not so fortunate. Born out of wedlock, the child—no name was reported—was assigned to be Anthony Newton's servant until he reached twenty-one, should he live so long. Newton, in return, was paid for providing lodging, food, and clothing. The town of Watertown found that Edward Sanderson's poverty presented a problem. Sanderson was unable to maintain his family and apparently was unemployed, and the town believed it would be difficult to support the Sandersons out of its own coffers. The town's selectmen debated whether they had the necessity and the means to supply the family, but decided against, for "it would not tend to the good of the children for their good eaducation & bringeing up soe as they may be usefull in the comon weall or them selves to live comfortablly and usefuly in time to come." Their solution was to apprentice two of the children to "honist famelleys," thus freeing the town of financial responsibility.[18]

There is no indication whether Edward Sanderson agreed with the town's solution, but he had no choice. Families might balk, but ultimately towns prevailed. On 12 January 1680, the selectmen of Dorchester ordered Francis Bale to appear before them so that they might inquire of his "outward Estate." Learning of his financial condition, they "advised him to dispose of two of his Children." When he replied his wife would not agree, they "p'swaded him to p'swad his wife to it." At Boston, the selectmen forbore such subtlety. On a single day in March 1672, they ordered a dozen families to "dispose of theire severall Children . . . abroad for servants." If the families would not comply, they threatened that the "Majestrates and Select men will take theire said Children from them, and place them with such Masters as they shall provide accordinge as the law directs."[19]

The Billington and Eaton families of Plymouth exemplify the connections between being poor and marginal and having to place their children into apprenticeships. Both families arrived on the *Mayflower* in 1620, but that was one of their few distinctions. Francis and Sarah Eaton brought their infant Samuel with them. Sarah died during the first winter, and Francis remarried, only to have his second wife die. He married Christian Penn as his third and last wife, and together they had three children before he died in 1633. The following year Christian married Francis Billington, who with his parents, John and Ellen, and a brother had also sailed on the *Mayflower*. John Billington was a ne'er-do-well from the start, and in 1630 he was hanged—the first Englishman executed in Plymouth Colony—for murdering John Newcomen. Governor William Bradford commented that Billington "and some of his had been often punished for miscarriages before, being one of the profanest families amongst them; they came from London, and I know not by what friends shuffled into their company."[20]

In addition to the four children Christian brought with her, she and Francis Billington in fairly rapid succession had eight more children. Beginning in poor circumstances, the growing family remained on the economic and social margins of the colony. Soon, the colonial government intervened. In 1636 the "Governor & Assistants, with his mothers consente" apprenticed the eight- or nine-year-old Benjamin Eaton to the widow Bridget Fuller for fourteen years and the sixteen-year-old Samuel Eaton to John Cooke for seven years. By 1643, Francis and Christian Billington were compelled to place four more of their children with other families. The first child of their marriage, Elizabeth, was put to service in 1642 when she was six and continued in that capacity until the age of twenty. Her younger brother Joseph was an apprentice by the age of five, when he attempted to escape to the comforts of family and home. Officials admonished his parents for receiving him and threatened them with having to sit in the stocks should they do so again. His stepbrother Benjamin Eaton, who had just completed his own indenture and was living at home with his mother and stepfather, was reprimanded for encouraging Joseph to leave his master, and he too was threatened with the stocks. It was fitting that when Benjamin Eaton married in 1660, his wife Sarah Hoskins had completed her servitude only a few years before. She was six when she had been sent from home.[21]

* * *

When Herodias Long first married, she was "taken" by her husband-to-be, and they wed in an Anglican chapel. We know no more about the "courtship" for her second marriage (although it does appear that her property was kept in her name), and the ceremony was the exchanging of words of commitment before some friends in their home. Perhaps her third marriage satisfied the legal requirements of New England colonies and followed more typical practice.

Introductions usually preceded courtship. Potential partners might meet each other in a variety of ways. Most New England towns were small enough that children and adults alike were well aware of fellow townsfolk. They visited one another and assisted each other in their daily tasks. Although most group activities involved members of the same sex (for example, men helping and working for one another in the fields, women assisting in childbirth and exchanging goods and produce), boys and girls accompanying their parents probably were acutely observant of each other. Harvest time, as in England, provided greater opportunities for establishing and strengthening social relations and greater temptations. The town of New Haven was so concerned about "much sin Committed at times of husking indian Corne" that it ordered that no single persons could meet "upon prtence of husking indian Corne" after nine o'clock at night without a parent, master, or designate being present.

During the early years of settlement, people from the same areas of England would remain in contact, even if they lived in different towns. Scattered but communicating kin, sometimes by letter and sometimes in person, might introduce young men and women. This was particularly true of people, such as merchants and ministers, whose occupations required travel. People of all backgrounds and from different towns could meet each other when they journeyed to the market days and fairs of such towns as Boston, Watertown, Salem, Plymouth, and Hartford. Edward Johnson in his *Wonder-Working Providence* commented that the residents of Malden "are much straitned in their bounds, yet their neerness to the chief Market Towns, makes it the more comfortable for habitation." Days when town militias trained, when the courts met, or when elections occurred also were times of social gatherings—so social that the young scholars of Harvard College were forbidden to attend without permission of the College President or a tutor. Sunday was the day set aside for public worship, but it too was a time for social interaction. Between morning and afternoon services, there was ample opportunity for social exchanges, pious and otherwise. Thursday lectures, when people were more likely to attend another congregation's meeting, offered additional occasions. Some young people didn't wait for services to end, and either went outside or were "disorderly" inside. Town after town found it necessary to station responsible men at meetinghouse doors to prevent all but those with "necessary occation" from leaving and to supervise the conduct of children and youth. Most of these directives were aimed at boys, but it is hard to imagine that there weren't wayward girls as well.[22]

Regardless of a wide variety of ways of meeting potential marriage partners, young men and women seldom had full control, let alone authority, about whom they would marry. At the very least, parental consent was required. John Hubbell and Abigail Burt, for example, were whipped by court order in Springfield for making "promises of Marriage" after her father had prohibited such a union. In some cases, parents arranged the entire match. Although parents at all social and economic levels may have been involved in matchmaking, remaining records point primarily to prominent families. Hugh Peter dangled "a Neere Cossen" before John Winthrop for any of his sons. She was described as the daughter of a Justice of the Peace "as handsome as any in the Country,

200 *li* for present and hopes to have 100 *li* more." Anticipating that Winthrop wouldn't nibble, Peter speculated about a Thomas Reade. John Endicott, her guardian, opposed Peter's brokering, at least for the time
being. He wrote Winthrop that his ward didn't want to marry "as yet"
and "confesseth . . . herselfe to be altogether yet unfitt for such a condition, she being a verie gerle and but 15 yeares of age." Besides, when a
prospective husband was suggested to her, "shee said shee could not like
him."[23] Here was the other side of the equation. Young men and women
were not to marry without their parents' consent, but neither could they
be forced to marry against their will. They might not love a partner in advance, but at least they had to find the person acceptable.

The negotiations between parents and offspring can be seen in the saga
of John Winthrop's niece, Lucy Downing. At one point, she was going to
marry Thomas Ayers, but, as her mother wrote, "he had not yet art
enoughe to carye his ship, so they turnd backe." Apparently, the senior
Lucy Downing fancied metaphor for explaining that a potential son-in-
law was not yet financially independent. Before the younger Lucy had
forgotten Ayers, she found herself pursued by William Norton, the
younger brother of the Reverend John Norton. Although her suitor was
"verye fayer," she had some objections that were forwarded to his
brother. When the objections were resolved, her father Emmanuel Downing began the serious negotiations. Norton's prospects as a merchant
were promising, and the details of house, land, furniture, bedding, and all
that was needed to set up comfortable housekeeping must have been
worked out—typically the husband's family provided land and a house
and the wife's family gave movable goods, and occasionally land, of comparable worth. All appeared to be arranged, but at that point Lucy let it
be known to her friends that John Harwood had captured her affections.
The Nortons were offended, and the Downings were embarrassed and
concerned that they would be viewed with "unjust suspisions of our in-
forcement of her to mr. norton." In the end, all was resolved and Lucy
and William married and had a long life together.[24]

Ordinarily before parents or guardians and often the prospective partners would agree that a marriage was feasible, they had to determine
what each family could offer the couple. All concerned expected a rough
equivalency of contribution: horses and houses, linens and land, perhaps
even cash. Although early New England did not have the fixed class
structure of England, New Englanders were not believers in the equality
of humankind. There were recognized differences of status and wealth,
and marriages based on the parity of gifts bestowed on couples reflected
those differences. When Michael Wigglesworth, the minister of Malden,
married his servant after his first wife died, he was rebuked for his

choice.[25] The proper order was for Billington to marry Eaton, Downing to marry Norton, not Wigglesworth to marry Mudge.

Once all the arrangements had been concluded to everyone's satisfaction, the couple became formally betrothed; that is, a contractual agreement to marry existed. They then had to publish publicly on two or three occasions, depending on the colony, their intent to wed. If no one presented reasons why they should not marry, a civil ceremony typically at the bride's home followed at least two weeks after the first announcement. A magistrate officiated. A minister's offering a prayer or an exhortation was deemed appropriate; but a minister before the loss of colonial charters in 1684 could not preside over a marriage ceremony. Puritans, in John Winthrop's words, "were not willing to bring in the English custom of ministers performing the solemnity of marriage." Marriage was not a religious sacrament, but a civil contract. Its function was to oil the wheels of legal process—paternity, inheritance, and such—not to pave the way to heaven. But it also was the joining together of a man and a woman and their families, and that could be celebrated. Samuel Sewall wrote that after Daniel Quincy and Anne Shepard wed in 1682, the guests ate cake, drank wine and beer "Plentifully," and filled Thomas Brattle's "great Hall" (where the ceremony had occurred) with song.[26]

The last requirement was for the couple to consummate the union. The inability or unwillingness to have sexual relations was one of the few accepted reasons for granting a divorce or, in the case of there being no consummation, an annulment. Somehow the pathbreaking work of Edmund Morgan, more than half a century ago, has not displaced the popular notion that New Englanders were puritanical in matters of sexuality. We too readily forget that they generally were an agricultural people with large families and cramped quarters. In all meanings of the term, they were an earthy people, who from an early age were familiar with and amused by the antics of animals in season and not-so-mysterious night sounds in their chambers at home. To their minds, sexuality was an essential part of being human, but it should be confined to marriage.[27]

* * *

As with so many mores, there was a wide gulf between ideal and practice. To this extent, Herodias Long was a person of her time. Yet the violation of these mores could risk more than community disapproval (a serious punishment in seventeenth-century New England), for many sexual offenses had been legislated as crimes. The punishment for adultery was severe. Although whippings, brandings, fines, and the wearing of the letter *A* or the letters *A.D.* were typical sanctions, death also could be administered for the offense in Massachusetts Bay, Connecticut, and New Haven.

One of only three occasions when capital punishment was inflicted involved James Britton and Mary Latham. After being rejected by a young man she loved, the eighteen-year-old Latham determined to marry the first man who would have her. Contrary to her friends' advice, she married "an ancient man who had neither honesty nor ability, and one whom she had no affection unto." Almost immediately, she began consorting with several young men who plied her with wine and gifts in exchange for sex. Among them was James Britton. He had always thought that people who testified against themselves to be fools, but a combination of "a deadly palsy" and a guilty conscience led him to confess his relations with Latham and other women. Latham's married state posed a serious problem, and the magistrates of Massachusetts Bay summoned her to return from Plymouth where she then lived. When confronted with Britton's testimony and a witness who claimed to have seen the two of them grappling on the ground, she acknowledged Britton's attempt but denied he had been successful. Although some of the magistrates thought the evidence weak "because there were not two direct witnesses," the jury found them guilty. She then confessed and named twelve other men, two of whom were married, as sexual partners. Five of the twelve were detained; because the condemned Latham was the only witness, however, they were not prosecuted. On 21 March 1644, the colony of Massachusetts Bay executed Mary Latham and James Britton.[28]

Adultery more commonly appeared in the record when an aggrieved spouse was suing for dissolution of a marriage. Implicating oneself of adultery and requesting a divorce was ineffective unless the other spouse joined in the petition. The sexual activity of married people outside of marriage was an area with a double standard. Whenever the case was criminal, one of the defendants always was a married woman. Possible combinations included a married woman with a married man or a married woman with a single man, but never a married man with a single woman. In divorce proceedings, there were instances where a wife initiated a suit against a husband who had dallied with a single woman; in the vast majority of the cases, however, the husband claimed to be the offended party, and he instigated the separation.

John and Sarah Williams of Barnstable are a good example. On 5 June 1672, Susanna Turner was fined £8 for committing fornication. She accused John Williams of being the father of her baby, but there wasn't sufficient evidence to convict him. Beginning in July, nevertheless, he began to pay child support of two shillings per week, and that continued until October when Isaac Turner, the brother of Susanna, discharged Williams from the responsibility. In July of the next year, Williams once again was in court, this time seeking a divorce from his wife. Sarah Williams had committed adultery and had borne another man's child. The divorce was granted, and Sarah "by her breach of wedlocke cutt off her selfe from any right henceforth to the pson or estate of the said John Williams, her late husband, and doe heerby likewise alow him libertie further to dispose of himselfe in marriage if hee shall see cause for the future soe to doe." When John apparently engaged in adultery, Sarah remained silent, at least at court. But when Sarah turned the table, John sued for divorce.[29]

New England courts applied punishments for fornication—sexual intercourse between unmarried persons—more equitably. The most compelling evidence of the "crime" was the birth of a child. To that extent, women were at a disadvantage; but whenever paternity could be established, men received as severe a punishment as women did. In one instance, John Ewen was fined, and Ruhamah Turner was not charged—a most unusual turn of events. For a first offense, a fine of £5 per person was typical. If it were a second offense, whipping was the usual sanction. In some cases, should the couple marry, all would be forgiven. When Mary Hitchcock in New Haven was given that option, she refused to marry Richard Matticks, and they both were whipped.

But married couples were not immune. If a baby were born suspiciously early, the couple would be charged and both partners would be fined. A distinction may have been made should conception occur between betrothal and marriage. William Gifford and his wife were fined £5 each for fornication before marriage or contract, while Thomas Cushman (but not his wife) was fined £5 for fornication before marriage and after contract. More likely, circumstances not revealed by the records were the difference. How else do we explain at the same Plymouth court session William Rogers but not his wife being found guilty of fornication "before marriage" and given the choice of a £5 fine or being whipped, Mary Adkinson but not her husband being found guilty of fornication "before marriage and contract" and fined £3 (which her father paid), while Jabez Snow and his wife were fined £10 together for fornication "before marriage"?[30]

Any glance at court records or a comparison of marriage dates and the dates of the birth of first children—even allowing for premature births—reveals that premarital intercourse was not unusual. In England during the late sixteenth and seventeenth century nearly one-fifth of women were pregnant on their wedding day. Such a high figure was not reached in New England until midway through the eighteenth century, when in some towns premarital pregnancy rates rose above 40 percent of all marriages. During the seventeenth century in New England villages the figure probably was between 5 and 10 percent. It may have been somewhat higher in larger towns such as Boston where there were more servants and more transients. New Englanders, like the rest of humankind, were a sexual people, but on the whole they remained chaste before marriage and faithful as spouses.[31]

* * *

Sexuality combined with marriage at a young age and relatively good health produced large families. Herodias Long's eight to ten children were somewhat greater in number than was usual in New England, but none of her neighbors would have considered hers an especially large family. Even had her first husband not taken their children with him (thus reducing the number of people residing together), eight to ten children in the same household were only a few above average. Households, moreover, were revolving institutions. Newborns might join a family at the same time their oldest brothers and sisters were preparing to leave home and establish their own families. The usual pattern for women during their fertile years was to give birth every two to three years with the spacing becoming greater with the woman's increasing age. Of course, there were variations: a woman whose newborn infant died might give birth again within a year and yet later have a gap of five years or more between births. Women born in New England before 1650 on average bore their last child at age thirty-seven and, all told, gave birth to seven children. Those who lived to forty or older, having escaped an early death from childbirth, disease, or mishap, typically had their last child near age forty and gave birth to eight children. Occasionally, a woman as old as forty-five had a baby, but childbirth beyond that age was rare.[32]

The birth of a child didn't necessarily enlarge family size, for infant mortality was high, regardless of where a person lived in the seventeenth century. Although the rate of infant mortality cannot be established with certainty, the consensus of historians is that one child in ten died before its first birthday. My own investigation places the figure at 13 percent for males and 12 percent for females. Even these rates were lower than in England, where for the period 1600–1649 they were 16.2 percent for males and 12.3 percent for females, or in France where they approached 25 percent for all infants. The years between one and four also were critical, with an additional 9 percent of boys and 7 percent of girls dying. The death rate declined during the remaining years of childhood, but by the age of seventeen nearly 28 percent of the population had died. By contrast, well over 25 percent were dead in England by the age of ten and over 30 percent by the age of fifteen; in France 50 percent had died by age twenty. Boys in New England, as elsewhere, were somewhat more susceptible to disease and accident than were girls, yet the numerical advantage males have over females at birth was not completely eliminated.[33]

* * *

In seventeenth-century New England, as in England, these parents and children lived in nuclear families. Two generations under the same roof was the norm, but there were variations. Despite discouragement from colonial authorities, young single men might live alone or with another single young man or two. Young single women, however, lived with families: their parents', their guardian's, or their master's. A young couple might reside with the husband's family even as long as to the birth of a child. In later years, a widowed parent might dwell with the family of a son or a daughter. Over the course of a lifetime, an individual might experience different household arrangements, but the nuclear family was most common. Even within the nuclear family, there might be the addition of a servant or two. The one variation that didn't occur was married siblings living in the same household. There might be combinations of more or less than two generations, but parallel nuclear families did not reside together.[34]

Although extended families were not standard, nuclear families stayed in close contact with one another. Kinship networks were important for emotional and economic support. During the Great Migration kinship groups traveled in the same ships and settled in the same towns. Gifts of land and inheritances kept family members in close proximity, although those distances would lengthen later in the century as family land in the longer settled areas became inadequate to support all members of a growing population. Family members provided mutual support in the fields and houses of New England towns and villages: harvesting crops, exchanging produce and cloth, assisting with births. Kinship connections aided merchants in intercolonial and transatlantic trade. Marriage bonded previously unrelated families and expanded what historian Roger Thompson calls "these daisy chains of kinship."[35]

* * *

The ideal of the New England family as expressed in law and sermon was a patriarchy where the husband/father was head of the household. New Englanders had transported the concepts of male superiority and female subordination with them when they crossed the Atlantic. John Winthrop, when commenting on the mental illness of Ann Hopkins, wife of Governor Edward Hopkins of Connecticut, explained the origins of her infirmity as a result of "giving herself wholly to reading and writing." As Winthrop and others perceived gender, men and women had different capacities. In regard to Ann Hopkins's unfortunate condition (and what could just as easily have been said of Anne Hutchinson or any other woman who didn't know her place), he mused in his *Journal:* "if she had attended her household affairs, and such things as belong to women, and not gone out of her way and calling to meddle in such things as are proper for men, whose minds are stronger, etc., she had kept her wits, and might have improved them usefully and honorably in the place God had set her." Public affairs were proper for men, but not for women. Men could vote, hold office, serve on juries. Women were not eligible for any of those responsibilities.

Although women were supposed to be men's spiritual equals, even in the relatively tolerant environment of Rhode Island husbands could curtail their wives' religious activities. That colony's order that no one should be prevented or punished for acts of conscience was tested when "one Verin" refused to allow his wife to attend religious meetings so frequently as she wanted. Roger Williams and other political leaders sought to censure him, but "one Arnold" (almost certainly the powerful and wealthy Benedict Arnold of Providence) reminded them that it was God's ordinance that wives were subjects to their husbands. Despite the clamor that wives would "cry out" against religious constraints imposed by their husbands, Verin was spared censure on the disingenuous basis that he had acted from conscience.[36] Most husbands, almost certainly, were more like George Gardiner, who did not prevent his Quaker wife from witnessing her faith, than like Verin; yet seventeenth-century New England was a place where women were less free than their fathers, brothers, husbands, and adult sons.

The family by tradition and religious precept was patriarchal, but there was room for great variation, dependent upon the personalities of the spouses within individual families. Some families had authoritarian and unloving husbands and timid wives, others had domineering wives and compliant husbands. But most, it seems, were composed of a balance between affectionate partners, each of whom had distinct, though frequently overlapping, areas of responsibility. In general, men spent their days in fields or shops while women dwelled in houses and adjacent gardens. Both contributed to the family economy, though often in different ways. These were not fortified boundaries, however. Each spouse was present where needed. In particular, women might be found working in fields, running taverns and inns, and during a husband's absence maintaining a shop. In addition to rearing children, making and mending clothes, tending fires, growing vegetables and herbs, preparing food, functioning as daughters to both sets of parents, as sisters to siblings, and as lovers to husbands, women served, in the historian Laurel Ulrich's phrase, as deputy husbands. When decisions had to be made about distributing or selling land, supervising servants, educating children, husbands and wives conferred and reached agreements together. Husbands might believe that women in general were inferior to men—and misogynist views were widespread—but when it came to their own wives, they were more apt to use expressions of affection and partnership. Stephen Bachiler, for example, referred to his wife, who had just died, as "my deare helper and yoke fellowe."[37] In the hierarchy of the family, men were the titular heads, and husbands and wives were both superior to their servants and their children.

* * *

Childrearing was not reserved exclusively for women. Moral and religious instruction, discipline, preparation for adult roles—all of these were the responsibilities of both parents. One of the first decisions the couple had to make was the name of their newborn infant. As they had done in England, New England parents often named their offspring after themselves and grandparents and occasionally after aunts and uncles, thus tying their children to family lineage. The names of the children of Samuel and Hannah (Hull) Sewall illustrate the practice. Their firstborn, John, was named for Hannah's father. Next was Samuel, followed by Hannah, both named for their parents. Their fifth-born, Hull, took Hannah's maiden name. Henry, the sixth-born, was given the same name as Samuel's father. Their seventh-born, Stephen, had the same name as one of Samuel's brothers. Ninth-born, Judith, was named for Hannah's mother and grandmother, while their twelfth-born, Jane, during her brief month of life held the same name as Samuel's mother and one of his sisters. The last and fourteenth child also was named Judith, perhaps for her sister who had died earlier as well as for Hannah's relations. One of the remaining five children died almost immediately after birth and may not have received a name. The other four were named Elizabeth, Joseph, Mary, and Sarah.[38]

Two other New England naming practices are evident among the Sewalls' children. When a child died, it was not unusual for parents to give the same name to a succeeding child. The Cambridge minister Thomas Shepard wrote in his autobiography that "my wife on the Sabbath day, being April 5, 1635, was delivered mercifully of this second son Thomas, which name I gave him because we thought the Lord gave me the first son I lost on sea in this again, and hence gave him his brother's name." To use a name a second time (sometimes a third) was not a sign of callous disrespect or a lack of love for the dead child but rather a way to maintain connections with the family past and, at least in Shepard's case, with God. If anything, reusing a name preserved a memory. The second New England naming practice was the use of biblical names. All of the

Sewall children who were not named for family members received scriptural designations. Elizabeth, Joseph, Mary, and Sarah were all traditional English names, but they also had biblical reference. In his diary, Sewall made quite clear that Joseph received his name "in hopes of the accomplishment of the Prophecy, EZed. 37 and such like: and not out of respect to any Relation, or other person, except the first Joseph."[39]

The Sewall children were born between 1677 and 1702, but the frequent practice of naming children for biblical figures was a characteristic New England convention beginning with the first generation (see appendix E). What was distinctive about the custom was not that biblical names were used (that was typical throughout the English-speaking world) but the frequency of the practice. Among the early emigrants to New England the most common names in order of frequency for males were John, Thomas, William, Richard, Robert, Samuel, Henry, Edward, George, and James, and for females were Mary, Elizabeth, Ann, Sarah, Margaret, Jane, Alice, Hannah, Martha, and Susanna. Several of these names, such as the most popular John, Thomas, Mary, and Elizabeth, had the dual advantage of English tradition and biblical reference, but many—William, Richard, Robert, Henry, Edward, George, Margaret, Jane, and Alice—were exclusively British.

By contrast, the most popular names of the migrants' children born in New England between 1620 and 1650 (the first generation of English children) in order of frequency for males were John, Samuel, Joseph, Thomas, Nathaniel, Jonathan, James, Benjamin, William, and Isaac; and for females, Mary, Elizabeth, Sarah, Hannah, Abigail, Rebecca, Martha, Ann, Lydia, and Ruth. Of the traditional English names without biblical reference, only William still appeared among the top ten, and it slipped from third place to ninth place. Richard, Robert, Henry, Edward, George, Margaret, Jane, and Alice, dropped to much lower depths; the most popular among them, Richard, was in twenty-second place among males and appeared only .8 percent of the time. Every name that replaced them in the top ten had biblical reference.[40]

There can be little doubt that the religious values of many of the colonists influenced their naming practice and that, in general, New England was different in this respect from other English-speaking colonies and the mother country. But before we leap too far in the direction of New England exceptionalism and homogeneity, we must recognize that religious motivation (even among the pious Sewalls) was not the only ingredient in New England recipes, nor were all New Englanders Puritans. Large families provided New Englanders with increased opportunities for innovative naming while still preserving family naming traditions. Firstborn sons, for example, were more likely to be given traditional English names than were their younger brothers. The core eight English, male names of John, Thomas, William, Richard, Robert, Henry, George, and James demonstrate the point. 61.6 percent of the English, male emigrants held those names while only 38.2 percent of their New England–born sons were so named. Like many broad averages, the 38.2 percent does not tell the whole story: 48.7 percent of firstborn sons had core English names, but only 30.2 percent of second-born sons, 24.4 percent of third-born sons, and 12.7 percent of fourth- and later-born sons received those names. In addition, firstborn sons were more tightly clustered by a few popular names and had less variety for their number than did their younger brothers: 34.8 percent of firstborn sons were named John (did anyone dare go into a crowded room and shout "John"?) and 62.1 percent were named John, Samuel, Thomas, Joseph, or Nathaniel. By contrast, only 30.4 percent of fourth- and later-born sons held one of the top five names for their birth order: Joseph, Benjamin, Samuel, Nathaniel, or John.[41] In short, religion played a prominent part in naming practice for many New Englanders, but so did family tradition and the opportunity for innovation afforded by large families.

* * *

The object of childrearing among New England families was to prepare their children for adulthood. For many this meant preparing their children for salvation; for all, it meant preparing their children for work. During their first six years or so, children were given few responsibilities, and boys and girls were reared together and similarly. Beginning around the age of six, boys put aside their gowns of childhood and dressed in clothes New Englanders considered appropriate to adult males. Except for size, there was little difference between the clothing for young girls and adult women; females wore the garb of childhood and subordination throughout their lives. At this same time, mothers began to teach their daughters domestic skills and fathers began to teach their sons agricultural methods or the skills of a trade. Children were treated not so much as little adults but as emerging adults. As children grew older, they were given increased responsibilities; full adult responsibilities were not thrust upon children at the age of six. Although twenty-one was the age when men became eligible for political and economic rights, adolescents gained some adult rights and responsibilities at sixteen. Then young women could consent to marriage, and young men were eligible for militia duty. Most young adults, particularly men, had to postpone independent adulthood for many years. Until they were given or earned land or other means for an independent livelihood, young men were dependent on parents or masters, while young women remained dependent upon parents or masters until they married. As a result of the shortage of labor, some men had to wait until a father died, but most were provided with gifts of land or goods prior to inheritance.[42]

* * *

It was fortunate that most parents bestowed gifts upon their sons and daughters, for life was long in New England. Unlike the Chesapeake where life expectancy was short and family life therefore unstable, parents in New England typically lived until the maturity of even their youngest children. If a person escaped death to the age of twenty, the chances for a long life were good. Both men and women in seventeenth-century New England could reasonably expect to live into their sixties: the mean age at death for men was 63.4 and for women 60.1. One-quarter of the adult population, men and women alike, lived to the age of eighty. During the first fifty or sixty years of English settlement, the age structure of New England was younger than that of England. There simply were fewer old people proportionate to the rest of the population. The resulting impression was paradoxical. The settlers and their children constantly confronted death—death of infants, death of children, death of young adults, death of the middle-aged—but less frequently during the first half-century death of old people. All the while a majority lived to old age, and a good number lived to a very old age, even by the standards of postindustrial societies. Their experience taught them that life was short and fragile; the longevity of those who survived childhood proved otherwise.[43]

Death brought grief to the survivors and perhaps prompted people to review their spiritual condition; it also, however, created the necessity of dividing an estate. When Nicholas Busby died in Boston on 28 August 1657, he had lived in New England for twenty years and he left a prosperous estate worth £973—well above average. He had long been a weaver in Norfolk before, at the age of fifty, he with his wife, Bridget, and other family members traveled to New England. They first lived at Watertown, where as a member of the church and a freeman of the colony he attained prominence and twice was selected to serve as a selectman. But he was used to a more cosmopolitan environment. Although Boston was much smaller than Norfolk (second in size among English cities only to London), it was more urban than Watertown. In 1646, he abandoned farming, and they moved to Boston where he became a merchant of dry goods and continued his trade as a weaver.[44]

Busby's will was straightforward, unremarkable, and afterward uncontested. He chose Bridget as the "Executrix," and she received "my dwelling house wherein I live, dureing her life, and all my household Stuffe plate & money." The Watertown farm was to be sold "if she will

consent thereto," and she was requested to distribute the proceeds to leg-
atees, keeping whatever was left over for her own maintenance. The eldest, surviving son John, who lived in England, received £70 in addition to
£30 that had been given to him the previous year, "Phisicke" books, a
cloak, and one of two looms (if he came to New England for it). The only
son living in New England, Abraham, was given £60, the promise of the
Boston house and land after Bridget's death, divinity books, and a loom
and weaving tools. Anne Nickerson, the eldest daughter, received £50
and the "thicke Bible." Her sister Catherine Savory, who had never left
England, inherited £40 in addition to what had been sent the previous
year, and "the bible in my Hamper." The youngest daughter Sarah
Grout, who may have been a favorite, was bequested £65 and the "Best
Bible." The remainder of the estate went to Joseph Busby (£20), a grand-
son whose father had died, Sarah Grout (£10), a granddaughter, and
William Nickerson, a weaver and husband of Anne Nickerson, who inherited a loom, if John Busby didn't claim it.[45]

New England practice determined that widows were to receive no less
than one-third of an estate, and by that standard Bridget Busby was well
treated. After £315, books and Bibles, looms and weaving tools, and a
cloak were deducted, at least half of the £973 estate remained, but with a
proviso. Although she possessed the house, she did not fully own it. She
did not have the authority to sell it, for it already had been set aside for
Abraham. Similarly, although the farm couldn't be sold without her consent, it is difficult to construct a way she could have raised the required
funds bequested to other family members without selling it. She had been
Nicholas's partner; when it came to property, however, she clearly was a
junior partner with a minority interest. At the time of Busby's death, she
was seventy-three years old, and all of their children were adults. Had she
been younger and their children minors, she might have been given full
control of the estate, with the understanding that gifts would be distributed to their sons and daughters when they married or reached adulthood. Under those circumstances, a young widow had to be cautious.
Should she remarry without a prenuptial contract, all of the estate legally
would belong to her new husband. She would have to choose between
contractually setting aside some or all of her estate for the children of her
first marriage or trusting that her new husband would be just.[46] As it was,
this was not a consideration for Bridget Busby.

Typically, an eldest son inherited a double portion, but John's residence in England reduced his share. Although youngest sons sometimes
received disproportionate bequests, Abraham's position as the only son
living in New England apparently boosted him to chief beneficiary. The
terms of the will gave each of the daughters lesser shares than their

brothers, and ultimately this may have been how the children of Nicholas and Bridget Busby were treated. There exists the possibility, however,
that as the recipients of wedding gifts and other earlier grants, all of
their offspring, with the exception of Abraham, received comparable
portions. At the time, Abraham was the only unmarried child, and he
may not have been given any means for independence previously. Two
years later, he married Abigail Briscoe.[47]

When Bridget Busby died in July 1660, her will was not greeted with
similar harmony and equanimity. William and Anne Nickerson contested
their share. On the face of it, there should have been few surprises. John
Busby and Catherine Savory, both still in England, received £20 and £10
respectively. Anne Nickerson and Sarah Grout inherited almost identical
furniture, linens, and household goods. The Nickersons' children had
£24 set aside for them, while £20 went to the children of Sarah and John
Grout. The two New England sons-in-law were each given a gold piece
worth twenty shillings. And the executor, Abraham, received the house
and its gardens and whatever else remained after funeral expenses.[48]

William and Anne Nickerson had married in Norfolk in 1627, when
he was twenty-three and she eighteen. Before they left for New England
ten years later at the same time as her parents did, they had four children
and he (like his father-in-law) pursued the trade of a weaver. In New England without the initial resources of Nicholas and Bridget Busby, they
were more successful at producing children than at making a living. Continually on the move, they kept seeking opportunity through weaving
and attempted land speculation. Two years before Nicholas Busby's
death, William Nickerson purchased land from Indians in Plymouth Colony without approval of colonial authorities; that one illegal act set off
nearly twenty-five years of controversy before a modest settlement was
made. In the meantime, there were mouths to feed and children to establish as independent adults. They received a fair share from Busby's estate
as had the others, but in their minds they deserved more. In March 1657,
Anne Nickerson went to Boston to assist her dying father. She stayed
with him and her mother until his death, and between then and her
mother's death three years later she helped her mother day and night.
During that time, the Nickersons borrowed £65 from Bridget Busby, and
they contended that in return for Anne's service, after the £24 was set
aside for the Nickersons' children, her mother had intended to forgive the
remainder of the debt.[49]

When Abraham Busby, as executor of Bridget Busby's estate and chief
beneficiary, attempted to collect the outstanding debt, William and Anne
Nickerson refused to pay. He proceeded to take his brother-in-law to
court. He had a written copy of the debt Nickerson had incurred, but

Nickerson had no evidence other than his wife's word to support his position. The court found for Abraham Busby and ordered Nickerson to reimburse the estate. Nickerson appealed, but was rebuffed by the court a second time.[50]

* * *

Not all New Englanders experienced family life in the same way. There were differences between families based on such variables as wealth, gender, status, family size, life span of parents, and place of residence. Some families were dysfunctional and at times brutal, while others were close-knit and affectionate. But for better or worse, it was a rare New Englander who didn't live within the structure of a family, either as a parent, a child, or a servant. Almost all adults married and generally married young, and in comparison to the Chesapeake they lived longer, had larger, more stable families, and had more of their children survive to adulthood—thus resembling England more closely than did the southern colonies. These patriarchal and generally two-generation families were the core of New England life. At their best they provided affection, instruction, discipline, and security. Families taught gender roles, guiding boys to be men and girls to be women. Together with ministers, they instilled religious beliefs and values in their children. Their public hierarchy mirrored the culture: men above women, parents above children, masters above servants, superiors above subordinates. Yet within the privacy of the home, some husbands and wives came close to companionate marriages of near equals. Decisions from childrearing to expenditures were made jointly between "yoke fellowes." Families were central to the material well-being of their members, from sustenance to legacies of land, goods, and connections, and they acted for various levels of government by providing discipline. Herodias Long may have undergone greater extremes and variety in her family life than did most of her New England cohorts, but like them from birth to death her existence was maintained and structured by family.

~ 6 ~

LUSTY YOUNG MEN AND
WICKED WOMEN

Samuel Ford was every middle-aged New Englander's nightmare. He was "aboute sixteene yeares" in May 1655, when New Haven town authorities brought him before the court, charging him with four separate offenses. The most serious of the allegations was the near killing of George Smith's young son. One Sunday that spring, Ford's father, Timothy, had told him to tend the cattle. Rather than follow his father's bidding, he wandered toward George Smith's house, where he came upon Smith's son and another boy pulling a bucket of water on a sled for a calf. The sled was little more than a board attached to a rope, but it was enough to tempt Samuel Ford to mischief. Grabbing the rope, he made a noose at one end and threw it over the boys' heads. Probably intending to torment the two by making them into his own beasts of burden, he soon turned the prank into a more deadly game. The older boy escaped his harness, but Smith's son, who was only five or six, found the rope tightening around his neck. When he attempted to flee, Ford strengthened his grip, forcing the boy to fall. Unable to call for help, the boy merely groaned, but the sound reached his nearby sister who shouted at Ford to stop. Caught or jolted to his senses, Ford loosened the rope, and the boy was spared. For the next three days, he wore rope marks on his neck, testifying to his ordeal.[1]

The other offenses were less life-threatening but no less disturbing to New England sensibilities. On another occasion, Samuel Ford went to a neighbor's house, where his mother was visiting. His greeting to her was, "now you are got a gossiping together, is my dinner ready." "You saucy boy," she responded, "who speake you to." With no less insolence, he replied, "you get a gossiping together, and when my father and I come to dinner, wee cannot have it." In later centuries, such an exchange might be perceived as bantering, teen-age self-absorption, or a stinging step along the prickly path of independence, but at least one neighbor who witnessed the scene, Goodwife Hodgkins, was neither amused nor tolerant of disrespect for parents. She exclaimed to Samuel's mother that if he were her son and too big to control she would send him to the governor or marshall. When Goodwife Hodgkins brought the charge before the court, Ford's protective mother defended him as best she could.[2]

At this same court session, Robert Meaker presented another example of Ford's "unmannerly cariag." One day while Meaker was driving a calf along a path, Ford attempted to block its passage. Upon Meaker's complaint and threat to tell his father, Ford "turned up his breech & bid him kiss it." Last, Samuel Ford was charged with making fires in the woods on a fast day. Timothy Ford tried to defend his son by explaining to the court that he had sent Samuel and another son to watch the cattle. Because it was a cold and rainy March day, he gave his approval for them to build a fire. Claiming that one fire was not enough "for theire comfort," they constructed a second. The court reminded the father that he had a building where they could have been more comfortable with a single fire, but Timothy Ford responded that it was "littered with straw aboute calves." Exasperated by Ford's taking his son's side, the court countered that there was another and larger building where the fire could have been built. At that point, Ford "confest he corrected his boye for makeing them fires on the fast day."[3]

The court found Samuel Ford guilty and sentenced him to be "seveerly whipped publiquly, that he may take heed of such courses hereafter, and others also may be warned by this example." Ford's "miscariages" merited punishment, but his underlying attitude that connected the four offenses was his undoing. He demonstrated a lack of respect for his neighbors, for his mother, and for the standards of the community. His breaking of the sabbath, a fast day, and the Fifth Commandment were disturbing, and the court used the occasion to dissuade others from behaving similarly. Young people had to be tamed; if a family could not fulfill its obligations to discipline and control its own, then the government would assert its own authority.[4]

Ford may have been involved in additional scrapes during the following years, but he didn't appear before the court again until 1664, when he was twenty-five. The complaint against him was "gross publike disorder & to the dammage of some persons": he was suspected of splitting some new posts and tearing down a section of fence. The evidence was circumstantial. He had been seen walking down the west lane with an axe one Saturday evening. At the time, all posts and fences were sound. By the next morning, the damage had occurred. Ford protested his innocence.

He acknowledged that he had carried an axe after claiming it at Isaac Beecher's place but denied responsibility for the vandalism. Two friends, John Thomas Jr., and Samuel Tharpe, testified that they had seen him on west lane and that he had behaved himself. The authorities pressed Ford further, and he admitted that the axe belonged to his brother-in-law, Nathaniel Tharpe. This was potentially incriminating evidence, for Samuel Whitehead, George Ross, John Winston, and the marshall had placed Tharpe's axe in the "markes of the posts" and it had "suted the markes to a hayres breadth as near as they could judge." In days before the manufacture of standardized tools, each implement had its own individuality. This was not the first time that fences had been damaged, and Ford's earlier comments suggested he knew who the culprits were. Edmund Dorman testified that "in hay time" he had heard Ford say as much. The court decided that there was sufficient evidence to keep pursuing the matter at their next session, and Ford was required to post £5 bail for his appearance.[5]

Between court sessions, the magistrates inquired further of the three friends, and in the course of examination John Thomas Jr., confessed. According to Thomas, Samuel Tharpe was the chief participant but Samuel Ford had been involved as well. The new posts had been split, because a man named Thompson, the owner of the posts, had taken a load of wood that belonged to Tharpe and a load of "pallisadoes" that belonged to Ford. The three of them then had ventured to John Alling's land, where Tharpe split his posts and all of them pulled down his fence. Again, this was an act of retribution, for Alling had been the cause of Tharpe earlier having had to sit in the stocks. When in court Ford was presented with his friend's testimony, he denied its accuracy. Even when the court warned him "to take heed that he did not goe on provoaking god, not knoweing how soone he may be called to give answer for those things," he was unmoved. Eventually, he admitted he was present at the incidents but claimed that Samuel Tharpe had dismantled the fence. Tharpe, for his part, disputed Ford; when asked if he had cut off the ear of Alling's horse, he stated he hadn't. When asked the same question, Ford also denied involvement. Bail then was set for Ford and Tharpe, and they were required to appear at the next court.[6]

Samuel Ford ignored the summons and forfeited his bail of £5. Samuel Tharpe ran away but was apprehended. When brought to court, he was contrite, and he confirmed Thomas's version of the events. They had struck Thompson's posts because he had taken Tharpe's wood and Ford's "pallisadoes," and they had felled Alling's fence because he "used to medle & be busie with young men." Tharpe, who was fined £3, must have been referring to Alling's pursuit of youthful misdeeds. Alling's vigilance was not deterred. A year and a half after the trial, while on watch with Ephraim Pennington, he apprehended five young men and women, including Samuel Tharpe and Elizabeth Thomas (John's sister), making a great deal of noise at the home of Benjamin Bunnill and his wife, who were absent at the time. John Thomas Jr., the most cooperative of the three, had to pay the modest fine of forty shillings.[7]

And so ended Samuel Ford's life of "crime." In 1674, he married Elizabeth Hopkins, and together they had at least four children. He remained in New Haven—even becoming a proprietor in 1685—for the rest of his life, dying there on 2 June 1712, at the age of seventy-three.[8]

* * *

Ford was not the only young man in seventeenth-century New England to find himself on the wrong side of the law. To hear the alarmed voices of several early immigrants, the land was alive with Samuel Fords. William Bradford lamented that most of the passengers from the *Fortune* in 1621 were "lusty young men, and many of them wild enough." Edward Johnson reflected on 1628 when "a mixt multitude" of servants arrived. They, "having itching desires after novelties, found a reddier way to make an end of the Masters provision, then they could finde meanes to get more." Nathaniel Ward in 1635 was saddened by the presence of "such multitudes of idle and profane young men, servants and others." He believed that the leadership had not sufficiently screened would-be migrants; and if they did not improve the process, they would be no better off than had they remained in England. They would have traveled from "the snare to the pitt."[9]

There was cause for such concerns. Some young people, particularly young men, engaged in a variety of illegal practices, ranging from assaults and murder to illicit sexual behavior to drunkenness, gaming, and bawdy singing.

The seaport town of Marblehead had an abundance of single young men, and it is no coincidence that one-fourth of all violent crimes for Essex County in the seventeenth century occurred in that unruly place. In Plymouth, the first duel between Englishmen in New England was fought in 1621 by two unmarried servants, Edward Doty and Edward Leister. Suffering minor wounds, they nevertheless were "adjudged by the whole company [of Plymouth] to have their head and feet tied together, and so to lie for twenty-four hours, without meat or drink." Fortunately for them, the governor released them after a painful hour "upon promise of better carriage."[10]

Many, if not most, of the fights and other assaults involving young men followed bouts of drinking and were directed at each other. But, on occasion, the violent act was sober murder. In 1638, Arthur Peach, described by Bradford as "a lusty and a desperate young man," killed a Narragansett. In debt and afraid of being punished for having "got a maid with child," Peach convinced Daniel Cross, Thomas Jackson, and Richard Stinnings—each an apprentice or servant—to escape their masters and join him in making a fresh start in the Dutch colony of New Netherlands. Along the way in the territory of Rhode Island, they stopped for a rest. While they were smoking by a fire, a Narragansett trader laden with cloth and wampum appeared. Peach invited the man to join them for a smoke, and he accepted. It soon became apparent that Peach, who had been a soldier in the Pequot War, was not being sociable. His companions objected when he told them he intended to kill and rob the Indian, but he spat out, "Hang him, rogue, he had killed many of them." With Cross, Jackson, and Stinnings offering no other resistance, Peach ran his rapier through the unsuspecting Narragansett, and the four of them left with "five fathom of wampum and three coats of cloth." Once the English had gone, the wounded Narragansett staggered home, only to die a few days later. Before his death, other aggrieved Narragansett brought Roger Williams to interview their dying comrade. Soon thereafter, they captured the four fugitives and took them to Williams. After negotiation with authorities of Plymouth and Massachusetts Bay, Williams sent the captured men to their home jurisdiction, Plymouth. Pressed by Bay magistrates fearing an Indian uprising if justice was not meted out, a reluctant Plymouth government brought Peach, Jackson, and Stinnings (Cross had escaped to Piscataqua) to trial. The jury found them guilty, and they were executed on 4 September.[11]

Women too could be murderers, and N. E. H. Hull finds that in Massachusetts between 1673 and 1774 homicide was the most frequent serious crime charged to females (though women still trailed men by a substantial number). While men most typically killed their victims away from their farms and shops, women almost always murdered within the home or its near environs and their victims usually were their own newborn infants or children. Unmarried women overwhelmingly were the chief perpetrators of infanticide, as they attempted to eliminate evidence of births out of wedlock.[12]

Among sexual offenses, the most common committed by young men and women was fornication. Colonial records are replete with cases of single men and women as well as young married couples who engaged in premarital intercourse. The act was contrary to moral standards, but it also had economic consequences. If a child were born and the mother had not wed nor was able or willing to name the father, the financial burden of child support potentially fell upon the town. If the father were known but he or both parties were servants and therefore without financial means, the situation was complicated further. Dorothy Temple, a servant of Stephen Hopkins, bore a child fathered by the executed murderer, Arthur Peach. Hopkins might have supported the child and extended Temple's indenture. Instead, he negotiated an arrangement with John Holmes where he paid him £3 "and other consideracons to him in hand payd" in exchange for Holmes taking on the indenture. A less honorable option that Hopkins forbore was to release Temple as his servant and to place the responsibility for her and her child's maintenance elsewhere. Single young men also were punished for adultery with married women, rape and attempted rape, masturbation, bestiality, and sodomy. Apart from fornication, it was rare for an unmarried woman to commit a sexual offense. One exception was the "lude behavior . . . uppon a bed" between Sarah Norman, wife of Hugh Norman, and Mary Hammon. Only the married Norman was reprimanded for "her unchast behavior" and "divers lasivious speeches by her allso spoken."[13]

In seventeenth-century New England eating and drinking for the body's sustenance was approved practice, but there were clear limits to making merry. Wine and beer were traditional beverages, and as long as their consumption didn't lead to drunkenness or excessive idleness all was well. If a person wished to drink an alcoholic beverage, the typical place for such refreshment was one's own home. But New England towns also designated establishments where travelers, strangers, and others could take meals and beverages and, quite typically, spend the night. Anyone could frequent these inns and taverns, but they were particularly good gathering places for young people, many of whom were servants. To reduce misbehavior and temptation, towns and colonies regulated ordinaries. No one could sell wine, beer, or liquor without a license, and few towns licensed more than one or two ordinaries. Not only could a person be punished for drunkenness, but the tavernkeeper could be fined for allowing people to drink too much, or to stay too long (usually half an hour to an hour was the limit), too late (generally after nine at night), or during religious services.[14]

Despite the regulations, ordinary keepers continually were brought before magistrates for infractions, and more often than not the infraction involved young people making merry. Stephen Hopkins, the master of Dorothy Temple and a Plymouth innkeeper, indirectly may have contributed to her pregnancy. On 2 October 1637, he was fined forty shillings for "suffering servants and others to sit drinkeing in his house (contrary to the orders of this Court,) and to play at shouvell board, & such like misdemeanors." The seriousness of his offense was compounded by the violation having occurred on a Sunday—before, during, and after the meeting. Sundays not only were God's day; they also were days when servants and others were free from ordinary labor. Similar infractions occurred throughout New England. In New Hampshire, the level of drunkenness, quarreling, and fighting had led to such disorder one June day in 1659 that the court felt compelled once again to spell out its restrictions on ordinaries. In 1664 the selectmen of Dorchester attempted to avoid the problem altogether by deciding not to allow an ordinary to be created "about, or neere unto the Meeting house."[15]

Young people quickly discovered that ordinaries were not essential for an evening of wine and song. And who needed an ordinary if you had neighbors like Thomas Langden and his wife? In 1650 at New Haven, Langden was charged with "disorderly Intertaining of young men in his house at unseasonable times in the nights to drinke wine, strong watter, and take tobacco." He also led his company in "filthy corrupting songs." As far as Langden was concerned, he had done nothing wrong. He was only being hospitable, and "if they were in old England," he argued, "they could sing and be merry." That was exactly the point, as the authorities saw it. They weren't in old England, and they didn't want to replicate the mother country. Because it was only a first offense, he was fined twenty shillings. Two years later, Langden was back in court, this time on his wife's behalf. She apparently wanted to make her home as welcome for young women as for young men, for she was accused of "disorderly inviteing Mr. Cranes maide in the night to her house to eat a sacke posset, with an intent to have her meete a young man there, with a purpose to drawe on a treaty of marriage, without parrents or masters consent." Although this was a second offense for the couple, Langden's wife's promise to mend her ways kept their fine to twenty shillings again.[16] And so it went.

Not only youthful transgressors alarmed older New Englanders; they also were uneasy about young men seeking a larger voice in public affairs. Even one individual, such as Henry Vane, had posed problems; large numbers of young men were more serious yet. Only in his early to mid-thirties himself, Roger Williams in 1636 wrote John Winthrop of the dilemma facing the fledgling settlement at Providence. Although the middle-aged residents needed the labor of single, young men, they were disturbed that the young hands were "discontented with their estate, and seeke the Freedome of Vote allso, and aequalities etc." Williams questioned Winthrop about the propriety of establishing community standards for the admission of new inhabitants. The screening of new residents proved to be one New England solution to controlling young people. The older townsmen of Roxbury had a different problem with their young men. When Joseph Weld, who was captain of the town's militia, died in October 1646, a vacancy opened. The young men of the militia wanted to elevate lieutenant George Denison, "a young soldier come lately out of the wars in England." "The ancient and chief men of the town" preferred Hugh Prichard. Prichard was a freeman, a requirement for the position, while Denison was not, and Prichard received at least twenty votes more than Denison. But the young men felt that one of their own had been slighted and, as John Winthrop put it, "were over strongly bent to have their will, although their election was void in law." The matter went to the General court, who found in favor of Prichard.[17]

* * *

Assaults, sexual misbehavior, drunkenness and carousing, attempts to enlarge political clout—such activities had to be curtailed, and middle-aged New Englanders instituted a series of laws and regulations with that end in mind. In part the Mayflower Compact was directed toward rebellious young men. Confronted by the "discontented and mutinous speeches" of "strangers" who contended that they were free to act as they wished because the patent applied to Virginia and not to New England, the leadership constructed a compact of all adult male settlers. By bringing young and middle-aged men alike "into a Civil Body Politic," they gained the promise of "all due submission and obedience." John Carver, William Brewster, Edward Winslow, Miles Standish, and William Bradford all signed the compact, as did Moses Fletcher, John Goodman, Thomas Williams, Richard Clarke, and John Alden.[18]

Just as the Mayflower Compact, while directed at all residents, had an underlying intent to control young men, so did laws against idleness and regulations on time spent in ordinaries. The Massachusetts Bay law against idleness, for example, on its surface was all-inclusive in its statement that "no person, Housholder or other shall spend his time idlely or unprofitably," and without specifying young people it singled out "common coasters, unproffitable fowlers and tobacco takers." The law when applied ordinarily combined idleness with other offenses, such as playing shuffleboard or cards, drinking, singing, and dancing, or staying at an ordinary too long; these activities disproportionately involved young men and, occasionally, young women. The townspeople of Plymouth were less oblique about the objects of their concerns, when they instructed their selectmen "to call such younge men or others as live Idelely and disorderly to an accompt for theire mispending theire time in ordinaryes, or otherwise and to take Course for their Reformation as shalbe by them thought meet."[19]

If laws against idleness, drunkenness, and other disorders pertained to the entire population, many of the punishments and preventive measures were aimed specifically at young people. In Rhode Island, authorities seeking to stop irreverent behavior on the sabbath took the positive step of instructing the towns "to alow what dayes they shall agree uppon for their men servants maid servants and children to recreate themselves, to prevent the incivilities which are amongst us exercised on that day." Others used more severe means to supervise and control their younger residents. When Plymouth first distributed land in 1623, it made grants to families and "ranged all boys and youth under some family." Whether those "boys and youth" were required to live with families is unclear, but there is no doubt that their economic interests were tied to families—an unhappy circumstance for the young men, who "did repine that they should spend their time and strength to work for other men's wives and children without any recompense." By 1668, Connecticut (1636), New Haven (1656), Rhode Island (1656), Plymouth, and Massachusetts Bay went further and legislated that all single persons had to reside with families. Even without laws on the books, colonies placed youth with families throughout the period. Jedediah Lambert was a rebellious son, and in 1638 his own father brought him to court. The court determined that Lambert should live with another family; and if his father couldn't find him a home, the court would do so. With legislation, towns acted more vigorously. In the single month of April 1669, the town of Dorchester warned twenty young men that they must submit to "famely Govrnment." These laws continued in effect throughout the century. Only because of Captain Moses Mansfield's intervention in 1686 did New Haven town authorities allow John Hancock to live in a house by himself. Although they waived the law on his behalf, they warned him that the privilege existed only "untill they shall see caus otherwise to order."[20]

Being required to live with a family was restrictive, but being placed into servitude was harsher yet. For "having lived an extravagant life," Thomas Higgins was required to serve John Jenny for eight years as an apprentice. Web Adey, on the other hand, was caught in a double bind. On the one hand, he was charged with working on two Sundays, yet on the other he was accused of "disorderly liveinge in idlenesse & nastynes." His punishment was to sit in the stocks and to place himself with a master. Adey, at the time, owned his own house and land, and the court ordered him either to sell or lease it. As is apparent in Adey's case, one did not have to be a youth to be subject to forced servitude. Jonathan Phillips was twenty-three when the Watertown selectmen questioned him about his "loosse living." They informed his mother that unless she better controlled him or put him under someone else's supervision, they would apply the law. Three months later, Jonathan Phillips, Samuel Benjamin (who then was twenty-eight or twenty-nine), Joshua Bassum, and John Knopp were ordered to place themselves with "some honest maisters for a yeare."

Two years after this injunction, Watertown authorities continued to inquire how these young, but aging, men were spending their time.[21]

Even if young men were working hard, supporting themselves, living unblemished lives, and managing their own shops, local authorities wanted them under supervision until they were twenty-one. Suggesting that it questioned both whether a person had mastered his craft with only three or four years of apprenticeship and whether such a young person was capable of governing and instructing others, the town of Boston in 1660 ordered that no one younger than twenty-one and with less than seven years' apprenticeship could open his own shop. They contended that such practice "threatens the welfare of this Towne." Was the "threat" to Boston's welfare the fear of shoddy products or the prospect of young men and boys living in dangerous enclaves? Probably both. For whatever reason, in 1664 the aspiring but underage cooper, Josiah Clarke, was forced to close his shop and complete his indenture.[22]

In the eyes of many, if not most, New Englanders (and certainly of the colonywide and local leadership), fathers and masters served similar functions, particularly as providers of instruction and discipline. Rhode Island made the connection quite clear. No young man, whether a son or a servant, was to have "absolute freedome untill the age of twenty-one years." In a series of regulations, they made no distinction between "sonne or servant" or between "parents or master." Whoever supervised young men were responsible for their conduct, and they could be fined for their son's or servant's breach of the peace. That was the same approach taken in Massachusetts Bay. The section on children in the Bay's *Lawes and Libertyes* laid out identical responsibilities for parents and masters. They were to instruct their children and apprentices to read, to know the capital laws, to understand religious principles, and to undertake "some honest calling, labour or imployment." If parents or masters were incapable of maintaining discipline, appropriate authorities were empowered to place the children or apprentices in other homes.[23]

No matter how vigilant, parents and masters couldn't oversee every minute of their charges' lives. Observant neighbors might assist, and one of the duties of each town's nightly watch was to spot and report disorderly conduct. Not only were watches to discover noise and disruption stemming from "danceing, drinckeing, Singinge vainlie &c," but also to inquire why any young men, young women, or "women or other persons, not of knowen fidellitie" were out walking after ten o'clock at night. To ensure that the watch didn't contribute to evening revels, assignments paired young men with older men. In the words of the *New Haven Town Records*, for example, watches were constructed so that "young and looser persons be as much seperated as may be: and that in each watch, with each young and less satisfying person, another more antient and trusty be joyned." In addition to parents, masters, neighbors, evening watches, magistrates, and local authorities, churches oversaw New England's youth. The historian Roger Thompson connects permissive parents and wayward young people with the revival of proposals for a half-way covenant. "One result of its passage in 1662," he claims, "was to bring a greatly augmented number of adolescents under the jurisdiction of church discipline."[24]

If disruptive or suspicious young people could be prevented from admission to towns or forced out when already present, the towns' problems would diminish. There are hints that such motives contributed to the policies of admission and warning out of seventeenth-century New England towns. Little more than a year after Roger Williams' inquiry of the propriety of townwide standards for the admission of young men, the nearby town of Portsmouth passed the regulation that "none shall be received as inhabitants or Freemen, to bild or plant upon the Island but such as shall be received in by the consent of the Bodye, and do submitt to the Government that is or shall be established, according to the word of God." Referring to Ipswich, the Reverend Nathaniel Ward wrote that they had imposed standards to judge who should receive lots. He regretted the policy had been too late to prevent awards of land being given to "many ill and doubtfull" persons, who "came in drinking and pilferinge." Later in the letter, he made it clear that the objects of his fears and contempt were the "multitudes of idle and profane young men, servants and others."[25]

* * *

Were Ward and his middle-aged cohorts overreacting? Were the young men (and to a lesser extent, the young women) of seventeenth-century New England a threat to society? There can be no doubt that some of New England's younger members contributed to the turmoil of the times. From murder to assault to drunkenness to fornication, young New Englanders were participants in all types of defined crime. Wherever there were high concentrations of single young men, there was an above-average incidence of crime or disorder. Yet such behavior was not unexpected. Most, if not all, societies have had to find ways to check the exuberance and sometimes antisocial actions of adolescents and young adults, and it is entirely possible that older generations exaggerated the level of disturbance. Perhaps envy of youthful energy and emerging power and a desire to retain their own place in society as much as actual incidents contributed to middle-aged fears of the young. That possibility is buttressed by the claims of some early New Englanders that the number of disruptive events was relatively few. Thomas Lechford, no apologist for Puritan authorities, wrote in a book published in 1642: "Profane swearing, drunkennesse, and beggars, are but rare in the compasse of this Patent, through the circumspection of the Magistrates, and the providence of God."[26] Any survey of seventeenth-century New England court records uncovers numerous young defendants, but neither their number nor the nature of their crimes was unusual in the English-speaking world. If anything, incidents such as drunkenness and premarital intercourse occurred less frequently than elsewhere.

The response of New Englanders to youthful offenders, in part, merely repeated English practice. The requirement that single persons live with families, for example, had English precedent from at least the 1560s.[27] What was unusual about New England laws was not that they sought to control young people (particularly young men) but rather their extent and the zeal with which they were enforced.

Middle-aged New England alarm may have been set off by the extraordinary proportion of single young people relative to the general population. In the period between the landing of the *Mayflower* in 1620 and the death of John Winthrop in 1649, nearly 27 percent of all New England colonists were between fifteen and twenty-four; males in that age group constituted 28.5 percent of the male population. By comparison, not quite 18 percent of the mother country's population were in that age range. Not only was the age structure of the New England population skewed toward the young; one-third of the adult males who migrated to New England before 1650 were single, young, and without family connection in their new land. Although after midcentury the ratio of males and females became more balanced and although time and longevity produced increased numbers of graying New Englanders, untypically large families kept the proportion of young people unusually high.[28] Young New Englanders behaved no worse, and probably better, than their peers in England did, but their extraordinarily large numbers fueled middle-aged imaginations with their potentially damaging force.

Perhaps what is most distinctive about these laws for supervising and restraining the young is their connection to a national covenant. The Puritan leadership believed it had made a compact with God to maintain a moral order. Puritans wanted government to regulate human behavior in line with scriptural injunctions. When the possible engine for those ends, Parliament, had been suspended in 1629, they were prompted to leave their native land.[29] Now in New England, they meant to enforce God's way, to keep their end of the bargain. Those who were not Puritans—disproportionately young men—had to be held to the same standards as everyone else, and the vitality of the young in general had to be channeled in moral directions.

* * *

There was one other segment of the population who received unusual attention from New England authorities: late-middle-aged women with strained family relations or no family at all. Those among this group who were without living sons and were from lower social ranks were most likely to be charged and prosecuted for witchcraft. In part, because they lacked willing, able, or living male protectors, these women were particularly vulnerable to accusations of all types from neighbors and other townsfolk. Equally important, these were people on the margins of family control. They often had had conflict with whatever family members remained, and these domestic eruptions oftentimes coincided with disputes with neighbors. When they challenged their place in society (through harsh words, an unwillingness to accept authority, the medicinal powers of a midwife, the unusual economic resources of a widow without male heirs, or even occult practices), they posed a threat to the expected gender, social, and church order.[30]

Fascination with the Salem episode of 1692 has led succeeding generations to exaggerate the importance of witchcraft in seventeenth-century New England. For most of the century, concerns about witches in their midst only arose sporadically, and even then authorities seldom brought defendants to trial and found them guilty. The historical significance of periodic charges of witchcraft comes more from what it tells us about New England society than about the accused. Although it is true that New Englanders perceived witchcraft primarily as a female crime, that is no more evidence of misogyny than the comparable opinion that murder and assault by virtue of their being viewed primarily as male crimes indicates societal contempt for men. Men and women alike could be threats to the social order, and in the seventeenth century, when family controls were not sufficient or were not present, the legal system filled the void, regardless of the gender of the accused.[31]

What the maverick Samuel Ford, the servant Dorothy Temple, and the accused witch Bridget Oliver had in common was weak, if not nonexistent, family supervision—a condition most typical of young men and women and of older women. The unusually large proportion of unattached young men during the first few decades of settlement compounded the problem. Those authorities, who controlled the law and its enforcement during the seventeenth century, were not so much warring on the young as youths nor on older women as women; rather, they were attempting to restrain that part of the population who, in their minds, were most likely to violate God's law and social order.

~❧ 7 ❧~

ECONOMIC BEHAVIOR
AND BELIEFS

Wwhen Robert Keayne died in 1656, he was one of New England's
wealthiest men; he also was one of its most unpopular. His
lengthy will, written between 1 August and 15 November
1653, with a brief addendum attached in mid-December, was his legacy,
his defense, and his revenge.

Combative throughout his life, he had clawed his way from a humble
background to affluence. Born a short distance from London at Windsor
in 1595 to a butcher and his wife, he was apprenticed to a London merchant from the age of ten to eighteen. Two years after his indenture concluded he was made a member of the Merchant Tailors' company. His
rise was rapid to the status of gentleman, and by 1623 he had become a
member of the Honourable Artillery Company of London, an organization more useful for its social and business connections than for military
preparation. Keayne attained his prominence by hard work and hard
dealing, and he acquired associates, perhaps some friends, and certainly
some enemies, along the way. He was among the merchants—Puritans
and those sympathetic to the Puritan cause—who financed the Plymouth
Company and the Massachusetts Bay Company.[1]

At some point he became a Puritan himself. Whether he acquired his
piety prior to those investments is not known. It is entirely possible that
his intense ambition awakened his awareness that avowed religious beliefs might ease his entry into particular merchant circles. Perhaps merely
the association with Puritan merchants opened his eyes to a religious life.
His marriage to Anne Mansfield in 1617 may have stimulated his interest in the Bible and Puritanism, for her sister was married to the Reverend John Wilson, who later became the pastor of the church in Boston.
Although there was little that was simple about Robert Keayne, he may

simply have become a believer. Regardless of what prompted his religious concern, before he, his wife, and their only surviving child, Benjamin, left for New England in 1635, he had become a genuine Puritan. His books on Scripture and religious subjects rested peacefully close by his account books. He recognized the centrality of justification, but he was comforted that God's blessings also indicated the eternal fate of one's soul.[2]

New England was a natural destination for an English Puritan in the 1630s, and Boston was an attractive settlement for an ambitious merchant with Puritan sensibilities. By the mid-1630s thousands of migrants were entering New England through Boston annually; most of them came with too few provisions, and none of them were or would become self-sufficient. Food, clothing, building materials, tools, animals, and all types of manufactured goods had to be purchased. Some of these items were produced locally, but there was a heavy dependence on imported goods, and few individuals had the capital, credit, and connections necessary for trade. London had provided Keayne with the opportunity for advancement, yet he remained a minor, though well-to-do, merchant. At Boston he could become a major figure, and he quickly took advantage of the circumstances.[3]

As he prospered economically, he became a pillar of the town of Boston and of the colony of Massachusetts Bay. In 1636 he joined his brother-in-law's church. He was appointed or elected to a variety of political offices, including repeated election as a selectman in Boston and as a deputy in the General Court. When the supporters of Wheelwright and Hutchinson were being disarmed, the General Court required them to relinquish their weapons at Keayne's home. He was the founder of the Ancient and Honorable Artillery Company in New England, and he imagined himself a military man. In 1652, his public life culminated with his appointment as judge of a county court.[4]

While he was writing his will in 1653, he could reflect on his prominence and good fortune. He had begun adult life with few advantages. Other than apprenticing him, his parents had done little for his advancement, providing him neither with land nor with other means for a livelihood. Through diligence, energy, and ambition he had struggled to financial, social, and political eminence. He was among the fortunate, and he believed himself to be a beneficiary of God's providence.[5] And yet he wrote this will a bitter, defensive, and vengeful man.

It is unlikely that the general populace revered any of the early merchants. Seeking profits and needing to offset shipping costs, they demanded higher prices than in England. Controlling the availability of goods and charging what the market would bear, they offered their fellow colonists the option of meeting their prices or doing without. Such merchant behavior easily bred resentment. Keayne may have been no more opportunistic than his brothers in trade, as he later would claim, but there was something about him—perhaps a cold calculation, perhaps too much steely joy in driving a hard bargain, perhaps too obvious an ambition to gain at others' expense, perhaps a mean spirit—that attracted contention. He may have won grudging acknowledgment of his success and ability, as his frequent elections would testify, but he also earned the animosity of those who dealt with him or who heard of his dealings.[6]

Keayne's siding with his brother-in-law, John Wilson, during the Antinomian episode in 1637–1638 was an admirable, even courageous, act of family loyalty, but it separated him from the vast majority of the members of the Boston congregation, including nearly all of the city's merchants. His support of the embattled Wilson, while hardly endearing him, probably could have been forgiven and forgotten. The designation of his home as the depository of the arms of the defeated defenders of John Wheelwright and Anne Hutchinson, a central and logical site, could not. His being brought before the General Court and his congregation on charges of improper trade practices in the following year was no coincidence.[7] Here was retaliation—for high prices, for a mean spirit, and for contributing to the downfall and humiliation of his fellow parishioners.

His troubles and unpopularity did not end in 1639. What followed was a series of public and private controversies. The most famous involved Mistress Sherman and her wayward sow, and the dispute erupted into charges of theft and slander, meriting the attention of the General Court. The unforeseen consequence of the case, as a result of the magistrates' supporting Keayne and of the deputies' agreeing with Sherman, was the division of the court into a bicameral legislature. The last tribulation occurred in 1652 when, after the General Court found him guilty of repeated drunkenness, he was forced to relinquish his judgeship.[8] Bitter and angry from these humiliations, he lashed out at his antagonists in his last will and testament.

Most wills in seventeenth-century New England consisted of only a page or two. Their ordinary purpose was to settle accounts and to distribute property. Occasionally, other wishes, such as how children should be educated or how a surviving spouse should be cared for, were included. Keayne's was no ordinary will. It contained 50,000 words, and it not only distributed property but also defended the activities of his life and attacked his detractors and opponents—real and potential.[9]

Recipients of his large estate were many. He provided the one-third widow's share for his "dear and loving wife," Anne, in the belief that it would be a "large and comfortable maintenance for her." In addition, she inherited her pick of books from his library, a silver beer bowl, "one feather bed and bedstead with a feather bolster and one pillow, two white blankets, one rug, two pair of sheets, two pillowbears, with a pair of curtains and valence suitable to her own use." He curiously added that these last gifts be "not the best of all that I have in my house but the . . . second or next to the best of all, if there should be any material difference between them." Later in the will, Keayne made clear that his wife's share was not for her free disposal, for he designated how her estate should be divided at her death: one-half for their son, one-fourth for their granddaughter, and one-fourth for Harvard College. What in fact Anne Keayne received for her self alone were the proceeds from her share. Those she could use for her "best benefit and use as long as she lives." Whatever remained after her expenses she could put aside "to distribute amongst her friends when she dies."[10]

Keayne also designated their adult son, Benjamin, to be a recipient of one-third of the estate. The bulk of Benjamin's inheritance was to be in land and houses, the better to lure him back to New England from England. Keayne believed his son "may do as well if not better [in New England] than in any other part of the world that I know of, [unless] the times should much alter." Besides, the shrewd merchant argued, should Benjamin sell the land, he would only obtain half its potential value. Like his mother, Benjamin was to receive his choice of the books as well as "a treatise on the sacrament of the Lord's Supper" and "3 great written paper books upon the exposition of the Bible upon this expectation and request that he would carry on the same work in manner as I have began, which will be a work of his whole life." In a seeming sentimental mood, Keayne bequeathed a keepsake that was not in his personal possession: a "great gold emerald ring that was my wife's father's and [is] now in my wife's keeping."[11]

Having fulfilled his obligations to his immediate family, he felt justified in disposing of the remainder of his estate "as I please." What followed was a long list of beneficiaries—thirty-seven persons in all—including family, friends, associates, former servants, current servants, and slaves. He also provided for a number of public works. He left funds for a water conduit, a townhouse that was to serve many public functions (including a marketplace, meeting rooms, storage for grain, a library, and an armory), the Artillery Company, the free school, the church primarily for the "relief of the poor members," and Harvard College.[12]

Not satisfied with designating gifts for worthy recipients, Keayne created a parallel world of those not worthy of bequests; and he named them in his will. In earlier wills, he had set aside a legacy for the Reverend John Eliot and his project of educating Indians, but since then Eliot had attempted to return to a group of Indians lands that Keayne and some partners had purchased and surveyed. People should not expect to challenge Keayne without retribution. Justice required an eye for an eye. What was offered could be withdrawn, and so it was. There was a lesson the merchant had for Puritan divines: "I would make it my request to the reverend elders of this country not to be too stiff and resolute in accomplishing their own wills and ways, but to hearken to the advice and counsel of their brethren and to be as easily persuaded to yield in civil and earthly respects and things as they expect to prevail with any of us when they have a request to make to us for one thing or another, lest by too much stiffness to have their own wills and way they hinder many good works that may be profitable to them_elves and to the whole country."[13]

Quite pointedly, he excluded two relatives from the fruits of his estate. Although he gave ten pounds to the two children of his wife's brother, John Mansfield, he refused to give anything to his brother-in-law and his wife. For many years, Keayne had supported Mansfield by paying his debts, winning his release from prison, setting him up in trade, and bringing him to New England "when his life was in some hazard." According to Keayne, Mansfield had returned his kindnesses with "distempered carriage and unworthy behavior," with "complaints to our elders and others," and with "false accusations." The public reading of Keayne's will reviewing Mansfield's faults and his exclusion from the estate would be instructive to his brother-in-law and redemptive to Keayne. "Besides," he added, "I know I shall leave to my loving wife, his sister, a comfortable estate who I doubt not will be willing and ready to do somewhat for him if his carriage to her as it hath been to myself do not hinder it."[14]

His most stinging retribution was saved for his former daughter-in-law, Sarah Dudley. She not only had dishonored him but also had scandalized the church and wronged his son, for which the church had excommunicated her for "irregular prophecying" and "falling into odious, lewd, and scandalous uncleane behaviour with one Nicholas Hart." She had left his son and remarried and, to his mind, had shown "no change or unfeigned repentance." She might be lost, but the child of her marriage to Benjamin Keayne, Hannah, could still be saved, and Robert Keayne fought to keep the child from her mother. Hannah should not live in her mother's home nor receive any education from her. Her grandmother and her father were to provide for her upbringing. Should both of them die before Hannah reached adulthood, John Wilson and his wife should rear her. If the child before she came of age were persuaded to give any of her legacy to her mother, she would be cut off from her inheritance except for "her maintenance and education during the time of her minority."[15]

Even his beloved Artillery Company was not spared from his scathing pen. Keayne compared his company with the London company, and it fell short. He expected smart maneuvers and a variety "of firings and charges." Spectators would be entertained, potential members would be encouraged to join, and the participants would be better prepared for future exigencies. But in Boston, the Artillery Company exercised too infrequently and lacklusterly, was poorly outfitted and supported, and its number was declining. Had that not been the case, his gift would have been larger.[16]

In this universe of parallel worlds of worthies and unworthies, of good and evil, there was some blurring prompted by fears of slights, false accusations, treachery, corruption, and ingratitude. Anthony Jupe, Mary Jupe Morse, and Benjamin Jupe fell into this netherworld. They were the children of Keayne's sister, Grace Jupe, and they had become his wards when both of their parents died. At the time of the writing of the will, Anthony Jupe and Mary Jupe Morse were living lives of independent adulthood, but Benjamin Jupe still was a minor, "lame and dim-sighted," and under Keayne's supervision. The suspicious merchant provided one hundred pounds for the three of them, with forty pounds going to Benjamin because of his infirmity. But there was a catch. Should any of them "grow proud, stubborn, undutiful, or troublesome either to my wife or son" or cast aspersions, they would be disinherited. Perhaps Keayne was fearful they would question his management of their mother's estate or challenge their share of his legacy, or perhaps he was just typically distrustful of human behavior. For whatever reason, before he completed his lengthy and time-consuming will, he added a proviso nullifying gifts reserved for Mary Jupe Morse and Benjamin Jupe, because of "some just occasions of offense that since have been given to me."[17]

He was similarly prepared for other relatives or friends who felt neglected. Although he believed he had remembered all living relations, should anyone "by reason of kin or consanguinity to me" make a claim upon his estate, each was to receive ten shillings so as to "cut off any further claim." And should any of the listed beneficiaries "not be contented with the legacies by me given to them but shall by any means prove vexatious or troublesome to my executor," they would be treated like the Jupes. This applied to his designated public works as well. Disclaiming any "just cause" for apprehension, he nevertheless laid bare his view of the possible. Political power might shift. "Corrupt or prejudiced men" might concoct "pretences" to steal away his estate. If he could help it, the dark world would not alter his intentions. Should anyone attempt to contest the distribution of gifts so as to personally benefit, all public legacies "save only that hundred and twenty pounds that I have given to the school and poor in Boston" would become null and void.[18] His implied hope was that public officials and the citizens of Boston would have a stake in protecting the wishes of his will.

In one particularly bleak section, Keayne even showed his suspicions of his wife and son. Countering the possibility that they would be displeased with his generosity toward friends and public works, he argued that there was an ample estate for setting aside one-third for such purposes. "If I thought that either of them should apprehend otherwise," he contentiously reasoned, "I would not have done for them nor provided so liberally on their behalf as I have done, for I know what power I have to dispose of my own estate and if their parts should have proved far less I think they ought to have been contented."[19] Sadly, he included even those closest to him in his confined and grumbling world.

Distrust and defensiveness permeated Keayne's will from beginning to end. Reality, to his way of thinking, was a competitive battlefield. People were either friends or foes, and there were far more of the latter than of the former. He conceived he had "many enemies that will be ready to take any advantage" against himself. Even kin could not be trusted fully, for they, like everyone else, might turn on him. Despite his material success, Keayne believed that he often had been treated unfairly. He wrote of the unkindnesses he had experienced, the "unneighborly discourtesies," the "unchristian, uncharitable, and unjust reproaches and slanders since I came hither." On occasion, he characterized such behavior and intentions as evil.

As a result of this view of the world, he devoted a large portion of his will to defending his actions, his decisions, and his bequests. His gifts to the town for a conduit and a townhouse were not self-serving: they would benefit all and, besides, he would not be alive to profit by them. If anyone should inquire why he had not given such gifts earlier, he responded that he had provided charities throughout his life, although there had been times when gifts were not possible without jeopardizing his estate and his family. Probably still smarting from his conviction for drunkenness, he argued that his many account books and his volumes of note-taking on several worthy subjects proved he had "not lived an idle, lazy, or dronish life, nor spent my time wantonly, fruitlessly or in company-keeping as some have been too ready to asperse me." His large estate, which he calculated to be worth £4,000, did not result from oppressing others but grew in relatively small increments from many years of hard labor. He figured that he had averaged not quite £100 per year over the course of forty to fifty years. "A tradesman or merchant that hath a full trade may get a 100 lb. a year above his expenses and a great deal more very honestly," he asserted, "without hurting his own conscience or wronging those that he deals with at all." The fact that he had undervalued his estate as only £1,000 for purposes of taxes, he glossed, was a common practice throughout the world, and he did "not think a man is bound in conscience to make known his whole estate and suffer himself to be valued to the uttermost extent thereof if he can honestly prevent it." He was paying more in taxes in New England anyway than he would have in England. The last substantive paragraph in the will defended to his wife and "any other [who] should be offended" why he had selected his son rather than her as his executor. His list of explanations included: his son was now "of full age"; Benjamin, being a man, was more fit for the burdens than she; and this arrangement would avoid the difficulties and conflicts that might arise should she remarry.[20]

Keayne had been a subject of controversy while still in England, and as he acknowledged in his will, he attracted criticism for his business practices as soon as he began trade in New England. His combative nature had existed prior to his problems in 1639, but his public humiliation from accusations, censure from the court, and an admonition from the Boston church confirmed and reinforced any tendencies he may have had toward distrust, bitterness, and anger. Nearly one-fourth of his 50,000-word will attempted to exonerate him from the charges of that year, and nearly every word exhibited the festering wound that had never healed.

In November 1639, Robert Keayne was brought before the General Court, accused of overpricing his goods. Widespread complaints were voiced over "the oppression used in the country in sale of foreign commodities," and Keayne was singled out as being "notoriously above others observed and complained of." On previous occasions, friends, magistrates, and elders had admonished him privately for taking unfair advantage of the short supply and high demand, and he had promised to reform; still, his sharp practices continued. In this case, the court presented him with a series of examples of his gouging the public. Buttons, bridles, nails, and thread had all been priced well above what one would pay in London. His markups produced from 30 percent to more than 100 percent profit over his cost.[21]

Keayne's chief antagonist, a magistrate, claimed that he not only had charged excessive prices but that he also had altered his books to increase his oppressive gains further. Two or three years before, the complainant had purchased a few thousand six-penny nails at the rate of eight pence per pound. More recently (and shortly before charges had been pressed against him) when Keayne demanded payment, according to the aggrieved magistrate, he increased the cost by insisting upon ten pence per pound. The evidence was Keayne's account book where the figure "six" in "six-penny" had been changed to "eight" and the figure "eight" in "eight pence per pound" had been altered to "ten." Keayne was taken aback, and he had no ready explanation. Fortunately for Keayne, before the General Court reached its verdict, a man who had worked for the purchaser reminded Keayne that the six-penny nails had been exchanged for eight-penny nails. Rather than create a new entry in his account book, he had written in the new figures over the old ones. This revelation convinced "many if not most of the Court" of Keayne's innocence on that particular charge, although his accuser remained dissatisfied.[22]

On the charge of oppressive prices, the General Court found Keayne guilty, but there was a split among them on how large the fine should be. The deputies for the most part agreed that £200 was proper (according to Keayne, some argued for as much as £1,000 or £500 and some form of corporal punishment, "such as my man's standing openly on a market day with a bridle in his mouth") while the magistrates believed £100 would be an appropriate punishment. They eventually compromised on £200 with the understanding that Keayne would only pay £100 until the court had time for further deliberation at their next session.[23]

The magistrates' reasons for moderation reveal the struggle that was occurring in early New England over proper practices for the establishing of prices and wages. Keayne was not the only culprit. They believed it was "common practice, in all countries, for men to make use of advantages for raising the prices of their commodities," and in Massachusetts Bay there was the "like excess in prices" for "cattle, corn, labor, etc." There had been frequent attempts to set standards for goods and for labor, but they all had failed. When limits were established on the wages of carpenters and other essential artisans, they moved to less restrictive locales or took advantage of the cheap land and went into farming. Only higher wages would lure them back. When ceilings were placed on the price of goods, merchants refused to sell them at those rates. The desperation of buyers was stronger than the law, and higher prices prevailed. By 1639 the General Court had abandoned attempts to set prices and wages and had transferred the issue to town discretion. Few towns acted. Without having a specific law that Keayne had violated, many magistrates felt most comfortable with moderate punishment. And some of them were merchants themselves.[24]

With the conclusion of the General Court, the Boston church began proceedings against Keayne. Some sought excommunication. Others preferred a milder reprimand. Keayne tearfully repented for his covetous behavior and attributed his faults to "ignorance of the true price of some wares, and chiefly by being misled by some false principles, as 1. That, if a man lost in one commodity, he might help himself in the price of another. 2. That if, through want of skill or other occasion, his commodity cost him more than the price of the market in England, he might then sell it for more than the price of the market in New England, etc."[25]

Keayne's testimony prompted John Cotton to lecture before the Boston congregation on those "false principles" and on Christian business ethics. He argued for the traditional ideas of just price and moral economy. His was a balance between the absolute and the relative, between the community and the individual. Cotton contended that a person should not charge interest on outstanding debts. If a cargo was lost because of shipwreck or some other calamity, that was God's will and, therefore, the owner should not raise prices on other goods to recoup the deficit. Similarly, if a person bargained poorly on a transaction, he should not increase his prices on those goods to compensate. Ineptitude in one deal did not justify gouging in another. At the heart of Cotton's economic beliefs was opposition to the "false principle" that a person "might sell as dear as he can, and buy as cheap as he can." There were community standards governing prices that should not be violated.

Were this the whole of his views, Cotton's goals might be summarized as support of community values, harmony, and equity. But he implicitly and explicitly modified this stance in the direction of relativity and the individual. According to Cotton, the proper price for a commodity was not fixed forever but was established by what was "usual in the time and place, and as another (who knows the worth of the commodity) would give for it, if he had occasion to use." He wanted prices to be just, but he also recognized and accepted that they fluctuated dependent on time and place and on what a buyer would pay. God, as in all things, had a role in supply and demand. If there was a scarcity of a commodity, it was proper to raise prices because the shortage resulted from the hand of God. Cotton supported a moral economy that accepted supply and demand. His only unequivocal positions were his opposition to usury and to passing on merchant losses to purchasers.[26]

With Cotton's guidance, the congregation found a middle way between excommunication and exoneration. They admonished Keayne for his poor judgment and false principles. Within the year and following another public repentance, Keayne was restored to full church membership. Probably equally satisfying to the troubled merchant, the General Court reduced his fine to £80.[27]

Not satisfied was Keayne's tormentor who initiated a new charge. He claimed that his father many years before in England had given Keayne £200 for safekeeping and that Keayne had dishonestly retained it. The seemingly wronged man, a magistrate, demanded that the Boston pastors with all the elders should conduct a hearing, and they agreed. Keayne remembered that he had repaid the funds but initially could not find any evidence to support his disclaimer. Before the meeting with the elders, Keayne "by a singular providence of God . . . found a clear and full receipt in one of my books, to whom I had paid his 200 lb., where and by whose order." Rather than simply produce the paper and close the case, he chose to toy with his antagonist. At the hearing, there were passionate accusations and denials, but no evidence. The elders, perplexed by the impasse, agreed to Keayne's suggestion that he would look through his books for a receipt and then they would meet again. At the next meeting, Keayne prolonged the proceedings by asking his accuser whether he had any recollection of the £200 having been paid, and, as he anticipated, the response was a vehement denial. Finally, Keayne produced the receipt, and his adversary left in defeat. After his accuser's departure, the wily merchant told the group of elders that he intended to sue "for the slanders and injury that he had done to me," but Cotton cautioned him to postpone his suit until less volatile times.[28]

Keayne apparently never sued, but he used his will to state his case and, he hoped, to reclaim his fine and his reputation. Despite his public confessions and repentance, he argued he had done nothing wrong, at least by the standards of human beings. Before God he was a sinner and, like all humans, deserved divine censure. "Yet I dare not say nor did I ever think (as far as I can call to mind)," he continued, "that the censure [from the General Court and the church] was just and righteous from men." In his estimation, his prices were a fair markup; but the 1630s were a time of "all buyers and few sellers," and the buyers rose together in complaint. By the time of the writing of his will, he contended, many of those buyers had become sellers and their prices were considerably higher than he had ever charged.[29]

In short, Keayne was a seventeenth-century New Englander who supported early preindustrial, capitalist economics. He believed in supply and demand. He thought he should be free to charge whatever the market would bear. He practiced usury. He sought to maximize his gains. He perceived goods as commodities—abstractions with monetary value. As the historian, Bernard Bailyn, observed, he was a calculating man, as witnessed by his numerous account books. He conjured material objects into quantitative figures that represented profits and debits. That was how he viewed the world. In his will alone, he used the word "profit" or a variation of it thirty-five times. Although the word occasionally was a synonym for benefit, it typically meant a return on an investment or possession.[30] Among the purposes of his accumulation of wealth was the well-being of his family and his family's future; his life, however, demonstrates that he also chased material gain for its own sake as well as for the status and power it provided. His chagrin, in part, was that his wealth did not shield him from the jealousy and outrage of his neighbors. Although he wished to help his community and those less fortunate than himself, he primarily was an individualist who placed his own advancement before all else. He was both a Puritan and a Yankee. He welcomed God's grace and sought God's blessings, and he had difficulty distinguishing between the two.

* * *

Although, when it came to economic views and practices, Robert Keayne may have been in advance of most early seventeenth-century New Englanders, he was not an aberration. There were numerous fellow merchants, agents, and land speculators who shared the perch with him. They too pursued profits, kept ledger books, competed for gain, used credit, and charged interest. They simply weren't so notorious as Keayne.

The more prominent merchants in the early years of the New England colonies traded for furs and provided settlers with essential goods. As the crunch of the Great Migration ended in 1642 and with a declining fur trade, those involved in international trade searched for new markets and new opportunities. Hampered by New England's limited exportable products and by the citizenry's shortage of money, they became shippers as well as traders, and their ships sailed between many ports and anchored in as many harbors as there were potential profits. In April 1645, John Winthrop noted in his journal that "one of our [Massachusetts Bay] ships, which went to the Canaries with pipestaves in the beginning of November last, returned now, and brought wine, and sugar, and salt, and some tobacco, which she had at Barbadoes, in exchange for Africoes, which she carried from the Isle of Maio." Central to merchant success were honest business associates at a variety of these destinations. Always short of capital, these entrepreneurs needed credit, and they needed partners and agents they could trust. Typically, they established commercial relations with other Englishmen (often kin), for the common bonds of language and culture made such trade easier to arrange; nevertheless, they did not disdain foreign opportunities, even with their nation's enemies, if such transactions had a reasonable chance of success.[31]

Although there were traders and shopkeepers scattered throughout New England, the bulk of the international merchants resided in Boston, Salem, and Charlestown. They participated in politics throughout the seventeenth century. During the first years of settlement, their political influence was contained within their own towns, particularly in the office of selectman. By the end of the century, their power—like their fortunes—had enlarged, and they held colonywide offices and possessed the prestige and connections needed for swaying colonywide institutions and individual attitudes. What held them somewhat in check was their fragmentation. Although there were general areas of agreement, their competition with one another kept them from becoming a single force.[32]

* * *

Some merchants with investments in New England never left England, but placed the day-to-day operations of their enterprises in the hands of agents. On Richmond Island off the coast of Maine during the 1630s and early 1640s, John Winter managed the widespread interests of the British merchant Robert Trelawny. At least forty men and a few women were under Winter's supervision at any one time. Most were fishermen, but their number also included shipmasters, carpenters, coopers, and farmers for the raising of corn and livestock. With few exceptions, these were contracted workers, who typically agreed to three-year terms, fixed annual wages, and food, clothing, and lodging. They often were an unruly and uncontrollable lot. Winter constantly lamented their leaving before their terms were up and their poor working habits. "This is no Contry for loyterers," he observed, yet to his mind he was plagued with shirkers. "Our Carpenters heare worke very sparingly," he wrote to Trelawny, "but yett they must have great wages, & the[y] must not be spoken unto to hasten their worke." He had little recourse. If he should fire a worker, there seldom were suitable replacements available. If he could locate a skilled worker, the person demanded too high a wage. If he wanted to retrieve a person who departed before his contracted term had expired, he had little assistance, "being heare in a lawles Contry." What was he do to? As he conceived the situation, "heare is neather law nor government with us about these partes to right such wrongs, & I am but on[e] man." His wife was no more pleased. Few of the women were any better than the men. They lounged while she milked and kept the dairy, baked, brewed, mended clothes, and engaged in all the various tasks necessary to maintain the large company. After seven hard years, Winter pleaded for "a good woman servant," for his wife "hath worren out her selfe in labour."[33]

   That, of course, was Winter's perspective. Workers at Richmond Island often drew other conclusions. If they broke their contracts by running away or if they slowed their work or if they demanded high wages, there was just cause. Sometimes, Winter delayed paying their wages or reimbursing them for expenses. The quality of the food was poor, and clothing was not always adequate. And if Winter's company store could charge what the market would bear, why couldn't they demand as high a wage as would be paid?[34]

   At times Trelawny must have considered abandoning the effort. In letter after letter, Winter told him of the problems he was encountering. The fishing catch too often was below expectations; the supply of beaver was declining as was demand in London; winter, wolves, and Indians were killing their hogs; the Indian trade had disappeared; and it was difficult receiving payment for debts from the local English population. As Winter characterized the situation, "the most part of the dwellers heare ar[e] good buyers but bad payers." At least the fishing (despite poor catches) remained profitable—and there was the land that Trelawny continued to accumulate.[35]

* * *

For a predominantly agricultural population, there was no possession more valuable than land. Even the nonfarmer Robert Keayne had most of his assets in land. At a time of fluctuating prices and an uncertain money supply, Keayne found land to be a secure investment for future sales and current rents, which compensated for its not being so profitable as other ventures. As the population grew, however, land (particularly in developed areas) became increasingly valuable, and many a New Englander found a rewarding sideline in land speculation. In some instances, the acquisition of undeveloped land was an investment in one's family's future. Sons and daughters (especially sons) and grandsons and granddaughters would have land to make possible the independent livelihood of their own families. Yet there were others, the speculators, who acquired land as an asset to sell to the highest bidder; their holdings typically were widely scattered as compared to the consolidated land of the family patriarchs. The major speculators negotiated with Indians and others, wheeled and dealed with government officials, surveyed boundaries, and settled thousands and thousands of acres. They contributed to developing the land in English style, for better and worse. Although the most prominent players were affluent and powerful members of the New England elite, more ordinary colonists tried their hand at the land game as well. At least two of Herodias Long's husbands were land speculators—one well to do and influential, the other less well placed. John Porter, her third husband, was one of the seven shareholders of the Pettaqamscut Company that purchased twelve square miles of land in what would become southwestern Rhode Island. George Gardiner, her second husband, purchased 1,000 acres of that land in 1663, which built the foundation of his family's eventual wealth and probably ignited the combustible series of events leading to his separation from Herodias Long and her marriage to John Porter.[36]

* * *

Merchants, agents, and land speculators were not the only New Englanders who attempted to profit through a market economy. During the period of the Great Migration, particularly from 1630 to 1640, it seemed as if anyone who had anything to sell—whether it be a commodity or labor—

tried to take advantage of the unusual circumstances. Robert Keayne, though greedier and more mean-spirited than most, shared an acquisitive *mentalité* with the general population. Early capitalist values permeated merchant, farmer, artisan, and laborer alike. Only servants and slaves were unable to participate in the competition for material gain.

People migrated with minimal possessions but some ready cash. Their needs were great, and, at least at first, they had the means to purchase. Houses had to be constructed, livestock acquired, trees felled and fields plowed, food and beverages bought, cloth, shoes, household goods, and tools purchased and sometimes repaired. At first, there was too much to be done without assistance. The fortunate brought their own servants, but even they ordinarily required additional help. These immigrants were at a disadvantage until they settled with houses built and crops planted, and they complained of the exploitative conditions. But they could look forward to thousands of new migrants, and last year's buyers became this year's sellers. They objected to oppressive prices and wages when they had to acquire goods and labor, but they relished the opportunity when they were on the supplying end.[37] Few New Englanders during this disruptive decade opposed a market economy on ideological grounds. Their complaints and their applause were relative to their situation.

All of this changed with the coming of the English Civil War. Migration diminished to a bare trickle. Demand and prices declined. Cash, which had been as plentiful as new immigrants, returned to England in payment for imported goods. Soon there was little circulating currency to purchase goods. Debts had to be paid off with products, produce, and labor; new goods had to be purchased in similar fashion. New England entered into a barter economy.

The immediate consequence of these changes was a depression. "Corn would buy nothing," John Winthrop wrote in his journal on 2 June 1641, "a cow which cost last year £20 might now be bought for 4 or £5, etc., and many gone out of the country, so as no man could pay his debts, nor the merchants make return into England for their commodities, which occasioned many there to speak evil of us."[38] The long-term consequences were adjustments to the conditions that would prevail throughout the remainder of the seventeenth century. Merchants struggled to find ways to profit, and they and land speculators retained their capitalist ways. Servants and slaves remained in dependency and near them were tenant farmers and fishermen. Life was more complicated for farmers who owned their own land (the bulk of the population) and artisans. Those close to the commercial towns and international markets continued to pursue profits when possible, but they easily could be caught in a local, limited economy. The more distant from broad markets the more a farmer focused on subsistence, supplemented by surplus. Opportunity rather than ideology determined a person's *mentalité*. People settled for competency rather than chose it. Perhaps in the eighteenth century and in the early nineteenth century when confronted by industrial capitalism people clung to competency, but that was not the case in the seventeenth century. The interpretation of "from Puritan to Yankee" offers a false dichotomy; both were present and important from at least the 1630s.

* * *

Some working people remained in a dependent situation, at least for a fixed number of years. A minority, yet substantial portion, of the early migrants came as servants. They had sold their labor for a number of years in return for passage to New England and their maintenance. While indentured, servants were members of their master's household and were under the direct supervision of their master and his wife. At best, the relationship could blossom with respect and affection, much like the affinity for a loved son or daughter in a family. The end of service might be rewarded with gifts of goods or land, and particular skills might have been acquired. Cordial relations might continue after the indenture was completed, and years later a servant might be remembered in a will. At worst, a servant might experience the horrors of a dysfunctional family, with the attendant abuse including the withholding of food and clothing, beatings, and even death. Whether it be a loving or a dysfunctional family, masters and mistresses attempted to regulate their servant's behavior throughout the day, not just during working hours. Servants' rights during their term of service were little different from those of slaves; being English, however, they could easily assimilate during and after their indentures.[39]

Unlike the history of other British colonies in North America, indentured servitude did not last long as a significant institution in New England. When those who came with the Great Migration completed their terms, they soon started their own households or left New England. There were sporadic but few replacements for them. Although labor was needed, most New Englanders did not have the means to purchase full-time, year-round labor.[40] The soil and climate were not conducive to large, specialized commercial crops, as was the case to the south. Servitude soon became an institution limited to providing welfare for the offspring of poor families, control of previously unsupervised young men, and occasionally training for apprentices.

Sometimes, a former servant might exist in the netherworld of neither landowner nor servant and would hire out. In the early years of settlement as in John Winter's Maine, such an arrangement could be lucrative, and a person with diligence could amass sufficient funds to attain independence. Less fortunate were those who through bad luck, limited skills, or lack of discipline became perpetual laborers or hands. They found work in the larger towns or on the farms of absentee owners. In a land where surplus crops were exchanged for goods and produce, few farmers had the funds to hire full-time hands. Instead, they worked their sons and exchanged labor with neighbors when necessary. The historian Ann Kussmaul's comparison of servants and laborers in England applies to seventeenth-century New England: "To be a servant was to be a potential farmer, but to be a labourer was to be a realized failure."[41] Laborers sold their time whenever possible; dependence, even with a bleak future, was preferable to starvation.

Most desperate of all were slaves. Following the Pequot War, there was human bounty to distribute. New England authorities sent male, Indian children to Bermuda, but the women and girls were "disposed aboute in the townes." A minor feeding frenzy took place as various prominent colonists vied for the captives. Israel Stoughton requested "the fairest and largest that I saw amongst them" and other "squaws" for associates. The Reverend Hugh Peter, on behalf of himself and John Endicott and unaware that boys already had been sent to Bermuda, wrote John Winthrop that they "would bee glad of a share viz: a yong woman or girle and a boy if you thinke good." Fearful of the mistreatment these slaves already were receiving, Roger Williams promised three Indian women that "if they would stay at my howse and not run away" he would attempt to secure them for himself.[42]

African slaves were present in New England as early as 1639, if not sooner. The voyager John Josselyn told of at least three who were owned by Samuel Maverick in October of that year. Residing at Maverick's home as a guest, Josselyn was startled by an African woman's "very loud and shril" singing outside his bedroom window one morning. When he went outside to find what was troubling her, she spoke only in her native tongue but conveyed her grief through gestures and facial expressions. Discussing the matter with his host, Josselyn learned that she once had been a queen and that Maverick, wishing to breed slaves, had attempted to force "a Negro young man" upon her. John Winthrop's brother-in-law, Emmanuel Downing, also envisioned possible profits and a solution to the labor shortage by the use of African slaves. He suggested to Winthrop that Massachusetts Bay should war on the Narragansett. Putting a religious gloss on his scheme and understanding his relative, he argued that an English victory would curtail devil worship and that the Indian captives could be exchanged for "Moores." Slavery, in Downing's estimation, was the only way they would thrive and "see this great Continent filled with people." Besides, he concluded, "you know verie well how wee shall maynteyne 20 Moores cheaper then one Englishe servant."[43]

Not all New Englanders agreed with Downing. In 1652 Rhode Island legislators attempted to end the practice of slavery. They passed a law that limited bondage of blacks and whites to no more than ten years or to the age of twenty-four, if a person was first enslaved younger than fourteen. Having salved their consciences, they instituted a halfway deterrent as a penalty: a fine of £40, half of what the Massachusetts Bay General Court charged Robert Keayne for excessive prices. Forty pounds was a substantial sum, but people who were willing to pay that fine could own slaves indefinitely. Whether there were people who paid the fine or whether the law was unenforced, slavery, though on a small scale, continued in Rhode Island. In Boston, town officials placed bounds on slave activities. Probably more to protect local artisans than to hinder slavery, they prohibited the use of slaves in any craft activity or manufacturing. When Thomas Deane in 1661 attempted to use his slave as a cooper, he was ordered to desist.[44]

The number of slaves in New England during the seventeenth century was less than 1 percent of the population. Edward Randolph estimated in 1676 that there were "not above 200 slaves" in the northeastern colonies.[45] Restricted in activity and few in number, most slaves worked fields of absentee owners or served as domestics. Their owners typically were wealthy merchants and pious ministers, and to a certain extent slaves were household ornaments—tributes to the wealth or prestige of their owners.

* * *

Somewhere between servants and slaves on the one hand and independent artisans and farmers on the other were fishermen and tenant farmers. These were people without the means for independence, yet not so wretched as to sign an indenture nor so unfortunate as to be enslaved. Most fishermen did not own their boats, let alone have the international connections for marketing their catches. Their usual practice was as a company of fishermen to make arrangements with an outfitter to rent a boat or boats and to receive necessary supplies for their work. In return, they were obligated to give their catch to the outfitter, who would deduct his expenses and pay them their shares based upon previously agreed rates. They did not control the tools of production, but neither were they employees. They were clients. The more fortunate fisherman might earn enough over time to acquire his own boat and perhaps a few acres and a house. Less frequently, a fisherman might become an outfitter himself and avoid the perils of the sea, if not of the market. In the latter part of the century, merchants began to purchase deep-sea fishing vessels and to hire crews, and fishermen began to sell their labor to the highest bidder rather than tie themselves to particular patrons.[46]

Tenant farmers had similar client-patron relationships with owners of land. A basic arrangement for the use of land required the tenant farmer to pay rent and taxes, perhaps deforest a fixed number of acres, and construct some sort of building. Even so, the farmer had to have seed and farm implements. Lacking those and possibly wanting livestock to raise and the use of oxen or horses for plowing, he might enter into a client-patron arrangement similar to fishermen and outfitters. The tenant farmer in that situation was obligated to give a portion of his animals' offspring or his crops to his patron rather than attempt to sell or exchange it on a more open market. For some who were young, poor, and without family support, this was a beginning toward propertied independence. For others, this was an inescapable way of life.[47]

* * *

Many of the immigrants, such as the large number of weavers from East Anglia, had been artisans in England. In New England, they found it more difficult to make a living from the full-time practice of a craft. Most towns needed a wide range of goods but could not support the full-time employment of many artisans—perhaps a miller, perhaps a blacksmith, but few others. The greatest demand for trades was in the seaport towns, where the populations were larger than in rural communities and where there was active maritime commerce. Coopers, shipwrights, shoemakers, and carpenters were far more likely to be found in Boston than in Billerica. Those who continued to practice their crafts throughout New England typically supplemented their incomes by farming. More likely, they were primarily farmers, as were most male New Englanders, who owned their land and who augmented their earnings however they could.[48]

Not even New England farmers were self-sufficient. They depended on the assistance of others and the exchange of goods and produce. Economic decisions were made with both subsistence and surplus in mind. What a family could grow, raise, and manufacture provided a substantial core, but survival, comfort, and accumulating land, cash, and goods for offsprings' futures depended on participation in an exchange economy. The decision of what proportion of family economic activity should be devoted to subsistence and what proportion to surplus was based on skills, opportunities, goals, and attitudes.[49]

It may be that the ideal of competency—with its implicit goals of material comfort and economic independence—played a part in forming the decision. There can be little doubt that the colonists sought material comfort. If given the choice between warm housing and a drafty hut or tent, between substantial meals and meager rations, between sufficient clothes and rags, between amenities and bare necessities or worse, seventeenth-century New Englanders chose comfort over asceticism or poverty. But comfort was a term relative to a person's aspirations and opportunities. If the choice were between moderate prosperity and affluence, the answer is less clear-cut. Robert Keayne believed he was leaving his wife and son "comfortable" estates, and it is easy to imagine that his sense of comfort had no bounds. In his will, he used the word "comfort" or a variation forty-four different times. What was comfortable to Keayne was unbelievable luxury to other settlers.[50] And yet would any New Englander have turned down a fortune such as Keayne's and settled for moderate prosperity?

In the seventeenth century, New Englanders sought profits and partici-pated in a market economy. They bargained for higher prices of goods and labor if they were selling and for lower prices if they were buying. They created marketplaces and fairs in Boston, Dorchester, Duxbury, Hartford, New Haven, Plymouth, Providence, Salem, and Watertown for the exchange of goods and livestock, and the bulk of the seventeenth-century English population lived close by those towns. Outside of those organized markets, people negotiated with merchants, shopkeepers, landowners, and anyone else wanting to engage in a transaction.[51]

Increased opportunities for market behavior, however, didn't mean that everyone could or would participate. Even if people had unlimited material aspirations, there were checks on what they might do, such as the location of their residences. When Edward Johnson surveyed the var-ious towns of early New England for his readers (often potential colo-nists), he commented on their commercial possibilities: the marketplace of Charlestown, the shops, warehouse, and markets of Boston, the iron and lead of Lynn, the timber of Hingham, the cattle of Ipswich, and so on. New Haven was plagued by "their remotenesse from the Mattachu-sets Bay, where the chiefe traffique lay." Dedham was in a better location near Boston, "whose coyne and commodities allures the Inhabitants of this Towne to make many a long walk."[52] The more remote a farm, the smaller its potential market and the more likely its owner would be con-fined to the trade of his neighbors. Affluence—so unlikely, if not impos-sible for those removed from regional or international markets—was not worth dreaming about, but one could hope to purchase cheap land and prepare for one's progeny's future.

Living within trading distance of a market town was no guarantee of success. A person had to have the means to profit. A tenant farmer near Springfield was much more restricted in opportunity than the farmer who owned his land in Dorchester. An artisan with his own tools and experience was better able to benefit than the unskilled laborer at the mercy of whoever would hire him. And religious scruples could inhibit a person's behavior. Not only religious divines, such as John Cotton, questioned certain market activities. In his conversion narrative, John Fessenden confessed to Thomas Shepard that in England he "was tempted to sell on the Sabbath day and so I resolved not to sell on that day and the Lord kept me from it. And then I heard sin of using many words in bargaining. . . . And to buy as cheap as I could and sell as dear as I could was my sin." Most New Englanders would have respected Fessenden's dilemma, but they would have found a way to combine piety and profit, and there is no record whether Fessenden maintained his marketplace reservations after his admission to the Cambridge church. Responsibilities to family and kin most likely more than religious considerations hampered market activities.[53] A needy relation could divert marketable produce, and haggling over price was inappropriate no matter how irritating the relative.

And then there was the other prong of competency: independence. Would a person have traded his independence for improved comfort? There is no easy answer to that question; independence, like comfort, had many levels. No one in seventeenth-century New England was absolutely independent nor self-sufficient. Everyone was dependent to one degree or another on other people. What one could aspire to or hope to retain was the economic independence coming from the ownership of the means of production, whether that be land or tools. This possibility was startling: while the idea of independence may have been long-standing, the reality of independence was new for most New Englanders. Few had owned their land outright in England. Perhaps the reverence for economic independence was not so ingrained as it later was with New Englanders in the late eighteenth century and the early nineteenth century when they were faced with industrial capitalism. And in the seventeenth century, farmers did not have the option of farm families in the nineteenth century when it could be more materially comfortable to work for someone else in a city. The issue was moot. Independence and comfort were complements, not choices.[54] To lose independence was to diminish material comfort. Tenant farmers, servants, laborers, and fishermen were evidence of that reality. For members of those groups, the choice was not comfort or independence but rather dependence and survival versus dependence and desperation. Better to be a client or a servant and survive with the hope of future independence than to be at the mercy of a town's kindness and without hope. Better yet to own land.

* * *

Almost all of the analysis thus far has pertained to male economic behavior and attitudes. But what of women? In general, there were gendered spheres of labor. Women typically worked in the house and the adjoining garden while men toiled in the fields, but this division of labor depended on season, circumstances, and occupations. Except for domestic tasks, such as cooking, and midwifery, men might pursue almost any type of work. Conversely, "almost any task was suitable for a woman," the historian Laurel Thatcher Ulrich writes, "as long as it furthered the good of her family and was acceptable to her husband." If a crop needed to be harvested and labor were scarce, a woman would work in the fields by her husband and sons. If a shopkeeper or merchant were away, his wife as "deputy husband" would manage the business. Running an ordinary required both men and women. When James Leonard's wife died, his license for his ordinary was revoked, since he no longer was "soe capeable of keeping a publicke house, [and] there being alsoe another ordinary in the towne." Similarly, Alice Thomas (presumably a widow) was approved "to sell wine, beer & keepe a house of publique entertainmt provided Wm Norton take the care of the government of the house."[55]

Work in seventeenth-century New England was a family affair, and women were an integral part of the household economy. What needed to be done to advance their family's economic well-being, women did. To that extent, we can assume that women shared the economic attitudes and goals of their husbands. Whether a merchant's wife, a fisherman's wife, or a farmer's wife, she was no more comfortable than her husband and she would have sought her family's advancement and future every bit as much as her husband. If market behavior benefited her family, she supported her husband's negotiations. If fixed prices kept her family from misery, she advocated such restrictions.

Although women were essential parts of household economies, that role did not prevent a separate, gendered economic sphere. Garden produce and manufactured goods such as cheese, butter, and yarn that were not taken to market could be exchanged with other women. Work such as midwifery also could be exchanged for goods. There may have been a hierarchy of obligations among neighboring women. When Rachel Ramsden, who was twenty-three and just two years married, went to Alice Bishop's house on an errand, Bishop asked her to "fetch her som buttermilke at Goodwife Winslows, and gave her a ketle for that purpose, and shee went and did it."[56] Whether Ramsden gladly assisted her older neighbor or whether her age and former poverty (she was one of Francis and Christian Eaton's offspring) compelled her to oblige is unknown. Just as uncertain is the nature of economic exchange among women. Because the activity occurred within a community, were there relatively fixed values that were observed or did women haggle over price or equivalent value of goods and services?

Competency was primarily a male aspiration; while women could share in material comfort, opportunities for independence were severely limited in a patriarchal society. Women might sacrifice for their husband's and sons' independence (and for themselves, to the extent independence was intertwined with comfort), but the most they could hope for their daughters was comfort. Widowhood was one of the few opportunities for female independence. If their one-third share was of sufficient size, widows who did not live with offspring, such as Anne Keayne after Robert's death in 1656, were economically independent for the typically brief period until they remarried. Sometimes widows ran their own businesses, particularly ordinaries and cookshops. Of the thirty-two people authorized by Boston officials in 1674 to sell wine, beer, strong water, and cider indoors in an ordinary or outside in a cart, eight were women, at least four of whom were widows.[57]

* * *

Although a scant majority of emigrants during the 1630s came as Puritans, almost all transplanted English people—merchant, farmer, and laborer alike—brought acquisitive, market-driven values with them. That economic frame of mind had predominated in England perhaps from the thirteenth century but certainly from the late sixteenth, and it was not abandoned on New England soil. Reformed Protestantism reinforced rather than opposed that *mentalité*. The focus on the individual and disciplined behavior connected Protestantism and early capitalism.[58] But with the end of the Great Migration and the resulting depression, opportunities diminished and behaviors changed to fit the new conditions. In the years that followed attitudes and actions responded to circumstances, and the same person could use a variety of strategies in the course of a lifetime. Acquisitive aspirations surfaced when opportunities allowed, but many had to settle for competency and some struggled simply to survive. Servants and slaves continued to be part of a patriarchal and hierarchical system. For a fixed period for servants and perhaps indefinitely for slaves, their every activity was monitored and their well-being was dependent on the disposition of their masters. Tenant farmers and fishermen were more independent, but their economic activity was checked by patron-client arrangements. Farmers who owned their land (and there was diversity within this group depending upon the location of farms), artisans who controlled production, land speculators, and merchants more freely participated in a mixed market-exchange economy. They sought profits as well as subsistence; they aspired to higher status as well as to family advancement; they sold and purchased goods for cash as well as making exchanges; and they viewed the world as commodities to be traded as well as God's domain.

❧ 8 ❧

SCATTERED LIKE SWEDES

New England Towns

In May 1669, when the General Assembly of Rhode Island declared Westerly the fifth town of the colony, nothing about the settlement resembled traditional visions of a New England town. There was no central cluster of houses and house lots watched over by a meetinghouse. There were no active villagers gossiping and bartering in shops and marketplaces. There were neither harmonious peasants nor communitarian idealists happily working the soil as loving neighbors. There was nothing about the area that in later centuries might be referred to nostalgically as quaint. Westerly was a "town" without a core. The only ideology that held it together was a common and competitive greed for land. Captain John Mason of Connecticut described the inhabitants as "a people that will come under noe government, neyther civill or eclesiastic; they beinge already in dispersed corners like the Swedes, soe that there is noe likelyhood of any tollerable Christianlike society to be settled amongst them."[1]

Rhode Island founded Westerly as a means to anchor its claim to disputed territory. When Roger Williams secured a patent from Parliament in 1644 for the towns of Providence, Portsmouth, Newport, and Warwick, and for the land owned and occupied by the Narragansett, Rhode Island was not yet a political entity. By the time monarchy was restored in England in 1660, much had changed. The four towns had joined together as Rhode Island and Providence Plantations, and they continued to claim the land south of Warwick and between the Pawcatuck River and Narragansett Bay. The strong Narragansett sachems, Miantonomi and Canonicus, had died, and a power vacuum resulted, producing uncertainty and conflict among the Narragansett and leaving them vulnerable. Massachusetts Bay proclaimed prior jurisdiction over Pequot country (which, it argued, included land west *and* east of the Pawcatuck River), as part of their booty for conquering the Pequots, and it created a paper town astride the Pawcatuck, Southertowne, to bolster their words. A group of land speculators, including Humphrey Atherton and John Winthrop Jr., through a series of shady maneuvers gained title to land within the Rhode Island patent. The southern land claims of the Atherton Company conflicted with part of the land acquired by a group of Rhode Island speculators known as the Pettaquamscut Company, one of whose members was Herodias Long's third husband, John Porter. To complicate this muddle further, an additional crew of Rhode Island speculators, including Governor Benedict Arnold, purchased title to land south of Warwick and west of the Pettaquamscut territory (called Misquamicut, later to become Westerly) and they actively sought settlers to protect their investment.[2]

The consequence was claim and counterclaim: the United Colonies versus maverick Rhode Island, outside land speculators versus Rhode Island land speculators, the Atherton Company versus Rhode Island, Southertowne settlers versus Misquamicut settlers. Usually this was a battle of words, but occasionally adversaries asserted physical force. William Chesbrough, a sixty-six-year-old resident of Southertowne, testified that "about thirty six inhabitants of Road Island" were laying out lots within Southertowne boundaries on the east side of the Pawcatuck River. When he confronted them, Benedict Arnold and others answered that "they would not try their title any where but in Road Island, or in England." Angry Massachusetts Bay authorities ordered the constable of Southertowne to "apprehend all such persons" and to bring them before the colony's magistrates. Walter Palmer arrested Tobias Saunders, Robert Burdett, and Joseph Clarke and conveyed Saunders and Burdett to Boston. In response to charges of "forcible entry and intrusion into the bounds of Southertown," Saunders and Burdett contended that with the approval of the Rhode Island General Court they had purchased land from Indians and lawfully had begun constructing homes and farms. Their arguments were ineffective, and they remained in jail for a year until £100 each was raised as security.[3]

As if there weren't complications enough, the ascension of Charles II placed all land claims and charters in jeopardy, particularly if they had been acquired during the English Civil War or Interregnum. With greater concerns before it, Massachusetts Bay removed itself from the contested territory. Connecticut stepped into the breach and claimed the territory the Bay colony had vacated, both to advance its own territorial ambitions and to serve as a shadow advocate for the Atherton Company. Roger Williams was outraged. Writing to the deputy governor of Connecticut, John Mason, he reviewed his own influential role during the Pequot War, acquainted Mason with the fact that the Pequots did not live east of the Pawcatuck River, and reminded him of the Rhode Island patent that granted them the area. "However you satisfy yourselves with the Pequot conquest," Williams fumed, "you will find the business at bottom to be, First, a depraved appetite after the great vanities, dreams and shadows of this vanishing life, great portions of land in this wilderness . . . . This is one of the gods of New-England, which the living and most high Eternal will destroy and famish. 2. An unneighborly and unchristian intrusion upon us, as being the weaker, contrary to your laws, as well as ours, concerning purchasing of lands without the consent of the General Court."[4]

But soon the issue was outside of New England control. Both Connecticut and Rhode Island desperately needed new charters with royal assent, and new charters potentially could resolve the boundary controversy. Rushing to London as Connecticut's agent, John Winthrop Jr., skillfully presented his colony's (and less directly, the Atherton Company's) case. The resulting royal charter of 1662 drew Connecticut's boundaries from Massachusetts Bay's southern border to the Sound and from "Norrogancett River, comonly called Norrogancett Bay" to the Pacific Ocean. The way was prepared for Connecticut to swallow up New Haven colony and to acquire all of southwestern Rhode Island. New Haven soon capitulated, but Rhode Island fought back through its influential agent, John Clarke. After more than a year of tactical maneuverings, Clarke and Winthrop reached an agreement that established the Pawcatuck River ("which said River shall for the future be alsoe called alias Narrogansett, or Narrogansett River") as the boundary between the two colonies. In addition, they concurred that the owners and inhabitants on Atherton Company land could "choose to which of those Colloneis they will belong." In the Rhode Island charter that soon followed, Clarke successfully upheld the boundary of the Pawcatuck River but conveniently neglected to acknowledge the option made to members of the Atherton Company. According to the charter, the company was under Rhode Island's jurisdiction whether it liked it or not.[5] At worst, the investors could lose title to their land. At best, they would have to work out an accord with Rhode Island authorities.

Overseeing British colonial policy, the earl of Clarendon anticipated continued conflict and appointed a royal commission to investigate and resolve the various controversies surrounding Connecticut and recently acquired New York. Before the commission arrived, trouble already had erupted in Narragansett country. Twenty or more men from Southertowne (which became part of Stonington under Connecticut jurisdiction) crossed the Pawcatuck River, broke into James Badcocke's house, and carried him back across the river as a prisoner. The Rhode Island government protested to Connecticut authorities and suggested that representatives of the two colonies should meet to establish a boundary. In the meantime,

Rhode Islanders retaliated in kind. Pressure was placed on people living on Atherton Company land to pledge their allegiance to Rhode Island. When John Green instead took Connecticut's side, he was seized and brought before Rhode Island authorities, where he quickly recanted and was restored to Rhode Island protection. Although both colonies made halfhearted attempts to negotiate, each found reasons to delay, and no progress was made.[6]

This was the climate the royal commissioners surveyed when they visited the area in late winter 1665. They were appalled by the situation. From John Porter's home in the Pettaquamscut region of the contested territory, they declared that for the time being the king would resume jurisdiction and Narragansett country would be known as the King's Province. Rather than being a setback for Rhode Island, the order put them in a strong negotiating position: Rhode Island authorities were appointed as the magistrates and justices of the peace for the area. The chief loser was the Atherton Company, whose transactions with the Indians were disallowed. Residents were required to leave within the year. When one of the royal commissioners, Richard Nicholls, who had not been present, later intervened, the action against the Atherton Company was rescinded.[7] All other decisions remained in place. The way was prepared for a resolution between Connecticut and Rhode Island. Should Connecticut accept the Pawcatuck River rather than Narragansett Bay as its eastern boundary, should Rhode Island recognize Atherton Company holdings as legitimate, should the Atherton Company in return acquiesce to Rhode Island sovereignty, the controversy could have concluded. Of course, all three contingencies would have to occur almost simultaneously, and of course they didn't.

Recriminations and hostile acts continued—a house was destroyed, a lot was laid out without authority, and so on—and neither colony, despite calls for meetings and the appointment of agents, found it desirable to negotiate. The sticking point was whether the Pawcatuck River, sometimes called the Narragansett River, was the boundary. Connecticut repeatedly claimed that the Narragansett River was Narragansett Bay, and Rhode Island countered that the Pawcatuck River and the Narragansett River were the same. They left little room for compromise.[8]

Four years after the royal commissioners' unsuccessful declarations, Rhode Island and Connecticut still had not met. At that point in 1669, Rhode Island tried a new tactic: it created a town on the eastern side of the Pawcatuck River. The place called Misquamicut became the town of Westerly, and Tobias Saunders and others were now townsmen as well as freemen. But calling an area a town didn't make it one. It remained a geographical designation for scattered settlers. Almost certainly, Rhode

Island authorities were aware of the charade, for at the same session of the General Assembly they agreed to send agents to meet with Connecticut.[9] Westerly was not so much a bargaining chip as a means of legitimizing Rhode Island aspirations.

Finally, on 14 June 1670, representatives from both colonies met at New London. The Rhode Island delegation insisted that all negotiations be in writing, and for three days communiqués were exchanged. But all was for naught. Connecticut continued to argue that the Narragansett River was their eastern boundary and that the river and the bay were the same. Rhode Island, unwilling to relinquish its southwestern territory, referred its adversaries to the 1644 patent, the 1664 charter, and the royal commissioners' determination of the King's Province, all of which set the Pawcatuck River as the boundary. The problem, as the Connecticut agents (Governor John Winthrop Jr.'s eldest son, Fitz-John, was one of the three) well knew, was that their charter confused the Narragansett River with Narragansett Bay; although Governor Winthrop in his agreement with Clarke had acknowledged that "Pawcatuck" and "Narragansett" described the same river, they refused to deflate their territorial ambitions. Profitable lobbying by the Atherton Company also strengthened their resolve. The conference dissolved with matters worse than before.[10]

The following day, 17 June, both sides in their frustration opted for force. The Connecticut commissioners ordered the residents of Westerly (which they called Squamacuck) to "submit to the government" of Connecticut, and they authorized the constable of Stonington, John Frink, to gather the Rhode Islanders to hear the declaration. The Westerly citizens did not appear. Instead, Tobias Saunders empowered James Badcock as a constable to arrest those claiming authority over them. Badcock apprehended Frink and two other Stonington residents. Almost immediately, Badcock and Saunders were captured and brought before the Connecticut commissioners. The Connecticut agents had a deal. They offered Saunders a town office under Connecticut jurisdiction. Whether Saunders accepted is unclear, but both he and Badcock had to post bail to appear before magistrates at New London the following June.[11]

Rhode Island, as usual, protested, but the following spring they asserted their own strong-arm tactics. The General Assembly warned that Connecticut citizens, particularly from Stonington, who disrupted Rhode Island lives would forfeit any land they owned east of the Pawcatuck River and would face additional prosecution. Residents of Westerly who professed loyalty to Connecticut also would lose their land. Westerly victims who incurred damage would be reimbursed from the sale of confiscated property. Connecticut's response was to apprehend one of Westerly's officers, John Crandall. When Rhode Island objected, Connecticut replied that people in the disputed territory were supposed to choose which government they wanted rather than having it imposed, and they complained that their citizens were the ones being molested. The Rhode Island General Assembly defiantly held their next session at Westerly. Just prior to the meeting the constable, James Badcock, was requested to call all the local residents in. The much-abused Badcock, caught once again in an awkward position, refused. Nevertheless, twenty-two adult males attended the meeting and swore their fidelity to Rhode Island. Two of the four nonattendees, including James Badcock, reversed themselves the next day, and they too acknowledged the sovereignty of the king and the Rhode Island government.[12]

For all the melodramatics, little was gained. Once again, there was charge and countercharge. The tedious jousting was interrupted by King Philip's War, when English settlers abandoned the Narragansett region, but immediately after the war Connecticut and Rhode Island resumed their skirmishing. Not until 1728—nearly sixty years after Westerly was declared a town—did the two colonies eventually agree that the Pawcatuck River was their boundary.

*   *   *

Despite Westerly's unusual early history, it shared some characteristics with other New England towns. Border disputes were not limited to Stonington and Westerly but were common throughout the region. Most towns formed during the first fifty years of English colonization claimed huge amounts of land and possessed imprecise borders—perfect tinder for flaming words and fiery acts. Of the twenty-five Connecticut towns incorporated by 1675, the average size was slightly more than 100 square miles, ranging from the 50.6 square miles of Greenwich to the 224.1 square miles of Farmington. The Reverend Nathaniel Ward of Ipswich, concerned that Massachusetts Bay's generosity to its towns would discourage continued migration from England, asked John Winthrop in 1640 to curtail the practice. Ward told of "some honest men" of his town who knew of sixty-eight towns in England that together would fit into Ipswich. For his own part, he was aware of "neere 40 where I dwelt." Ipswich's adjacent town, Rowley, according to Ward, was even larger.[13]

The imprecision of town lines came from Indian purchases that occasionally overlapped and that were based on changeable physical features, from careless colonial grants, from sometimes unscrupulous land speculators, and from land-hungry settlers. Colonial governments overwhelmed by the illusion of a vast, unpopulated wilderness and desirous of expanding their jurisdiction often gave land that was not theirs to give and, for roundheads, were most cavalier in designating boundaries.[14]

Vague town borders contributed to conflicts between individual land-owners as their own properties were contested. Potentially provocative but ultimately a safeguard once property lines were accepted, fences protected crops from roving animals and lessened the likelihood of arguments between neighbors. Ezekiel Rogers, the minister of Rowley, thought the same solution could be applied to disputes between towns; in this case he was referring to the boundary controversy between his own town and Ipswich. Anticipating Robert Frost by three centuries, he wrote: "Touching the buisinesse of the bounds, which we have now in agitation; I have thought, that a good fence helpeth to keepe peace betweene neighbours; but let us take heede that we make not a high stone wall, to keepe us from meeting."[15] Rogers was correct that fences could reduce conflict; without prior agreement over boundaries, however, fences could be torn down as easily as they could be constructed. Many a New England fence was destroyed during the seventeenth century.

* * *

Just as the experience of boundary disputes linked Westerly with other seventeenth-century New England towns, so too did its scattered farms. By the time of Westerly's incorporation in 1669, there were few nuclear, open-field towns remaining. That was not the intent of some of the early English leaders nor of many of the first English settlers. Both John Winthrop at Massachusetts Bay and William Bradford at Plymouth wanted to establish single, unified communities, and they were disappointed when early colonists dispersed to several settlements. For the seven hundred people who sailed with Winthrop, conditions required that they form many groups rather than one. Poor sanitation and widespread sickness along with the fear that a single cluster of people was too easy prey for possible French attack drove them from the huts and tents of Charlestown to form seven towns within three months of landing. In succeeding years, following the arrival of more emigrants, additional towns were created, and substantial portions of three of the original towns' populations left Massachusetts Bay to establish Hartford, Wethersfield, and Windsor along the Connecticut River. New arrivals who had migrated with family members, friends, neighbors, and congregations often wanted to re-create the communities they had left as quickly as possible; others, prompted by a desire for more pastoral land for their animals and perhaps more breathing space from Bay associates, chose to migrate again.[16] Roger Williams, John Wheelwright, Anne Hutchinson, and other dissenters had no choice. They were expelled from Massachusetts Bay and forced to form new settlements or leave New England.

But even with the forces for dispersion, the individual towns could create close-knit communities. Each of them could group houses closely together. They could have common meadows, common herds, and common woodlots. Their town members could work several strips of land in outlying fields where neighbors jointly decided what to plant, when to plant, and when to harvest. There were many incentives for establishing such nuclear, open-field towns. Numbers of people living in close proximity watched over each other and provided protection from attack— whether by Indians, French, Dutch, or Satan—and neighbors offered psychological comfort to those reeling from dislocation and unfamiliar surroundings. In a new and threatening world, what could be more comforting than the reestablishment of familiar patterns? People who came from the areas of England where open-field villages were the norm and who had the numbers or clout to dictate the spatial arrangements of land distribution and farm practices created open-field towns in New England. During the lifetime of the first generation of residents of Andover, Dedham, and Rowley, for example, open-fields characterized their towns.[17]

The goals of protection from outside threats, of safeguarding the morality of the community, and of neighborliness did not preclude the placement of houses on unified, individual parcels of farmland. With farms in fairly close proximity to each other and the town center, that arrangement offered the advantages of community and farming practices familiar to those from English consolidated farms, such as were typical in East Anglia. Whether towns chose open-field or consolidated farm agricultural practices, or even some other variation, the Massachusetts Bay General Court attempted to require people to live close together. In 1635 they ordered that all people reside within half a mile of a meetinghouse. The forces for dispersion, however, were more powerful than the forces for unity, and in 1640 the General Court rescinded its failed policy.[18]

In some parts of New England, dispersion had been the practice from the beginning or as soon as land was divided. Plymouth colony never had open fields, and as soon as individual plots of land became available people scattered throughout the "towns." Small groupings of neighbors, living on consolidated farms, formed here and there, but they were parts of towns—villages and neighborhoods within townships—not entire towns. Individual, dispersed farms also was the agricultural practice of the settlements north of Massachusetts Bay. Similar to Westerly, most northern villages were more collections of family farms than town-centered communities.[19]

By 1660, most of the original open-field towns were changing to consolidated farm communities. Although such towns held vast acreage, early divisions of land were made in small strips relatively close to the town centers. Most of the land was held in reserve for distribution to

newcomers and for later divisions among the original landowners. In following years, new divisions by necessity were farther from the town nu-
cleus, and they tended to be larger individual parcels than at first. The
growth of population, primarily resulting from large families, and the desire to enlarge their estates compelled parents to seek land for their children and themselves, and they pressured town proprietors to release sections of unassigned territory. Residents began to trade, purchase, and sell
their separated strips and blocks of land so as to form consolidated holdings that eventually they could divide among their own offspring. Over
time, farmers grew weary of trekking to distant fields, and they moved
their houses to their farms. For some, dispersion proved more conven-
ient; for those who originally came from consolidated farms in England
the change returned familiar ways; for still others, the distance from
town center and from fellow citizens provided greater privacy and less
scrutiny.[20]

Separation from the town core was not free from disadvantages. Although residents on outlying farms avoided long walks from homes to
fields, they now had to trudge several miles to a meetinghouse for religious services and lectures once or twice a week. Tax revenues also
seemed to be spent more for the benefit of the central town than for its
peripheral neighborhoods. Groups of neighboring families and kin questioned whether it would be better to form their own town with its own
meetinghouse and minister and its own local government, and they negotiated, often heatedly, with original towns for separation. Wenham split
from Salem, Medfield from Dedham, and Malden from Charlestown.[21]
By the time of Westerly's incorporation, New England towns composed
of scattered, consolidated farms were the norm. Nuclear, open-field communities, never a majority in New England even before 1650, disappeared by the eighteenth century.

* * *

Although many town functions had antecedents in England, the town itself was an invention, not an inheritance. Parallels can be seen in the parish, the manor, and the village, but there was no institution in the mother
country identical to the New England town. Had Winthrop, Bradford,
and other leaders had their way, there would have been no towns; the colony and the community would have been one. But dispersion brought
multiplicity, and multiplicity created unanticipated responsibilities and
opportunities. Two tasks, the distribution of local land and the establishment of local churches, required immediate attention. Administrative and
governmental obligations—laying out and constructing roads and fences,
supervising animals, maintaining order, training militias, providing

schools, raising taxes—developed soon after. Town offices had to be authorized, and town officials had to be elected and appointed. Land agency, church, local government, community—together these separate but linked units formed most seventeenth-century New England towns.[22]

* * *

There were common features to New England towns, but there were significant differences as well. A quick glance might confuse Westerly with Stonington or Dedham with Andover, but even the briefest of glimpses would not mistake Westerly for Dedham or Dedham for Springfield or Springfield for New Haven or New Haven for Boston. While there were New England towns, *the* New England town never existed. Towns varied by economic behavior, community orientation, distribution of wealth, life patterns such as age at marriage and age at death, religious focus, population size, geographical features, even degrees of disorder. But if there wasn't a single type of town, were there enough similarities between groups of towns to justify designating types?

Numerous historians have struggled with that question with varying degrees of success. Depending upon one's criteria, there are a host of possible answers. Analyzing Connecticut, Jackson Turner Main discovers trading centers, agricultural villages, old towns, and frontier settlements, but he concludes that the differences were small and that the various towns all "belonged to the same basic species." Stephen Innes, looking for settlement zones rather than types of towns, takes a different approach and identifies three separate New England regions: "an urbanized coastal region, typified by Boston and Salem, a subsistence farming region comprised of towns like Dedham and Andover; and an area of highly commercialized agriculture, such as the towns of the colony's breadbasket—the Connecticut River Valley." Edward M. Cook, using a variation of central place theory for eighteenth-century New England towns, finds five types. "the city or urban center"; "the major county town"; "suburbs to the cities or . . . secondary centers in the rural counties"; "small, self-contained farming villages"; and "newly settled, struggling, and unstable . . . frontier towns."[23]

All three interpretations are useful and compatible models. My own conclusion, nearly identical to Cook's, is a variation of their leads. At one end are commercial towns with substantial international trade and at the other are frontier villages, generally isolated from other towns and founded late in the century. In between are secondary political and economic centers, towns subordinate to commercial towns and secondary centers, and agricultural towns generally established by midcentury and a moderate distance from centers.

These categories are hardly foolproof. They give the impression of permanency whereas individual towns were continually changing, and they suggest uniformity within type whereas there is variation even within the categories. Categories are constructs, not realities. They are alternatives to chaos and therefore satisfying to minds trying to make sense of the muddle of the past. But for all their limitations, they should refute the idea that a single generalization describes all New England towns.

Commercial towns. Boston was unlike any other settlement in New England. As a consequence of its geographical location jutting into a deepwater harbor and the circumstances that placed the government of Massachusetts Bay within its confines, Shawmut—without the intention of its early English residents—soon emerged as Boston, the political and economic center of all New England. It had the largest population, and upon disembarking most emigrants temporarily resided there before settling elsewhere. By the end of the first decade, its meetinghouse was too small, and even its spacious new meetinghouse could not provide seating (or standing) for the growing populace. By midcentury, almost all agriculture had left the peninsula and was replaced by shops, houses, warehouses, and wharves. As crafts and trade displaced food production, Boston by necessity established a symbiotic relationship with the countryside. Sailors, artisans, merchants, colonywide officials, seekers of government favor, goodwives, farmers bringing produce to market, tavernkeepers, laborers, and prostitutes, the godly and the godforsaken—all were attracted to Boston.[24]

Only one other town, Salem, came close to duplicating New England's central place. Over its first four decades, it gradually polarized into a commercial and crafts core and a farming hinterland. Once Wenham and Beverly established themselves as independent towns, the Salem peninsula in all meaningful ways became Salem town, much to the distress of the outlying and agricultural Salem village. Like Boston, Salem soon was dominated by merchants and artisans and sprinkled with sailors.[25]

Boston and Salem were more densely populated than other New England towns in the seventeenth century, which produced problems not faced by other communities. The threat of fire was chief among them. Where the burning of a house or barn was a threat to the lives and well-being of individual Dedham or Braintree households and possibly a neighbor or two, a fire in Boston or Salem potentially could destroy the entire town. Where Watertown required all householders to have ladders and New Haven insisted that chimneys be swept, Boston and Salem had elaborate plans for the controlling of fires, including the blowing up of houses in a fire's path so as to save the rest of the town. Watches in the two commercial towns patrolled the evening streets looking for suspicious people who might be plotting arson. Such precautions were warranted. In 1676, an accidental fire in Boston consumed fifty houses and a meetinghouse. The following year, on three separate occasions lighted candles were discovered on roofs but were extinguished before fire spread. The perpetrators remained unknown.[26]

Diverse and relatively large populations contributed to other differences in the commercial towns. Both towns had greater wealth and greater poverty than was typical elsewhere. By the standard of gini coefficients (a statistical measure of wealth distribution where 1.0 represents absolute inequality and 0.0 represents absolute equality) greater inequality existed in Boston and Salem than anywhere else in New England (see appendix F). They were the only towns where the gini coefficient was above .60 (.68 in Boston and .62 in Salem) and where the top 10 percent of residents controlled more than 50 percent of total wealth (60.6 percent of all Boston wealth was held by its top 10 percent and the Salem elite held 56.9 percent of its town's wealth). By way of comparison, the slave South as of 1860 and the industrial North in the late nineteenth century had gini coefficients greater than .80, and it was highly unusual for any village, even in the middle colonies, to have a distribution of wealth as low as .30.[27]

Even life events, such as birth, marriage, and death, differentiated Boston and Salem from most other towns. In Boston, men and women married earlier than New England averages, had smaller families, and died younger (see appendix G). In Salem, men married earlier while women married at average ages, but families were smaller than for New England in general, and both men and women died younger than regional averages. Higher levels of poverty, exposure to a broader range of diseases and a transient population, poorer sanitation, and a large concentration of maritime and mercantile occupations probably offered different life choices and made life riskier than in rural villages.

Secondary Political and Economic Centers. This group of towns served as centers of colonywide government (such as New Haven and Plymouth), held regular market days or fairs or was the chief trading town in its area (such as Hartford and Lynn), or was the home of an extraordinary individual who participated in international trade and had broad influence (such as William Pynchon's and then John Pynchon's Springfield and John Winthrop Jr.'s Saybrook). Unlike Boston and Salem, most of these towns had economies where agriculture was integral, if not dominant. Their merchants typically participated in regional commerce but had little experience outside of New England; quite often they were engaged in farming as well. Charlestown, which for a while came close to being

Boston's twin city, was the exception, with a number of merchants involved in broad commerce. The secondary centers tended to be more individualistic and competitive than communal and harmonious. Like the two commercial towns, these were the homes of land speculators. Also similar to Boston and Salem, none of these towns ever were nuclear, open-field communities.[28]

Wealth in most of these towns was more concentrated than anywhere in New England outside of Boston and Salem. Their gini coefficients were in the mid- to upper .50s, and the top 10 percent controlled more than 40 percent of their towns' total wealth. New Haven was the exception, with its wealth distribution more like subordinate towns.[29] The demographic experience of the residents of the secondary centers provided no consistent pattern, ranging from Charlestown, New Haven, and New London (which were similar to Boston and Salem with young marriages, relatively small families, and earlier than usual deaths) to Newport, Providence, and Saybrook (whose male residents married older and lived longer than most New England males).

Subordinate Towns. Subordinate towns were satellites of commercial towns and secondary centers. They fed Boston and Salem and provided food for trade. Pointed toward trade centers, they devoted a substantial portion of their land to commercial agriculture. Their general level of affluence, as measured by median wealth, tended to be higher than in other types of towns, and their wealth, as demonstrated by gini coefficients and the concentration of resources held by the top 10 percent, was spread more equally than in commercial towns and secondary centers. The towns close to Boston—Cambridge, Dorchester, Roxbury, and Watertown—were homes to several powerful individuals who often served as magistrates of Massachusetts Bay, and Cambridge hosted Harvard College. Although there was a variety of demographic experiences, the residents of these towns generally lived lives close to regional norms: men marrying near the age of twenty-five and women near twenty, and seven children per family. If there was any common departure from New England standards, it was they had the good fortune to live somewhat longer than average.[30]

The fishing villages of Gloucester and Marblehead are included in this category because of their economic subordination to Salem and Boston and because of Marblehead's proximity to Salem, but they were quite different from the other subordinate towns. These were the poorest of all the towns surveyed, and what little wealth they had was divided unequally. Young seafaring men notorious for their rowdy behavior populated Marblehead in particular. Gloucester, in comparison to Marblehead, had a higher proportion of families and an economy where fishing was complemented by farming. By the end of the century, Gloucester functioned more like an agricultural town of the following category.[31]

Agricultural Towns. Here finally are communities that resemble the stereotypical New England town. Many of these were subsistence villages that at initial settlement were laid out with houses and house lots clustered close to one another and to a meetinghouse and with outlying areas composed of open fields, common pastures, and common woodlots. All were incorporated no later than 1651, and the original settlers almost always were proprietors entitled to future divisions of town land. In general, their populations were small relative to all categories but frontier towns, and their trading spheres were local rather than regional. Although these towns were predominantly, if not entirely, agricultural, some of them supplemented their incomes with other products, such as lumber from Hingham and cloth from Rowley. Agricultural towns were not free from internal turmoil, but if utopian, harmonious communities are to be found, here is where to look.[32]

The tendency toward equal distribution of wealth may have promoted harmony. To be sure, there was social and economic stratification, but these towns, as measured by their gini coefficents, the percentage of wealth controlled by their top 10 percent, and the close correspondence between means and medians of probated estates, were the most equitable of all New England towns. Surprisingly, Dedham, defined by Kenneth Lockridge as a "Christian Utopian Closed Corporate Community," was one of the few exceptions, with a gini coefficient of .55 and 46.6 percent of the wealth held by its top 10 percent.[33] Perhaps its trading relationship and nearness to Boston influenced Dedham or perhaps the small number of probated estates (18) distorted its actual nature. Dependent on the acquisition of land, the people of the agricultural towns married somewhat later than their counterparts elsewhere in New England; needing farm workers, they had larger families than typical; and perhaps enjoying lives of fellowship with families and kin (and maybe even neighbors) and more protected from attack than people in frontier towns, they lived longer lives than most New Englanders.

Frontier Towns. The name for this group of towns is not intended to resuscitate Turnerian images but rather to designate towns located on the edge of English, not human, settlement. They typically were isolated from longer established towns, and all were founded in the last half of the seventeenth century. None of them began as a nuclear, open-field community. Like Westerly, which belongs to this category, they consisted of scattered, individual farms. Land speculators formed many of these settlements and often were absentee owners. Deerfield, for example, was the creation of a number of Dedham residents who hoped to profit by selling land, but not by living there themselves. In several instances, a church was a belated afterthought. Frontier towns provided opportunity for people with enough resources to purchase land, construct a house, and farm the soil, but who were too poor or too late to acquire property in well-established towns. The advantage was cheap land; the danger was vulnerability to attack by Europeans and Indians. These circumstances help explain the demographic experience of residents of frontier towns. Like citizens of agricultural towns, they married somewhat later than average for New England as a whole; they had the largest families compared with residents of any other type of town, but their lengths of life differed significantly. Men in Topsfield averaged over seventy years before death, while inhabitants of Deerfield and Hatfield were cut down at early ages by tomahawk and fire.[34]

* * *

Not only were there divisions by types of towns, there also were divisions by personal standing within towns. Some people were "proprietors" or "commoners." They held title to land and were eligible for future divisions of unassigned land. During the first few years in the original English towns, nearly all adult male landowners were proprietors. The population surge soon altered that practice. Fearful that remaining town land would all be given away to newcomers and wanting to preserve later allocations for themselves and their children, by 1635 proprietors began restricting their membership. "Agreed by the Consent of the Freemen (in consideration there be too many Inhabitants in the Towne & the Towne thereby in danger to be ruinated)," the Watertown meeting decided, "that no Foreainer comming into the Towne, or any Family arising among our selves shall have any benefitt either of Commonage, or Land undivided but what they shall purchase, except that they buy a mans right wholly in the Towne." Approved new people could purchase property, but they were not eligible for additional allotments unless they also had purchased a share in what had become a land company. As colonies granted large quantities of land to colony officials and other prominent men and as land speculators began acquiring chunks of territory, it became possible for a person to be a proprietor of several towns simultaneously. A proprietor need not be a resident. Although political rights, such as voting, might be eliminated for nonresident proprietors, their economic rights as owners remained.[35]

New England towns attempted to be closed communities. They determined who was eligible to live within their boundaries. They sought religious orthodoxy and moral behavior, but their bottom line was financial solvency. They did not want to admit people who would become dependent on town welfare. Even John Brown, who was born in Dorchester, was not granted automatic admission when he returned to help his parents. After first warning him out of town, local officials eventually relented and admitted him as an inhabitant. Those, like Brown, who passed the admission test were welcomed as permanent residents and were designated as "inhabitants."

The first inhabitants of the early towns generally also were proprietors with full economic and political rights. When towns limited the number of their proprietors, inhabitancy no longer guaranteed a stake in common lands, but it did make people eligible to purchase property and set up shops and manufacturing. Should they become ill, incapacitated, or simply impoverished, inhabitants were entitled to town assistance. Boston grew alarmed by "sojourners, inmates, hyred servants, journeymen, or other persons that come for help in physick or chyrurgery, whereby no litle damage hath already, and much more may accrew to the towne." By midcentury, Boston and other towns began protecting themselves from such responsibility. Before being admitted as an inhabitant, a person or the person's sponsor had to "give sufficient Security, whereby the Towne, may be freed and secured from all such costs and charges, as may thereby com upon it." Local officials could not be too careful. Cautious Salem authorities in 1676 accepted refugees, driven from their towns by King Phillip's War, after being assured they had provisions for one year. Perhaps they were trying to avoid the experience of Boston which after providing shelter for English victims petitioned the General Court for "such reliefe & redresse that noe particular Towne may be burdened thereby."[36]

Short-term residents with no town economic or political standing were "sojourners." Magistrates or selectmen had to approve even such temporary dwellers. The object was to discourage runaway servants, public charges, or disruptive people from settling. Town residents could have guests stay with them, but visits longer than a week ordinarily required official approval to avoid fines. Experience often led to such regulations. New Haven warned the sick Elisha Weeden out of town and placed him on a ship for England. When the ship was "lost," Weeden somehow returned and the town was stuck with him. To avoid similar charges but not wanting to discourage traveling merchants or visiting family members, New Haven established rules for temporary residency. Because sojourners usually received unfixed lengths of time for town privileges and because even deadlines could be forgotten or overlooked, they could become permanent residents by default.[37]

The consequence of these divisions into proprietor, inhabitant, and sojourner was a fragmentation of the towns. In 1659, for example, Dorchester town records reported separate meetings of the selectmen, the "generall" town, and the proprietors. Some Dorchester residents might have attended and participated in all three meetings, while others at the other extreme were eligible to attend and perhaps speak, but not vote, at only the general town meeting. These inequalities were additionally exacerbated by splits between church members and non–church members.[38]

* * *

New Englanders in the seventeenth century in part were connected by a common institution: their invention, the town. Although the family was the most central institution for New England lives, the town was the most important public institution. Life was lived at the local level. On occasion, colonywide power intervened, but more typically the critical decisions that shaped lives were made within the family or the town. More complex than a parish, manor, or village, the New England town nevertheless closely resembled English settlement patterns and differentiated the region from the Chesapeake colonies.

Immigrants brought traditional practices of land distribution, land use, and local governance with them from the mother country, but England was not uniform. Different areas had different traditions. And there was the rub. Although some New England towns were dominated in their early days by substantial numbers of people from the same area or even parish in England, no town was absolutely homogeneous. Try as people might to preserve old ways, negotiation still was necessary. Where towns were composed of migrants from diverse regions, conflict and compromise produced new forms; if conflict continued, families and friendly neighbors might move again. Populations initially were small, but the territorial bounds of towns were nearly beyond English imaginations. Seemingly boundless space, population growth, land greed, and English agricultural practices scattered New Englanders farther and farther from town centers. The ocean and rivers played their part as well. By connecting some towns to the larger world, waterways contributed to the development of diverse towns and varying opportunities.

The result was New England towns of many types, and different sorts of towns contributed to different experiences for their residents. Whether a person lived in a commercial town, an agricultural town, or a frontier town prompted different economic opportunities, aspirations, and behaviors. A Boston resident might actively engage in acquisitive, market-driven behavior, for example, while a Lancaster resident might accept competency as the most that was possible. Ranges of wealth, life expectancies, family size, diversity of population, educational opportunities—all of those were partially dependent upon the type of town in which a person lived. Within towns of all types there were additional divisions related to one's town status. A proprietor had greater access to land and to decision-making of various kinds than did either inhabitants or sojourners, and inhabitants had similar advantages over sojourners.

From a broad perspective, New Englanders shared a common institution that distinguished their culture; closer inspection, however, reveals a diversity of towns and town statuses that differentiated New Englanders from one another.

NEW ENGLAND IN THE SEVENTEENTH CENTURY

I t is time to put "Puritan New England" to rest. The problem with the characterization is not that it's wrong but that it's only partly right. It is far too exclusive and simplistic. Like "The Age of Jackson," "the Enlightenment," "Nazi Germany," and "Communist China," it disguises as much as it reveals. It offers the comfort of a phrase at the expense of complexity. It suggests homogeneity and uniformity and steers us away from diversity. It makes the dominant (not necessarily the majority) viewpoint the norm and treats other beliefs as aberrant. It focuses on only one characteristic of a people while ignoring others. It provides only one test by which to judge whether a person were typical or an outsider and thereby relegates most inhabitants of the region to a cultural trashcan.

Puritanism, certainly, was an important ingredient in the complex New England stew, but it should not be presented as its exclusive defining characteristic—the criterion by which New Englanders should be judged as insiders or outsiders. We too frequently take the beliefs and laws of the powerful (even when they are shared by many ordinary people) as the only way to determine whether one belongs to a culture or is a deviant. That approach continually has plagued Americans as a nation as one segment or another of the population has attempted to define our culture by a narrow orthodoxy. The lesson from New England is that in what appears to be the most homogeneous of early American regions there was a mansion with many rooms.

Even after removing Puritanism as *the* defining quality of New Englanders, there were few, if any, people in seventeenth-century New England who were typical in all other respects. George Walton was not a typical New Englander, nor was Herodias Long, Robert Keayne, or Anne Hutchinson. For that matter, no minister, such as John Cotton or Thomas

Shepard, fit the norm in all ways (their office alone made them different from most), nor did any deacon, selectman, carpenter, fisherman, farmer, midwife, or governor. Some were residents of small villages while others lived in market centers. Some occupied the highest stratum of society while others rested on various less elevated tiers. Some were disenfranchised while others were politically powerful. Some were prosperous while others were poor. Some were Puritans; more were not. Some were women while others were men; some masters, some servants; some parents, some children. Not even John Winthrop—first married at age seventeen, four times wed, and governor—was typical. Each of these people had some traits in common and some that were quite unusual. What has usually been interpreted as a homogenous culture was in fact, like most cultures, full of divisions. The people of New England experienced the world in different ways.

This game of sheep and goats is only useful to the point it helps us understand the diversity and complexity of life in seventeenth-century New England. It highlights differences and calls into question otherness if everyone to some extent was other. But if Puritanism did not provide the glue to hold New England together, if New Englanders were divided by status, gender, wealth, age, type of town in which they lived, occupation, religious beliefs, power, aspirations, opportunities, and ethnicity, were there any beliefs, values, structures, institutions, or characteristics of any type that bonded people? Was there *a* New England culture?

Whether one finds a coherent culture is largely dependent upon the lens being used. The wider the angle and the more distant the viewer, the more uniform and homogenous the subjects appear; conversely, as the focus narrows down, the differences loom larger. At one extreme all humanity is connected as the same species on the same planet. We all are born, most of us age, and we all die; we reproduce with each other. At the other extreme, the world is atomistic: all is individual, there are no connections. Cultures exist somewhere between those two real extremes. To argue for cultures is not to deny either broad humanity or genuine differences but rather to recognize that a middle world exists as well. Seventeenth-century New England as a coherent whole was in that middle place.

* * *

Notching down a few levels from the comprehensive end, one of the objects that comes into view is seventeenth-century English culture. People in this group spoke English. They accepted English laws and the English legal system. They were Christian, primarily Protestant. They lived in nuclear, patriarchal families and preferred local institutions. Their economic outlook was acquisitive, market-driven, and competitive. They aspired to owning private property. They believed that social order properly should be hierarchical, but their increasingly individualistic values were chipping away at those traditional structures. Thus far, New Englanders were no different from other English people. Although they become culturally separated from native peoples of New England, at this level they look the same as residents of England and of the Chesapeake. If we stop here, we have discovered what could be several important components of a New England culture but have not found that culture itself.

Zooming in more, New England becomes increasingly distinct, but not altogether different from the rest of the English-speaking world. Like the Chesapeake, New England was composed of new colonies. It was dependent on English support, yet, largely because of the great distance from London, for most of the century was essentially independent from English control. During the first decades of settlement, the age and sex composition of its population differentiated it from both England and the Chesapeake. Although it resembled the Chesapeake in having relatively few residents older than forty and in having an unusually high proportion of male settlers, most of the New England colonists arrived in family groups. Families provided greater continuity with traditional ways than is typical in colonial societies, but the large numbers of single unattached men produced the expected disorder when they were tightly clustered together as well as the fear of transgressions in the minds of authorities. Both New Englanders and residents of the Chesapeake lived close by Indians. Their early survival depended on cooperation with native peoples; nonetheless, despite public hopes and occasional efforts for creating biracial societies, the proximity of Indians primarily heightened a sense of English identity and separateness.

The physical environment of New England was more similar to England than to the Chesapeake. English emigrants did not stumble upon an alien land. Neither desert nor glacier nor tropics confronted them. The landscape presented several, seemingly familiar, faces: hills and flatlands, forests and meadows, seacoasts and interior, rivers and ponds, a variety of soils. Yet winters were colder than in England and summers hotter, the growing season was shorter, and there was an unusual abundance of trees, fish, and game—many new to English eyes. This was neither a new Eden nor an old England, but it had the potential to be a new England.[1] Trying to replicate their English past, settlers felled trees, coaxed English grains out of generally mediocre soils, raised English livestock, and created small family farms.

New Englanders would have liked to continue their acquisitive, market-driven ways of the 1630s, but the curtailment of heavy immigration and ready cash limited the possibility. Soil and climate didn't cooperate, and they were unable to produce a large-scale commercial crop, such as tobacco in the Chesapeake. Instead, they had to rely on a mixed economy. Ships, trees and their by-products, fish, livestock, and some grains could be sold in international and regional markets, and shipping became an enterprise in its own right. Capitalist values and behaviors most flourished where there was land speculation and commerce, but they often were latent elsewhere. The more removed from large-market opportunities, the more people had to participate in a subsistence-barter economy. Yet settling for competency was better than starving or being dependent on others. The mixed economies of New England and England more closely resembled each other than they did the single-crop economy of the Chesapeake.[2]

Seventeenth-century New England families were large and, as a result of the long lives of parents, stable (again similar to the mother country). The relatively low mortality rates for all family members and early marriages stimulated rapid population growth, and parental continuity provided for consistent discipline of offspring. With a climate and soil that did not easily produce commercial crops, not needing to augment their labor force with full-time, year-round workers, and generally lacking funds from highly profitable commercial crops, New England farmers plowed their surplus into more land rather than purchased labor. The Chesapeake with its high mortality rates and skewed sex ratio, by comparison, had small, unstable families and was unable to reproduce itself. Although Maryland and Virginia were blessed by soil and climate that produced the highly profitable, labor-intensive, nutrient-demanding crop of tobacco, they needed to import a labor force—at first indentured servants and later, when servants weren't available in sufficient numbers and proved potentially dangerous, slaves.[3] Demographics, climate, and soil rather than virtue made the difference.

Settlement patterns also separated New England from the Chesapeake. Although scattered more widely than myth would have it, the small farms, dwellings, and shops of New Englanders connected as towns and brought closer proximity than did the large plantations and county governments of the southern colonies. Regulating behavior when families failed or were ineffective, distributing land, mediating between neighbors, offering community, organizing churches, and supplying local government—towns had multiple functions that replaced the separate English institutions of parish, manor, and village.

Christianity was an important part of all the English-speaking world, but nowhere else was it as central to the culture nor as narrowly focused as it was in New England. Not only were almost all New Englanders Protestants, the vast majority were Reformed Protestants or shared that general worldview and thereby constituted the radical wing of Protestantism. As Puritans, Baptists, Quakers, Dutch Reformed, reformist Anglicans, and members of a variety of small sects, they sought a better world now and hereafter. Attempting to return to what they imagined the early Christian church to have been and seeking to establish and enforce what they considered God's law, they were evangelical, moralistic, and reformist. Not all of their values coincided perfectly. On the one hand, they wanted to maintain their sense of God's hierarchical order: rulers above subjects, clergy above laity, men above women, parents above children and servants, rich above poor. On the other, they believed that human beings ultimately were beholden to no one other than God, that salvation was exclusively a matter between the individual and God. They struggled to resolve the conflict but couldn't avoid the subversive force of their own beliefs.

Many of the leadership in New England, particularly those of the first generation, had a religious intensity that spilled out of church services and private prayers into laws and governance, and the new world environment encouraged innovations. Scriptural injunctions were particularly evident in criminal law, and women had a larger role in courtroom practice and more equitable treatment than was the case in England or would be the case in the eighteenth century. As Cornelia Hughes Dayton concludes for New Haven colony, the religious desire "to call all sinners to account—men and women, rich and poor" brought about increased impartiality until new royal charters, English governors and other appointees, and social change reasserted more uniform English legal culture.[4]

* * *

This then was the culture of seventeenth-century New England. To zoom any closer to the atomistic end is to find very real worlds of subcultures and individuals but no longer a coherent culture. It should be no surprise that historians who study the past at levels below culture should find diversity. Gender, level of wealth, occupation, degree of power, status, type of town, religious belief—all of these produce and produced different experiences and perspectives. Yet those differences occurred within a larger context: that of humanity and culture. There is no contradiction in an individual's not being typical and still being a member of a culture; it would be a rare person indeed who would be representative of all aspects.

This then was the New England of Herodias Long and John Winthrop, Robert Keayne and John Cotton, even of George Walton. They were not identical people. There were differences, some serious, between them. There were fissures in seventeenth-century New England. Yet even though Puritanism was not their common rock, there was a broader culture that made the English colonists one.

APPENDIXES

APPENDIX A. Wealth and Men's Church Seating: New Haven, 1656, 1662, 1668

Name	Church member	Date of death	Worth of estate (£)	Best seat
Benjamin Wilmot	No	1669	25	1 abv. door, 68
Richard Johnson	No	1679	39	bef. deacon, 62
William Bassett	Yes	1684	50	bef. little, 68
Andrew Low	No	1670	53	2 abv. door, 68
Henry Morrell	Yes	1665	71	5 bel. door, 62
John Tuttle	No	1683	79	7 long, 68
John Benham	Yes	1661	80	7 long, 56
Samuel Hodgkins	No	1663	86	5 bel. door, 68
Henry Lines	Yes	1663	91	bef. Rudderford, 62
Henry Hummerston	No	1664	98	1 soldiers, 62
Edward Camp	No	1659	100	9 stile, 56
Ralph Russell	No	1676	103	9 long, 68
Robert Hill	Yes	1663	107	8 long, 62
Ephraim Pennington	Yes	1660	112	bef. Gilbert, 56
John Wakefield	No	1660	115	6 stile, 56
Mr. Isaac Allerton	Yes	1659	118	1 cross, 56
Thomas Beaumont	Yes	1684	122	6 long, 68
Richard Hull	Yes	1662	122	bef. Gov., 62
Joseph Potter	No	1669	123	4 bel. door, 62
Edward Parker	No	1662	124	9 long, 62
Matthew Row	No	1662	130	8 long, 62
Robert Talmage	Yes	1662	131	7 long, 56
Thomas Powell	No	1681	139	2 cross, 68
John Peakon	No	1657	141	6 long, 56
William Russell	Yes	1665	142	3 cross, 62
Thomas Jeffries	Yes	1661	152	3 cross, 62
William Thorp	No	1679	152	bef. Gov., 68
Timothy Ford	No	1684	166	6 long, 68
Thomas Lamson	Yes	1663	167	9 long, 62
Francis Brown	Yes	1668	170	3 cross, 68
Jarvis Boykin	Yes	1661	173	7 long, 56
John Thomas	Yes	1671	174	1 abv. door, 68
Robert Pigg	No	1660	176	bef. Tuttle, 56
Phillip Leeke	Yes	1676	181	long wall, 68
William Thompson	Yes	1683	187	5 long, 68
William Potter	Yes	1662	190	5 long, 62
George Smith	No	1662	195	7 long, 62

Name	Church member	Date of death	Worth of estate (£)	Best seat
Edward Hitchcock	No	1659	196	5 stile, 56
Thomas "old" Wheeler	No	1656	200	8 long, 56
James Russell	No	1681	205	little seat, 68
John Thompson	No	1656	229	7 long, 56
Samuel Blackly	No	1672	231	9 long, 68
Richard Miles	Yes	1667	288	deacon, 62
Mr. William Gibbard	Yes	1663	290	2 long, 62
Mr. John Wakeman	Yes	1661	301	3 long, 56
Matthew Moulthrop	Yes	1668	304	4 long, 68
William Davis	Yes	1659	308	3 long, 56
Henry Lindall	Yes	1660	323	5 long, 56
William Judson	Yes	1662	326	3 long, 62
John Punderson	Yes	1681	327	1 cross, 68
Ephraim How	Yes	1680	353	1 gallery, 68
William Wooden	No	1684	360	9 long, 68
Robert Johnson	No	1661	366	bef. Gov., 56
William Andrews	No	1676	367	3 long, 68
John Sackett	No	1684	382	4 abv. door, 62
Thomas Morris	Yes	1673	391	bef. deacon, 68
Roger Alling	Yes	1674	394	3 long, 68
William Payne	Yes	1683	417	1 abv. door, 68
Joseph Nash	Yes	1678	419	5 cross, 56
Mr. Francis Newman	Yes	1660	430	2 long, 56
Matthew Hitchcock	No	1669	469	6 long, 68
Mr. Thomas Yale	Yes	1683	479	2 long, 68
Joseph Alsop	Yes	1691	490	1 gallery, 68
Jeremiah Osborn	No	1676	501	5 long, 68
John Harriman	Yes	1683	511	bef. deacon, 68
John Nash	Yes	1687	664	2 long, 68
Mr. Henry Rotherford	Yes	1668	862	1 cross, 68
Christopher Todd	No	1686	989	5 long, 68
Mr. Theophilus Eaton	Yes	1658	1515	1 long, 56
Mr. Nicholas Auger	Yes	1678	1638	1 cross, 68

Out of the 237 different men who were seated in 1656, 1662, or 1668, only the 69 named above have extant probate assessments of the worth of their estates. They are listed in the order of their estates' values. Many of these men were seated multiple times, and Best Seat indicates their most prominent placement in any of the three years. In 1662, the cross seats were referred to as short seats, but they are described here as cross seats. The number following the location under Best Seat represents the year of the seating. Some of the men who are listed as not being church members may have been so, but there is no remaining evidence establishing their possible membership. See pages 62 and 63 of chapter 4 for a discussion of the relative status of various seats.

Sources are: Dexter and Powers, *New Haven Town Records*, 1: 270–74, 510–13; 2: 219–21; Dexter, *Historical Catalogue of the Members of the First Church of Christ in New Haven, Connecticut;* "Abstracts of the Early Probate Records of New Haven," 121–35; New Haven Probate Record (microfilm); and Savage, *Genealogical Dictionary of the First Settlers of New England,* vols. 1–4.

APPENDIX B. Officeholding

	Governor		Dep. Gov.		Assistant		Deputy		Selectman		Town Clerk		Constable		Elder		Deacon	
	N	%	N	%	N	%	N	%	N	%	N	%	N	%	N	%	N	%
Governor	—	—	(13)	37.1	(21)	60.0	(12)	34.3	(2)	5.7	(0)	0.0	(0)	0.0	(0)	0.0	(0)	0.0
Dep. Gov.	(13)	39.3	—	—	(23)	69.7	(13)	39.3	(3)	9.1	(0)	0.0	(0)	0.0	(2)	6.1	(1)	3.0
Assistant	(21)	11.5	(23)	28.0	—	—	(98)	53.8	(16)	8.8	(1)	.5	(7)	3.8	(2)	1.1	(4)	2.2
Deputy	(12)	1.2	(13)	1.3	(98)	10.0	—	—	(125)	12.6	(53)	5.3	(46)	4.6	(25)	2.5	(95)	9.6
Selectman	(2)	.7	(3)	1.0	(16)	5.4	(125)	41.9	—	—	(32)	10.8	(38)	12.8	(11)	3.7	(42)	10.6
Town Clerk	(0)	0.0	(0)	0.0	(1)	.9	(53)	49.5	(32)	29.9	—	—	(9)	8.4	(1)	.9	(15)	14.0
Constable	(0)	0.0	(0)	0.0	(7)	3.6	(46)	23.7	(38)	19.6	(9)	4.6	—	—	(3)	1.5	(6)	3.1
Elder	(0)	0.0	(2)	2.9	(2)	2.9	(25)	36.8	(11)	16.2	(1)	1.5	(3)	4.4	—	—	(10)	14.7
Deacon	(0)	0.0	(1)	.4	(4)	1.4	(95)	34.1	(42)	15.1	(15)	5.4	(6)	2.2	(10)	3.6	—	—

These figures are based on my computer data of 12,318 males who migrated to New England or were born there by 1650 and who are not known to have died before the age of twenty. The first column contains four colonywide offices (governor [35, .3 percent]; deputy governor [33, .3 percent]; assistant [182, 1.5 percent]; and deputy [991, 8.0 percent]), three town offices (selectman [298, 2.4 percent]; town clerk [107, .9 percent]; and constable [194, 1.6 percent]), and two church offices (elder [68, .6 percent]; and deacon [279, 2.3 percent]). The numbers by each office indicate how many men are known to have held them and their percentage of all men. Succeeding columns show the correspondence between holding multiple offices. For example, thirteen men are known to have served both as governor and deputy governor, and they constitute 37.1 percent of all governors and 39.3 percent of all deputy governors.

APPENDIX C. Age, Wealth, and Officeholding

	Median age	Mean age	Range age	Median wealth (£)	Range wealth (£)
Governor	(13) 55	57.2	34–86	(5) 1069	103 ... 1440
Dep. Governor	(9) 58	57.6	44–70	(4) —	103 ... 2449
Assistant	(71) 41	44.0	22–72	(18) 888	103 ... 8446
Deputy	(338) 45	45.5	23–75	(111) 501	49 ...14000
Selectman	(49) 48	46.5	22–74	(45) 476	49 ...14000
Town Clerk	(21) 44	45.0	29–65	(15) 224	51 ... 8446
Constable	(35) 46	45.0	25–73	(31) 324	57 ... 7819
Elder	(6) 46	45.5	33–55	(9) 671	57 ... 2449
Deacon	(8) 47	47.3	34–58	(22) 359	49 ... 1145

The number in parentheses preceding median age and median wealth represent the number for whom there are data in all age categories and all wealth categories respectively. All age categories refer to age when first taking office.

APPENDIX D. Distribution by Decile for General Population

Number = 1017; Median 207; Range 1–14000

(101) Top Decile	897 ... 14000
(101) 2d	520 ... 895
(101) 3d	366 ... 515
(102) 4th	276 ... 366
(102) 5th	207 ... 276
(102) 6th	154 ... 207
(102) 7th	115 ... 152
(102) 8th	82 ... 114
(102) 9th	49 ... 82
(102) Bottom	1 ... 49

Sources for Appendix C and Appendix D come from the database discussed in note 11 of chapter 4, at the bottom of Appendix F, and the following: Charles William Manwaring, comp., *A Digest of the Early Connecticut Probate Records* (Hartford, Conn., 1902), "Abstracts of the Early Probate Records of New Haven," 1121–135; New Haven Probate Record (microfilm); Wills, Inventories, Etc. 1637 to 1685, County of Barnstable, microfilm; George F. Dow, ed., *Probate Records of Essex County, Massachusetts, 1635–1681*, 3 vols. (Salem, Mass., 1916–1920); Suffolk County Probate Records, vol. 5, microfilm; *Suffolk County Wills: Abstracts of the Earliest Wills Upon Record in the County of Suffolk, Massachusetts* (Baltimore, Md., 1984).

APPENDIX E. Male and Female Names

Name	N	%	Cum%	Rank N.E.	% N.E.
Male names, born in England (N=6412)					
1. John	1260	19.7	19.7	1	23.1
2. Thomas	779	12.1	31.8	4	7.2
3. William	669	10.4	42.2	9	2.5
4. Richard	378	5.9	48.1	22	.8
5. Robert	282	4.4	52.5	27	.6
6. Samuel	223	3.5	56.0	2	10.9
7. Henry	218	3.4	59.4	26	.6
8. Edward	206	3.2	62.6	23	.8
9. George	192	3.0	65.6	39	.4
10. James	176	2.7	71.0	7	3.0
240 additional names					
Female names, born in England (N=3187)					
1. Mary	521	16.3	16.3	1	22.9
2. Elizabeth	510	16.0	32.3	2	14.1
3. Ann[e]	291	9.1	41.4	8	2.5
4. Sarah	252	7.9	49.3	3	13.6
5. Margaret	122	3.8	53.1	24*	.4
6. Jane	107	3.4	56.5	32*	.2
7. Alice	92	2.9	59.4	31	.3
8. Hannah	83	2.6	62.0	4	10.9
9. Martha	74	2.3	64.3	7	2.8
9. Susanna	74	2.3	66.5	12	1.6
148 additional names					

* = tied with two other names

Name	N	%	Cum%	Rank Eng.	% Eng.
Male names, born in New England (N=3825)					
1. John	885	23.1	23.1	1	19.7
2. Samuel	416	10.9	34.0	6	3.5
3. Joseph	311	8.1	42.1	11	2.7
4. Thomas	276	7.2	49.3	2	12.1
5. Nathaniel	161	4.2	53.5	12	1.8
6. Jonathan	119	3.1	56.6	29	.5
7. James	115	3.0	59.6	10	2.7
8. Benjamin	114	3.0	62.6	19	.8
9. William	95	2.5	65.1	3	10.4
10. Isaac	73	1.9	67.0	22	.7
216 additional names					
Female names, born in New England (N=3430)					
1. Mary	785	22.9	22.9	1	16.3
2. Elizabeth	482	14.1	37.0	2	16.0
3. Sarah	468	13.6	50.6	4	7.9
4. Hannah	375	10.9	61.5	8	2.6
5. Abigail	152	4.4	65.9	16	1.4
6. Rebecca	111	3.2	69.1	11	2.1
7. Martha	96	2.8	71.9	9**	2.3
8. Ann[e]	87	2.5	74.4	3	9.1
9. Lydia	80	2.3	76.7	18	1.3
10. Ruth	73	2.1	78.8	31	.4
135 additional names					

** = tied with one other name

Town	N	Gini	Top 10%	Mean (£)	Median (£)
Commercial					
Boston	176	.68	60.6	638	210
Salem	166	.62	56.9	268	122
Secondary Centers					
Hartford	64	.59	44.2	687	323
Ipswich	120	.58	48.8	338	184
Lynn	59	.53	41.1	189	126
Newbury	69	.58	42.8	335	164
New Haven	72	.45	34.4	270	173
Subordinate					
Beverly	12			423	331
Dorchester	36	.49	36.2	475	279
Gloucester	18	.55	29.7	85	44
Marblehead	32	.60	47.4	105	70
Roxbury	22	.50	34.0	439	315
Salisbury	26	.42	30.4	223	217
Wenham	17	.46	36.7	186	131
Wethersfield	51	.50	32.3	397	221
Windsor	61	.52	43.0	336	184
Agricultural					
Andover	9			279	350
Barnstable	30	.56	45.3	242	106
Dedham	18	.55	46.6	277	140
Eastham	7			136	142
Farmington	15			223	182
Haverhill	25	.43	34.0	216	168
Hingham	15			234	230
Middletown	15			237	220
Rowley	43	.39	25.4	346	331
Sandwich	14			153	91
Yarmouth	20	.41	26.3	270	206

The seven towns without Gini coefficents and the percentage of wealth held by the top 10 percent had insufficient numbers for those calculations. Nevertheless, a rough sense of wealth distribution can be achieved by comparing the median with the mean. In general, the closer the correspondence, the greater the equality. These data are based on records only of males who were permanent residents and who were living in New England by 1650. Female records, which constituted only a small fraction of the total and which almost entirely represented widows, were not included, nor were records of transients, such as sailors who had died at sea or in port but who were recorded at ports of call. There were too few records for Frontier Towns to include them in this Appendix. Records for the Hartford District, New Haven, Essex County, and Suffolk County included both real and personal property, but Barnstable County only occasionally listed real property. On average in Barnstable County real property equaled 46 percent of personal property; therefore to equate all New England records I added that amount to Barnstable records. Massachusetts Bay records detailed indebtedness as well as assets, and I used net estate. For analyses of the flaws of probate records and imaginative suggestions for their effective use, see Gloria L. Main, "The Correction of Biases in Colonial American Probate Records," *Historical Methods Newsletter*, 8 (1974): 10–28, "Probate Records as a Source for Early American History," *William and Mary Quarterly*, 3d ser., 32 (1975): 89–99, and "Inequality in Early America: The Evidence from Probate Records of Massachusetts and Maryland," *Journal of Interdisciplinary History*, 7 (1977): 559–581; and Daniel Scott Smith, "Underregistration and Bias in Probate Records: An Analysis of Data from Eighteenth-Century Hingham, Massachusetts," *William and Mary Quarterly*, 3d ser., 32 (1975): 100–110. For a model analysis, see Jackson Turner Main, "The Distribution of Property in Colonial Connecticut," in *The Human Dimensions of Nation Making: Essays on Colonial and Revolutionary America*, ed. James Kirby Martin (Madison, Wis., 1976), 54–104. See Appendix D for a listing of the probate records used for this table.

APPENDIX G. New England Towns and Demography

Town	Age at marriage		Children per family		Age at death	
	N	Mean	N	Mean	N	Mean
Commercial						
Boston	56	24.0	312	6.0	163	61.2
	30	18.9	192	4.9	44	60.2
Salem	46	23.9	131	6.6	101	62.7
	16	20.0	72	5.9	29	52.6
Secondary Centers						
Charlestown	30	25.1	151	6.1	107	62.0
	25	20.9	105	5.6	61	61.8
Hartford	14	23.1	92	6.5	41	65.3
	6	20.2	33	5.5	13	68.0
Ipswich (m)	16	23.9	94	6.1	63	67.9
Newbury	27	25.7	86	6.9	60	64.6
	10	20.7	60	6.5	15	55.9
New Haven	23	24.0	118	6.2	45	58.9
	12	19.6	53	6.2	13	48.7
New London (m)	15	24.7	50	6.5	24	62.1
Newport	7	27.6	29	7.3	21	74.0
	5	16.2	15	5.4	5	54.4
Plymouth	12	26.8	39	6.2	21	75.1
	8	19.9	32	4.6	11	74.9
Providence (m)	5	28.8	24	6.2	11	70.1
Saybrook (m)	9	28.7	19	7.0	12	67.6
Springfield	14	25.4	58	7.0	20	65.2
	5	19.2	32	7.1	5	58.4
Subordinate						
Beverly (m)	5	23.2	18	7.6	17	68.4
Cambridge	36	26.3	111	6.7	91	65.8
	27	22.4	81	5.5	44	55.9
Dorchester	30	25.0	90	6.2	68	69.2
	19	19.0	69	6.4	37	70.9

Town	Age at marriage		Children per family		Age at death	
	N	Mean	N	Mean	N	Mean
Duxbury (m)	6	25.5	19	7.1	12	67.2
Gloucester	12	26.4	37	7.0	19	71.6
	8	19.4	28	5.4	10	64.8
Hadley (m)	8	24.5	40	7.0	23	62.7
Malden	15	24.8	36	6.2	29	65.9
	5	20.2	21	5.8	9	62.1
Roxbury	38	26.2	102	7.0	71	63.6
	15	19.6	68	5.9	30	59.8
Salisbury	6	25.0	37	6.1	14	54.4
	7	20.6	28	5.8	7	42.0
Watertown	46	29.2	139	6.9	110	66.6
	20	19.0	93	6.0	47	64.6
Windsor	30	24.5	103	7.1	38	65.0
	11	19.9	54	6.4	13	58.8
Agricultural						
Andover	16	26.9	27	8.1	23	73.1
	5	18.4	17	6.8	7	63.7
Barnstable	15	23.4	34	7.6	16	66.2
	12	19.2	27	7.0	9	50.0
Braintree	17	27.0	52	6.8	37	70.4
	9	18.9	35	6.2	13	58.1
Concord (m)	9	26.8	32	6.4	27	66.2
Dedham	17	26.4	63	6.6	26	68.0
	9	20.7	49	5.6	10	56.9
Eastham (m)	8	23.4	23	7.4	13	61.9
Exeter (m)	5	26.2	14	7.6	12	66.2
Farmington (m)	7	25.1	45	6.6	18	61.7
Guilford (m)	11	26.6	46	6.4	13	61.6
Hampton (m)	9	26.4	42	6.1	29	69.1
Hingham	26	25.3	68	7.4	36	68.9
	12	21.4	37	7.4	13	60.9
Marshfield	6	26.0	22	5.9	16	71.4
	5	18.8	16	6.8	8	58.5
Medfield (m)	6	24.0	24	7.0	9	70.9
Middletown	14	27.4	41	7.7	18	61.9
	7	19.7	24	6.3	7	70.4
Milford	10	24.7	44	6.6	20	56.4
	6	19.5	21	6.1	5	58.0
Northampton	18	24.8	63	8.1	31	65.7
	10	21.1	38	7.6	10	57.5
Reading	7	27.3	25	7.0	11	68.4
	5	21.6	15	5.4	9	72.8
Rowley (m)	6	24.3	25	6.6	16	64.0
Scituate (m)	13	27.3	49	6.2	21	66.1
Sudbury (m)	6	28.5	39	6.0	24	58.7

Town	Age at marriage		Children per family		Age at death	
	N	Mean	N	Mean	N	Mean
Frontier						
Billerica (m)	13	25.5	24	8.0	18	67.2
Deerfield (m)	7	23.6	17	6.3	10	43.7
Groton (m)	7	25.1	18	7.2	11	69.0
Hatfield	7	26.3	20	8.1	10	54.1
	5	22.6	12	7.3	5	35.4
Marlborough	14	27.0	26	7.4	17	67.4
	5	23.0	12	7.4	6	64.0
Newton (m)	6	29.3	21	8.3	17	67.1
Stonington (m)	7	26.0	14	7.5	17	63.7
Topsfield (m)	5	27.2	12	7.8	11	71.7

(m) = Based entirely on male data; female data inadequate.

All data derive from towns where people died. If there are not at least five records in each of the three categories for either males or females for a particular town, the town is not included. The first line of data by each town is numbers and means for males; the second line is numbers and means for females. The average age at death applies only to people who had attained at least age twenty. See note 11 of chapter 5 for sources.

NOTES

Introduction (pp. 1–4)

1. Cotton Mather, *Magnalia Christi Americana; Or, The Ecclesiastical History of New England, From Its First Planting, in the Year 1620, Unto the Year of Our Lord 1698*, 2 vols. (Hartford, Conn., 1853), 2:453; see also Richard Chamberlain, "Lithobolia, or the Stone-Throwing Devil," (1698) in George Lincoln Burr, *Narratives of the Witchcraft Cases, 1648–1706* (New York, 1914), 58–77.
2. James Savage, *A Genealogical Dictionary of the First Settlers of New England, . . . Who Came Before May, 1692. . .*, 4 vols. (Boston, 1860–1862; reprint, Baltimore, Md., 1965), 4:404; Nathaniel Bouton, ed., *Documents and Records Relating to the Province of New-Hampshire, From the Earliest Period of its Settlement: 1623–1686* (Concord, N.H., 1867), 132–133; Otis G. Hammond, ed., *New Hampshire Court Records, 1640–1692* (New Hampshire, 1943), 6, 49, 79, 107, 110–111, 118, 119, 137, 147, 148–149, 179–180, 193, 196, 208, 216, 245, 246, 307, 342, 359, 362, 270, 375, 380, and 391.
3. Hammond, ed., *New Hampshire Court Records*, 11, 60, 89, 98, 113, 122, 125, 127–128, 134, 141, 145, 149–150, 152, 161, 336, 338, 353, 489; Bouton, ed., *Documents and Records*, 215; Albert Stillman Batchellor, ed., *Probate Records of the Province of New Hampshire, 1635–1717* (Concord, N.H., 1907), 198, 233.
4. Hammond, ed., *New Hampshire Court Records*, 20, 83, 121–122, 129, 130, 189, 283–284; Savage, *Genealogical Dictionary of First Settlers*, 4: 404.
5. Hammond, ed., *New Hampshire Court Records*, 203, 308.

2. Relations Between Colonists and Native Americans (pp. 5–26)

1. The best review of the literature and analysis of the size of the Indian population of the New England region and the impact of the epidemics is Neal Salisbury, *Manitou and Providence: Indians, Europeans, and the Making of New England, 1500–1643* (New York, 1982), 22–30; for an analysis of the particular diseases plaguing New England Indians, see William Starna, "The Pequots in the Early Seventeenth Century," in Laurence M. Hauptman and James D. Wherry, eds., *The Pequots in Southern New England: The Fall and Rise of an American Indian Nation* (Norman, Okla., 1990), 45; the "sad spectacle" comes from William Bradford, *Of Plymouth Plantation, 1620–1647*, ed. Samuel Eliot Morison (New York, 1952), 87; for Massasoit's illness, see Bradford, *Of Plymouth Plantation*, 117, and Edward Winslow, *Good Newes From New England . . .* (London, 1624), in Alexander Young, ed., *Chronicles of the Pilgrim Fathers of the Colony of Plymouth, From 1602 to 1625* (Boston, 2d ed., 1844; reprint, Baltimore, 1974), 318–320.

2. *Mourt's Relation,* in Alexander Young, ed., *Chronicles of the Pilgrim Fathers,* 194; months later at Nauset, they met another sachem, Iyanough, whom they described as "not exceeding twenty-six years of age," *Mourt's Relation,* 215; the accuracy of their age assessments is tested by their reference to "an old woman, whom we judge to be no less than a hundred years old"—a possible, though not likely, attainment, ibid.; other evidence for Massasoit's age, though indirect, is that following his recovery he lived for nearly forty more years; also William Wood and John Josselyn commented on the longevity of Indians: Wood, *New England's Prospect* (1635), ed. Alden T. Vaughan (Amherst, Mass., 1977), 82, and Josselyn, *An Account of Two Voyages to New-England,* ed. Paul J. Lindholdt (London, 1674; reprint, Hanover, N.H., 1988), 93; Bradford died on 9 May 1657, and Winslow on 8 May 1654; for hereditary lines of sachems, see Bert Salwen, "Indians of Southern New England and Long Island: Early Period," in Bruce G. Trigger, ed., *Handbook of North American Indians: Northeast* (Washington, D.C., 1978), 15:167; for the disruption caused by the epidemics, see William Cronon, *Changes in the Land: Indians, Colonists, and the Ecology of New England* (New York, 1983), 88–90.

3. Salwen, "Indians of Southern New England," 171; the articles of the treaty are in *Mourt's Relations,* 193.

4. For a comparison of the age structure of English emigrants to New England with the population of England as a whole, see my "New England Mosaic: A Demographic Analysis for the Seventeenth Century," *William and Mary Quarterly,* 3d ser., 47 (October, 1990): 479–480; for a view that argues that the age structure of the two populations "virtually mirrored" each other, see Virginia DeJohn Anderson, "Migrants and Motives: Religion and the Settlement of New England, 1630–1640," *New England Quarterly* 58 (September 1985): 347–348 and *New England's Generation: The Great Migration and the formation of society and culture in the seventeenth century* (New York, 1991), 19–20; for the mortality of the Mayflower emigrants as well as the most thorough single work on New Plymouth colony, see George D. Langdon Jr., *Pilgrim Colony: A History of New Plymouth, 1620–1691* (New Haven, Conn., 1966), 14 and passim.

5. Salwen, "Indians of Southern New England," 160.

6. For the reasons for leaving Holland, see Bradford, *Of Plymouth Plantation,* 23–25; Francis Jennings, *The Invasion of America: Indians, Colonialism, and the Cant of Conquest* (Chapel Hill, N.C., 1975), 30.

7. Winslow's account of his visit to the dying Massasoit appears in his *Good Newes From New England.* Unless otherwise noted, all that follows on the trip is based on that source.

8. Winslow's first trip to Sowams is described in *Mourt's Relation,* 202–213. The quotes come from page 211.

9. For Corbitant's earlier hostility, see Bradford, *Of Plymouth Plantation,* 88–89 and *Mourt's Relation,* 219–222.

10. The sources do not give so detailed an account of Massasoit's house as is given here. The image of the house is drawn from: Wood, *New England's Prospect,* 112–113; Thomas Morton, *New English Canaan or New Canaan* (Amsterdam, 1637) with introductory matter and notes by Charles Francis Adams Jr. (Boston, 1883; reprint, New York, 1967), 134–138; Edward Johnson, *Wonder-Working Providence of Sions Saviour in New England* (London, 1653), ed. J. Franklin Jameson (New York, 1910), 162, and Roger Williams, *A Key into the Language of America.* (London, 1643), ed. John J. Teunissen and Evelyn J. Hinz

(Detroit, Mich., 1973), 108, 117–118, 122, 127–128, as well as Winslow, *Good Newes From New England*, 317–318. See also Starna, "Pequots in the Early Seventeenth Century," 38.

11. Thomas Weston to William Bradford, in Bradford, *Of Plymouth Plantation*, 106; Robert Cushman to William Bradford, March or April, 1623, in ibid., 107–108; the literature on the motivation for migration to New England is vast, and most of it focuses on the Great Migration to Massachusetts Bay between 1630 and 1642; the following works give a good sense of the range of arguments: Anderson, "Migrants and Motives," passim; Anderson, *New England's Generation*, 12–46; Virginia DeJohn Anderson and David Grayson Allen provide an enlightening debate in "Communications: On English Migration to Early New England," *New England Quarterly* 59 (September 1986): 408–424; T. H. Breen and Stephen Foster, "Moving to the New World: The Character of Early Massachusetts Immigration," *William and Mary Quarterly* 30 (April 1973): passim; Peter Clark, *English Provincial Society from the Reformation to the Revolution: Religion, Politics and Society in Kent, 1500–1640* (Sussex, Eng., 1977), 372–373; David Cressy, *Coming Over: Migration and Communication Between England and New England in the Seventeenth Century* (Cambridge, 1987), 74, 85, 87–88; Allen French, *Charles I and the Puritan Upheaval: A Study of the Causes of the Great Migration* (Boston, 1955), 99, 106, 114, 122, 131, 222, 231, 314; Langdon, *Pilgrim Colony*, 7–8; motives for Chesapeake migration are discussed in: James Horn, "Servant Emigration to the Chesapeake in the Seventeenth Century," in Thad W. Tate and David L. Ammerman, eds., *The Chesapeake in the Seventeenth Century: Essays on Anglo-American Society* (Chapel Hill, N.C., 1979), 94–95, and Horn, *Adapting to a New World: English Society in the Seventeenth-Century Chesapeake* (Chapel Hill, N.C., 1994), 16 and passim; Russell R. Menard, "British Migration to the Chesapeake Colonies in the Seventeenth Century," in Lois Green Carr, Russell R. Menard, and Jean B. Russo, eds., *Colonial Chesapeake Society* (Chapel Hill, N. C., 1988), 116–117 and passim; and Edmund S. Morgan, *American Slavery, American Freedom: The Ordeal of Colonial Virginia* (New York, 1975), 47, 84–86.

12. Bradford, *Of Plymouth Plantation*, 109; Winslow, *Good Newes From New England*, 296–298.

13. Bradford, *Of Plymouth Plantation*, 114–117; Winslow, *Good Newes From New England*, 327–328; Phineas Pratt, "A Decliration of the Afaires of the Einglish People [That First] Inhabited New England," *Collections*, Massachusetts Historical Society, 4th ser. (1858), 4:482–483.

14. Bradford, *Of Plymouth Plantation*, 115; Winslow, *Good Newes From New England*, 328–330.

15. Winslow, *Good Newes From New England*, 330–331.

16. Ibid., 309–312.

17. Ibid., 278–279, 293 n, 295, 335; Bradford, *Of Plymouth Plantation*, 111.

18. Winslow, *Good Newes Rom New England.*, 331–332.

19. Pratt, "A Decliration of the Afaires of the Einglish People," 483–485; Bradford, *Of Plymouth Plantation*, 117–118; Winslow, *Good Newes From New England*, 333–334.

20. Bradford, *Of Plymouth Plantation*, 98–99; Winslow, *Good Newes From New England*, 285–292. See John H. Humins, "Squanto and Massasoit: A Struggle for Power," *New England Quarterly* 60 (March 1987): 54–70. The reference

to a member of Squanto's "family" is perplexing, considering that all people in his village reportedly had died.

21. For example, see Hobbamock's reaction to the reported death of Massasoit, Winslow, *Good Newes From New England,* 316.

22. Winslow, *Good Newes From New England,* 330; for Squanto's capture and the colonists' retaliation, see *Mourt's Relation,* 219–223.

23. Introduction to Pratt's "A Decliration of the Afaires of the Einglish People," 475; Pratt, "A Decliration of the Afaires of the Einglish People," 476–487; Winslow, *Good Newes From New England,* 332–334; Bradford, *Of Plymouth Plantation,* 117–118. Pratt's petition was successful, by the way, for the General Court granted him three hundred acres.

24. Pratt, "A Decliration of the Afaires of the Einglish People," 479; Winslow, *Good Newes From New England,* 302.

25. For an analysis of the "conspiracy" that helped me considerably, see Salisbury, *Manitou and Providence,* 130–132.

26. Unless otherwise noted, the account of the Standish expedition is based on Winslow, *Good Newes From New England,* 336–342.

27. Pecksuot figured prominently in Pratt's account (although called Peckworth, he was almost certainly the same person); see Pratt, "A Decliration of the Afaires of the Einglish People," 479–483. It is difficult to know how much to believe Pratt, for he intertwined so much of Winslow's earlier published account into his own. Part of what Pratt attributed to Pecksuot, for example, Winslow identified as coming from Wituwamat; compare ibid., 481, to Winslow, *Good Newes From New England,* 338.

28. Ibid., 339.

29. Ibid., 341.

30. Ibid., 342, 343; Morton, *New English Canaan,* 253; Emmanuel Altham to Sir Edward Altham, September 1623, in Sydney V. James, ed., *Three Visitors to Early Plymouth: Letters about the Pilgrim Settlement in New England during its first Seven Years* (Plymouth, Mass., 1963), 31.

31. John Robinson to the Plymouth congregation, 19 December 1623, partially quoted in Winslow, *Good Newes From New England,* 339 n; Bradford, *Of Plymouth Plantation,* 118.

32. The following paragraphs on land ownership, land use, and the landscape are heavily indebted to William Cronon's book, *Changes in the Land,* passim but particularly 54–81; also see James Axtell, *The Invasion Within: The Contest of Cultures in Colonial North America* (New York, 1985), 155–157, 162–166; Philip J. Greven Jr., *Four Generations: Population, Land, and Family in Colonial Andover, Massachusetts* (Ithaca, N.Y., 1970), 61–62; William Haller Jr., *The Puritan Frontier: Town-Planting in New England Colonial Development, 1630–1660* (New York, 1951), 26, 81; Jennings, *Invasion of America,* 130; Karen Ordahl Kupperman, *Settling With the Indians: The Meeting of English and Indian Cultures in America, 1580–1640* (Totowa, N.J., 1980), 90–91; John Frederick Martin, *Profits in the Wilderness: Entrepreneurship and the Founding of New England Towns in the Seventeenth Century* (Chapel Hill, N.C., 1991), 127–128, 135; Carolyn Merchant, *Ecological Revolutions: Nature, Gender, and Science in New England* (Chapel Hill, N.C., 1989), 52, 62–63; Salisbury, *Manitou and Providence,* 33, 198, 238–239; Alden T. Vaughan, *New England Frontier: Puritans and Indians, 1620–1675* (Boston, 1965), 105–106.

33. For a survey of the impact of deforestation, see Cronon, *Changes in the Land,* 122–126; for comparative approaches to domesticated animals and the Indians' adoption of the practice, see Virginia DeJohn Anderson, "King Philip's Herds: Indians, Colonists, and the Problem of Livestock in Early New England," *William and Mary Quarterly,* 3d ser., 51 (October 1994): 601–624.

34. After more than a quarter of a century, Philip Greven's study of families, land, and population, still is fresh and compelling: *Four Generations,* passim; for land speculation, see Martin, *Profits in the Wilderness,* passim; for an analysis of life expectancy, family size, and population growth, see my "New England Mosaic," 488–489, 492, 494–497.

35. Although he is analyzing different people, different places, and different times, Richard White provides insights that are valuable for understanding encounters between peoples in New England as well as the Great Lakes region: White, *The Middle Ground: Indians, Empires, and Republics in the Great Lakes Region, 1650–1815* (New York, 1991); see Daniel K. Richter, *The Ordeal of the Longhouse: The Peoples of the Iroquois League in the Era of European Colonization* (Chapel Hill, N.C., 1992) for his analysis of the survival strategies of the Iroquois.

36. Cronon, *Changes in the Land,* 94; Merchant, *Ecological Revolutions,* 53–54; Kenneth M. Morrison, *The Embattled Northeast: The Elusive Ideal of Alliance in Abenaki-Euramerican Relations* (Berkeley and Los Angeles, Calif., 1984), 14; Neal Salisbury, "Indians and Colonists in Southern New England after the Pequot War: An Uneasy Balance," in Hauptman and Wherry, eds., *Pequots in Southern New England,* 82; for early comments on Indians and alcohol, see Josselyn, *Two Voyages to New-England,* 99, and Wood, *New England's Prospect,* 79–80; for skulking methods of warfare, see Benjamin Church, *Diary of King Philip's War, 1675–76* (Boston, 1716; reprint, Chester, Conn., 1975), 140.

37. Bradford, *Of Plymouth Plantation,* 25; Matthew Cradock to John Endicott, 16 February 1629, in Alexander Young, ed., *Chronicles of the First Planters,* 133.

38. For a comprehensive analysis of attempts by French, English, and Indians to convert the other to their own ways, see Axtell, *The Invasion Within,* passim; see also Jennings, *Invasion of America,* 233, 238; Kupperman, *Settling With the Indians,* 42, 78–79; Vaughan, *New England Frontier,* 234; for "praying towns," see Salisbury, "Red Puritans: The 'Praying Indians' of Massachusetts Bay and John Eliot," *William and Mary Quarterly,* 3d ser., 31 (1974): 27–54; for English law and Indians, see Richard I. Melvoin, *New England Outpost: War and Society in Colonial Deerfield* (New York, 1989), 36; Vaughan, *New England Frontier,* 192; for some examples of the law's application see, William Hammond to Sir Simonds D'Ewes, 26 September 1633, in Everett Emerson, ed., *Letters from New England: The Massachusetts Bay Colony, 1629–1638* (Amherst, Mass., 1976), 111–112; Franklin Bowditch Dexter and Zara Jones Power, eds., *New Haven Town Records, 1649–1662* (New Haven, Conn., 1917), 1:77 (hereafter *New Haven Town Records*); Nathaniel B. Shurtleff, ed., *Records of the Colony of New Plymouth in New England,* 12 vols. (Boston, 1855–1861), 4:51 (hereafter *Plymouth Colony Records*).

39. For Indian motives for joining praying towns and for resisting, see Salisbury, "Red Puritans," 34–37, 38–39; for the murder trial, see *Records of the Court of Assistants of the Colony of the Massachusetts Bay, 1630–1692* 3 vols. (Boston, 1901–1928), 1:52–54; for examples of verdicts favorable to Indians in

English courts, see *New Haven Town Records,* 1:125; *Plymouth Colony Records,* 5:6 and 22; *The Early Records of the Town of Warwick* (Providence, R.I., 1926), 89; Hubbard's comments come from William Hubbard, *The History of the Indian Wars in New England* (1677), ed. Samuel G. Drake (Roxbury, Mass., 1865; reprint, New York, 1969), 1:47.

40. For William Baker, see Roger Williams to John Winthrop, 10 January 1638, 28 February 1638, and 22 May 1638, in *Winthrop Papers,* 5 vols. (Boston, 1929-1947), 4:7, 15, 31; for "white Indians" see Axtell, *Invasion Within,* 302-327; for Iroquois mourning-wars and the acculturation of captives, see Richter, *Ordeal of the Longhouse,* 57-58, 65, 69; for an account of an eighteenth-century New England family's captivity and the acculturation of one member, Eunice Williams, see John Demos, *The Unredeemed Captive: A Family Story from Early America* (New York, 1994), passim; the famous "Narrative of the Captivity of Mrs. Mary Rowlandson" (1682), is in Charles H. Lincoln, ed., *Narratives of the Indian Wars, 1675-1699* (New York, 1913; reprint, 1952), 112-167.

41. For an example of English authorities commanding the appearance of a "plotting" sachem, in this case Metacom of the Wampanoag more than a decade before the war that bears his name, see *Plymouth Colony Records,* 6 August 1662, 4:25-26; for examples of various forms of Indian retaliation, see John Winter to Robert Trelawny, 23 June 1636, in *The Trelawny Papers,* ed. James Phinney Baxter (Portland, Maine, 1884), 86; *New Haven Town Records,* 1:177; Samuel Sewall, *The Diary of Samuel Sewall, 1674-1729* , ed. M. Halsey Thomas, 2 vols. (New York, 1973), 1:22, 24-25.

42. For interpretations of the Pequot War and its consequences, see Russell Bourne, *The Red King's Rebellion: Racial Politics in New England, 1675-1678* (New York, 1990), 41-84; Alfred A. Cave, "The Pequot Invasion of Southern New England: A Reassessment of the Evidence," *New England Quarterly,* 62 (March 1989): 27-44, and "Who Killed John Stone? A Note on the Origins of the Pequot War," *William and Mary Quarterly,* 3d ser., 49 (July 1992): 509-521; Laurence M. Hauptman, "The Pequot War and Its Legacies," in Hauptman and Wherry, eds., *Pequots in Southern New England,* 69-80; Jennings, *Invasion of America,* 178, 227; Salisbury, *Manitou and Providence,* 220, 224, 225; Salwen, "Indians of Southern New England," 173; Alan and Mary Simpson, introduction to Church, *Diary of King Philip's War,* 20. For the colonists' version of why they warred on the Pequots, see John Higginson to John Winthrop, May 1637, in *Winthrop Papers,* 3:405-406; Thomas Hooker to John Winthrop, May 1637, in ibid., 3:407-408; John Winthrop to Richard Saltonstall and others, ca. 21 June 1643, in ibid., 4:409; and John Hull, *Diaries of John Hull, Mint-master and Treasurer of the Colony of Massachusetts Bay* (Boston, 1857) reprinted in *A Library of American Puritan Writings, The Seventeenth Century,* vol. 7, *Puritan Personal Writings: Diaries,* edited by Sacvan Bercovitch (New York, 1982), 171.

43. For Metacom's request for an English name, see *Plymouth Colony Records,* 13 June 1660, 3:192. William Hubbard claimed that the title "King" was a pejorative term, yet the prominent Springfield resident, John Pynchon, refers to "Sachem Philip" and "King Philip" interchangeably four years before the war. See Hubbard, *History of the Indian Wars,* 1:52; and John Pynchon to John Winthrop Jr., 10 May 1671, in *The Pynchon Papers, Letters of John Pynchon, 1654-1700,* ed. Carl Bridenbaugh (Boston, 1982), 1:87. For historians' accounts of King Philip's War and its consequences, see Anderson, "King Philip's Herds,"

620–624; Bourne, *Red King's Rebellion*, passim; Jennings, *Invasion of America*, 228, 283, 297, 325–326; Douglas Edward Leach, *Flintlock and Tomahawk: New England in King Philip's War* (New York, 1958), passim; Jill Lepore, *The Name of War: King Philip's War and the Origins of American Identity* (New York, 1998), 3–170; Morrison, *Embattled Northeast*, 89; Simpson and Simpson, introduction to Church, *Diary of King Philip's War*, 18, 28; and Vaughan, *New England Frontier*, 312, 314, 323. For contemporary accounts, see Church, *Diary of King Philip's War*, passim; Hubbard, *History of the Indian Wars*, vols. 1 and 2, passim; and Charles H. Lincoln, ed., *Narratives of the Indian Wars*, passim.

3. "All Things Are Turned Upside Down Among Us": Religion, Power, and Order (pp. 27–58)

1. For the Wheelwright episode, see John Winthrop, *Winthrop's Journal "History of New England," 1630–1649*, ed. James Kendall Hosmer, 2 vols. (New York, 1908), 1:196–197; for the comparison of decision-making between the Boston congregation and the Salem congregation, see Thomas Lechford, *Plain Dealing: or, Newes from New-England* (London, 1642; reprint, New York, 1969), 38.
2. John Winthrop, "A Modell of Christian Charity," in *Winthrop Papers*, 5 vols. (Boston, 1929–1947), 2:282.
3. For hierarchical views of early New Englanders, see Stephen Foster, *Their Solitary Way: The Puritan Social Ethic in the First Century of Settlement in New England* (New Haven, Conn., 1971), 7 and passim; David H. Flaherty, *Privacy in Colonial New England* (Charlottesville, Va., 1972), 96; Kenneth Lockridge, *A New England Town: The First Hundred Years* (New York, 1970), 11; and Edmund S. Morgan, *The Puritan Family, Religion and Domestic Relations in Seventeenth-Century New England* (New York, rev. ed., 1966), 19. For the potentially subversive beliefs of Reformed Protestantism, in particular Puritanism, see Emery Battis, *Saints and Sectaries: Anne Hutchinson and the Antinomian Controversy in the Massachusetts Bay Colony* (Chapel Hill, N.C., 1962), 255; Foster, *Their Solitary Way*, 39; and David D. Hall, preface to Hall, ed., *The Antinomian Controversy, 1636–1638: A Documentary History* (Durham, N.C.; 2d ed., 1990), xi–xii, and *Worlds of Wonder, Days of Judgment: Popular Religious Belief in Early New England* (New York, 1989; reprint Cambridge, Mass., 1990), 10
4. For a more thorough analysis of the developing government of Massachusetts Bay in the 1630s, see Edmund S. Morgan, *The Puritan Dilemma: The Story of John Winthrop* (Boston, 1958), 84–114.
5. David D. Hall, in his introduction to a collection of documents on the Antinomian controversy and in the collection itself is persuasive that Cotton was the "major figure" in the affair: see Hall, introduction to Hall, ed., *Antinomian Controversy*, 4, and the collection; the characterization of Cotton as being "meek and cautious" comes from Larzer Ziff, *The Career of John Cotton: Puritanism and the American Experience* (Princeton, N.J., 1962), 80; for Cotton's attitude toward civil authority, see ibid., 97, 103; for the particular examples, see Winthrop, *Journal*, 1:124–125, 133–134, 143–144.
6. For the differences between pastors and teachers, see Ziff, *Career of John Cotton*, 83–84; for Winthrop's assessment of the successes of Cotton and Wilson, see Winthrop, *Journal*, 1:116; and for the gift of the heifer, see ibid., 1:128.

7. My attempt to define Puritanism in this and the following paragraphs requires a complete bibliography to acknowledge all the scholars whose works have influenced me. Let me instead note a few key works as a guide. Older but still useful books include: Perry Miller, *The New England Mind: From Colony to Province* (Boston, 1953) and *The New England Mind: The Seventeenth Century* (Boston, 1961; originally published 1939); Edmund S. Morgan, *Visible Saints, The History of a Puritan Idea* (New York, 1963); and Alan Simpson, *Puritanism in Old and New England* (Chicago, 1955). More recent studies include: Theodore Dwight Bozeman, *To Live Ancient Lives: The Primitivist Dimension in Puritanism* (Chapel Hill, N.C., 1988); Charles Lloyd Cohen, *God's Caress: The Psychology of Puritan Religious Experience* (New York, 1986); Stephen Foster, *The Long Argument: English Puritanism and the Shaping of New England Culture, 1570–1700* (Chapel Hill, N.C., 1991); Philip F. Gura, *A Glimpse of Sion's Glory: Puritan Radicalism in New England, 1620–1660* (Middletown, Conn., 1984); Hall, *Worlds of Wonder;* Charles E. Hambrick-Stowe, *The Practice of Piety: Puritan Devotional Disciplines in Seventeenth-Century New England* (Chapel Hill, N.C., 1982); Robert Middlekauff, *The Mathers: Three Generations of Puritan Intellectuals, 1596–1728* (New York, 1971); and Darrett B. Rutman, *American Puritanism: Faith and Practice* (Philadelphia, 1970). Two post-Miller guides to Puritan studies—Michael McGiffert, "American Puritan Studies in the 1960's, *William and Mary Quarterly,* 3d ser., 27 (1970): 36–67, and David D. Hall, "Understanding the Puritans," in Herbert J. Bass, ed., *The State of American History* (Chicago, 1970), 330–349—should be supplemented by Hall's more recent "On Common Ground: The Coherence of American Puritan Studies," *William and Mary Quarterly,* 3d ser., 44 (1987): 193–229.

8. The classic analysis of covenant theology is Perry Miller, "The Marrow of Puritan Divinity," in his *Errand Into the Wilderness* (New York, 1956), 48–98. That has been largely revised, if not replaced, by more recent studies. See particularly Michael McGiffert, "Grace and Works: The Rise and Division of Covenant Divinity in Elizabethan Puritanism," *Harvard Theological Review* 75 (1982): 463–502 and "From Moses to Adam: The Making of the Covenant of Works," *Sixteenth Century Journal,* 19 (summer 1988): 131–155; and Cohen, *God's Caress,* 47–74.

9. See the "Elders Reply" in Hall, ed., *Antinomian Controversy,* 61–77; for an extensive analysis of the issue of an active will in the process of salvation as it was debated in the controversy, see William K. B. Stoever, *"A Faire and Easie Way to Heaven": Covenant Theology and Antinomianism in Early Massachusetts* (Middletown, Conn., 1978); for the active preparation for faith and for repeated conversion experiences, see Cohen, *God's Caress,* 92, 94, 104; for renewed conversions, see Michael McGiffert's introduction to *God's Plot: Being the Autobiography & Journal of Thomas Shepard* (Amherst, Mass., 1972), 26. For Cotton's views, see *Sixteene Questions of Serious and Necessary Consequence, Propounded unto Mr. John Cotton of Boston in New-England, Together with His Answers to each Question* (London, 1644), in Hall, ed., *Antinomian Controversy,* 46–59, and John Cotton, "Rejoinder," in Hall, ed., *Antinomian Controversy,* 79–151. Janice Knight finds a fundamental difference between the two camps, with the stake being who was to define orthodoxy in early New England; see her *Orthodoxies in Massachusetts: Rereading American Puritanism* (Cambridge, Mass., 1994).

10. Despite some questionable assumptions about menopause and Hutchinson's behavior during the controversy, the most comprehensive study of Anne

Hutchinson and the Antinomian episode remains Battis, *Saints and Sectaries*. For an antidote to Battis's assumptions, see Lyle Koehler, *A Search for Power: The "Weaker Sex" in Seventeenth-Century New England* (Urbana, Ill., 1980) and "The Case of the American Jezebels: Anne Hutchinson and Female Agitation during the Years of Antinomian Turmoil, 1636–1640," *William and Mary Quarterly*, 3d. ser., 31 (1974): 55–78.

11. See "The Examination of Mrs. Anne Hutchinson at the Court at Newtown," in Hall, ed., *Antinomian Controversy*, 314; Thomas Weld's preface to John Winthrop, *A Short Story of the rise, reign, and ruine of the Antinomians, Familists & Libertines, that infected the Churches of New-England* (London, 1644), in Hall, ed., *Antinomian Controversy*, 207–208.

12. See Ziff, *Career of John Cotton*, 106–107.

13. Ibid., 114.

14. Morgan, *Puritan Dilemma*, 115–116; Battis, *Saints and Sectaries*, 106–107.

15. Winthrop, *Journal*, 1:182; Morgan, *Puritan Dilemma*, 167.

16. Thomas Shepard to John Cotton, in Hall, ed., *Antinomian Controversy*, 25–29. David D. Hall dates this letter February–June 1636, in his introduction to Hall, ed., *Antinomian Controversy*, 24–25. Hall's invaluable introduction and documents., which begin with Shepard's letter, greatly influenced my interpretation of the Antinomian controversy.

17. John Cotton to Thomas Shepard, in Hall, ed., *Antinomian Controversy*, 29–33.

18. "Peter Bulkeley and John Cotton: On Union with Christ," in Hall, ed., *Antinomian Controversy*, 34–42; Stoever, *"A Faire and Easie Way to Heaven,"* 65–66, 106, 113.

19. Winthrop, *Journal*, 1:196.

20. Ibid., 197.

21. Ibid., 201.

22. Ibid., 201–203.

23. Winthrop, *A Short Story*, in Hall, ed., *Antinomian Controversy*, 269–271; "Examination of Mrs. Anne Hutchinson," in Hall, ed., *Antinomian Controversy*, 319–326, 333–336; see Battis, whose ordering of the events at the time of the December General Court is most useful, *Saints and Sectaries*, 129.

24. Winthrop, *Journal*, 1:203–204; Battis, *Saints and Sectaries*, 134–136.

25. Winthrop, *Journal*, 1:204–205; Battis, *Saints and Sectaries*, 136–137; for church members walking out of the meetinghouse, also see John Cotton, *The Way of Congregational Churches Cleared* (London, 1648), in Hall, ed., *Antinomian Controversy*, 423.

26. "Questions of the Elders," in Hall, ed., *Antinomian Controversy*, 44–45; John Cotton, *Sixteene Questions of Serious and Necessary Consequence, Propounded unto Mr. John Cotton of Boston in New-England, Together with His Answers to each Question* (London, 1644), in ibid., 46–59.

27. "The Elders Reply," in Hall, ed., *Antinomian Controversy*, 61–77.

28. "Mr. Cottons Rejoynder," in Hall, ed., *Antinomian Controversy*, 79–151; the quotation appears on 140.

29. Battis, *Saints and Sectaries*, 141.

30. John Wheelwright, "A Fast-Day Sermon," in Hall, ed., *Antinomian Controversy*, 153–172.

31. Winthrop, *Journal*, 1:211–212.

32. Ibid., 213.

33. Ibid., 215, and 216 and 220 for the sergeants' "inaction"; for an analysis of the composition and background of the petitioners and other supporters of Cotton, Wheelwright, and Hutchinson, see Battis, *Saints and Sectaries*, 249–285.

34. Winthrop, *Journal*, 1:217–218, 219; Cotton, *Way of Congregational Churches Cleared*, 413–416.

35. Winthrop, *Journal*, 1:218, 226.

36. Ibid., 229.

37. Ibid., 230, 233–234; Cotton's position may be seen in John Cotton, *A Conference Mr. John Cotton Held at Boston With the Elders of New-England* (London, 1646), in Hall, ed., *Antinomian Controversy*, 175–198.

38. Winthrop, *Journal*, 1: 232; Cotton, *Way of Congregational Churches Cleared*, 407–408; Battis, *Saints and Sectaries*, 164–166; Ziff, *Career of John Cotton*, 133–134.

39. Winthrop, *Journal*, 1:232–235; Cotton, *Way of Congregational Churches Cleared*, 399–400, 408, 409–410, 422, 426–428; Battis, *Saints and Sectaries*, 167–173.

40. Winthrop, *Journal*, 1:239; Winthrop, *A Short Story*, 248.

41. Winthrop, *Journal*, 1:239; Winthrop, *A Short Story*, 250–251.

42. Winthrop, *A Short Story*, 252–255.

43. Ibid., 255–257; Winthrop, *Journal*, 1:240.

44. Winthrop, *A Short Story*, 257–261.

45. Unless otherwise noted, this account of the Hutchinson trial is based on "The Examination of Mrs. Ann Hutchinson at the court at Newtown," in Hall, ed., *Antinomian Controversy*, 312–348; for Winthrop's slant, see *A Short Story*, 262–276.

46. Attitudes toward revelation and foretelling the future were more ambiguous and complex than the magistrates allowed at this time. See Hall, *Worlds of Wonder*, 94–110.

47. Winthrop, *A Short Story*, 261–262, 276–277; Winthrop, *Journal*, 1:259; Battis, *Saints and Sectaries*, 209–212.

48. Winthrop, *Journal*, 1:258.

49. John Cotton to unknown, 1636, in Emerson, ed., *Letters from New England*, 197; Hall, introduction to "A Report of the Trial of Mrs. Ann Hutchinson before the Church in Boston, March, 1638," in Hall, ed., *Antinomian Controversy*, 350.

50. This account of the church trial is based on "A Report of the Trial of Mrs. Ann Hutchinson before the Church in Boston, March, 1638," in Hall, ed., *Antinomian Controversy*, 350–388.

51. For a discussion of Cotton's attempts to assist Hutchinson during the week between the two meetings of her church trial, see Battis, *Saints and Sectaries*, 243–244.

52. Gura, *Glimpse of Sion's Glory*, 4–5, 7–9, 20–21; Hall, *Worlds of Wonder*, 19; Rutman, *American Puritanism*, 112; Jon Butler, *Awash in a Sea of Faith: Christianizing the American People* (Cambridge, Mass., 1990), 55.

53. Gura, *Glimpse of Sion's Glory*, passim; Jonathan M. Chu, *Neighbors, Friends, or Madmen: The Puritan Adjustment to Quakerism in Seventeenth-Century Massachusetts Bay* (Westport, Conn., 1985), passim; and Carla Gardina Pestana, *Quakers and Baptists in Colonial Massachusetts* (Cambridge, 1991), passim; ; for assessments of how many people were church members, see Foster,

Long Argument, 151; David Thomas Konig, *Law and Society in Puritan Massachusetts: Essex County, 1629–1692* (Chapel Hill, N.C., 1979), 91; Benjamin W. Labaree, *Colonial Massachusetts: A History* (Millwood, N.Y., 1979), 91; Lockridge, *New England Town,* 31, and *Settlement and Unsettlement in Early America: The Crisis of Political Legitimacy Before the Revolution* (Cambridge, 1981), 24; Paul R. Lucas, *Valley of Discord: Church and Society Along the Connecticut River, 1636–1725* (Hanover, N.H., 1976), 139, 141–142; Robert G. Pope, *The Half-Way Covenant: Church Membership in Puritan New England* (Princeton, N.J., 1969), 233–236; Darrett B. Rutman, *Winthrop's Boston: A Portrait of a Puritan Town, 1630–1649* (Chapel Hill, N.C., 1965), 58; and John J. Waters, Jr., *The Otis Family in Provincial and Revolutionary Massachusetts* (Chapel Hill, N.C., 1968), 17; also see this volume, chapter 4, n. 19.

54. Samuel Sewall, *The Diary of Samuel Sewall, 1674–1729,* ed. M. Halsey Thomas, 2 vols. (New York, 1973), 1:135.

55. John Fiske, *The Notebook of The Reverend John Fiske, 1644–1675,* ed. and intro. Robert G. Pope (Salem, Mass., 1974), 3; for descriptions of the New England Way, see Johnson, *Wonder-Working Providence,* 217–218; Lechford, *Plain Dealing,* 18–25; and Morgan, *Visible Saints,* passim.

56. Fiske, *Notebook,* 10, 17; and Robert G. Pope, introduction to Fiske, *Notebook,* xv-xvi.

57. For transcriptions and summaries of specific relations, see Fiske, *Notebook;* Thomas Shepard, *Thomas Shepard's Confessions,* ed. and intro. George Selement and Bruce C. Wooley (Boston, 1981); and Mary Rhinelander McCarl, "Thomas Shepard's Record of Relations of Religious Experience, 1648–1649," *William and Mary Quarterly,* 3d ser., 48 (July 1991): 432–466. Although neither was a conversion narrative, the following also offer insight into the Puritan religious experience: John Dane, "A Declaration of Remarkabell Prouedenses in the Corse of My Life," *New England Historic Genealogical Register* 8 (April 1854): 149–156; and John Winthrop, "John Winthrop's Relation of His Religious Experience," *Winthrop Papers,* 3:338–344. For the importance of congregational speaking, see Patricia Caldwell, *The Puritan Conversion Narrative: The Beginnings of American Expression* (Cambridge, 1983), 79; and Cohen, *God's Caress,* 140, 161, 163, 176. For the Wenham debate about women speaking and the eventual reversal, see Fiske, *Notebook,* 4–5, 106, and 151; and Pope, introduction to Fiske, *Notebook,* xvii.

58. Pope, introduction to Fiske, *Notebook,* xvii.

59. Fiske, *Notebook,* 3.

60. Ibid., 17,19, 20–24, 31, 32–33, 38–40.

61. For a description of the division of town residents as communicants, children of church members, and nonmembers, see Pope, introduction to Fiske, *Notebook,* xx; for a brief but typically insightful survey of the degree of religious belief among English New Englanders, see Hall, *Worlds of Wonder,* 14–17.

62. Middlekauff, *The Mathers,* 55–57; Pope, *Half-Way Covenant,* 17–18.

63. Middlekauff, *The Mathers,* 56; Pope, *Half-Way Covenant,* 46–47, 85–86.

64. Pope, *Half-Way Covenant,* 43–74.

65. Ibid., 132–133, 139, 271; David Hall believes more church members supported the half-way covenant than opposed it, *Worlds of Wonder,* 153.

66. Pope, *Half-Way Covenant,* 134, 75–131, 253.

67. The deputies' report is quoted in ibid., 173.

68. Ibid., 174-175.

69. Hall, *Worlds of Wonder,* 15, 17, passim and "On Common Ground," passim; Rutman, *American Puritanism,* 112; Gura, *Glimpse of Sion's Glory,* 4-5, 7-9, 20-21, 92, 322-323.

4. The Eminent and the Mean: Social Stratification, Status, and Power (pp. 59-72)

1. Isabel MacBeath Calder, *The New Haven Colony* (New Haven, Conn., 1934), 90; Anthony N. B. Garvan, *Architecture and Town Planning in Colonial Connecticut* (New Haven, Conn., 1951), 143; Franklin Bowditch Dexter and Zara Jones Powers, eds., *New Haven Town Records, 1649-1662, 1662-1684,* and *1684-1769* (New Haven, Conn., 1917, 1919, and 1962), 1:115, 298-299 (hereafter *New Haven Town Records*).

2. Marian Card Donnelly, *The New England Meetinghouses of the Seventeenth Century* (Middletown, Conn., 1968), 15, 51, 95; *New Haven Town Records,* 1:98-99, 338, 431-433.

3. *New Haven Town Records,* 1:270-274, 510-513; 2:219-221.

4. Ibid., 1:176-177, 270-274, 510-513; 2:95, 219-221. John Coolidge similarly concludes that the meetinghouse in Hingham could not have sheltered the town's entire population, "Hingham Builds A Meetinghouse," *New England Quarterly,* 34 (December 1961): 455n.

5. Ibid., 1:242, 266, 505; 2:142; Isabel Calder considers "dignity, age, and estate" to be the most important criteria for seating, *New Haven Colony,* 90-91; Coolidge identifies "status in the community and age," "Hingham Builds A Meetinghouse," 457; Robert J. Dinkin concludes that "monetary worth and age were the two most important considerations, though such factors as high political office could also be influential," "Seating the Meetinghouse in Early Massachusetts," in Robert Blair St. George, ed., *Material Life in America, 1600-1860* (Boston, 1988), 410; and David Hackett Fischer reasons that "age, estate and reputation" were most important," with age often being the strongest of the three, *Albion's Seed: Four British Folkways in America* (New York, 1989), 180.

6. This paragraph and those that follow that analyze the New Haven seatings of 1656, 1662, and 1668 are based on *New Haven Town Records,* 1:270-274, 510-513; 2:219-221.

7. The most complete identification of New Haven church members was made by Franklin Bowditch Dexter, *Historical Catalogue of the Members of the First Church of Christ in New Haven, Connecticut, A.D. 1639-1914* (New Haven, Conn., 1914), yet he acknowledged that the list of admissions before 1685 was incomplete. For other estimates of what percentage of a town's or New England's population were church members, see Foster, *Long Argument,* 151; Konig, *Law and Society in Puritan Massachusetts,* 91; Lockridge, *A New England Town,* 31, 34, and *Settlement and Unsettlement in Early America,* 24; Lucas, *Valley of Discord,* 141-142; Pope, *Half-Way Covenant,* 236; and Rutman, *Winthrop's Boston,* 57-58, 146-147.

8. For a row-by-row analysis of the Hingham meetinghouse, see Coolidge, "Hingham Builds A Meetinghouse," 457-459.

9. Savage, *Genealogical Dictionary of New England,* 1:38; 3:261-262; Dexter, *Historical Catalogue of Members,* 8, 9; *Plymouth Colony Records,* 1:9-11;

"Abstracts of the Early Probate Records of New Haven, Book I, Part I, 1647–1687," *New England Historical and Genealogical Register,* 81 (April 1927), 121, 122, 127, 129, 130; and New Haven Probate Record, Connecticut State Library, State Archives (microfilm, reel 1).

10. Savage, *Genealogical Dictionary of New England,* 1:233; 4:348; "Early Probate Records of New Haven," 122; and New Haven Probate Record (microfilm, reel 1).

11. Savage, *Genealogical Dictionary of New England,* 1:165, 223; 2:224, 576–577; 3:23; 4:285, 350–352; Dexter, *Historical Catalogue of Members,* 2, 3, 5, 14, 15; "Early Probate Records of New Haven," 124, 127, 133; and New Haven Probate Record (microfilm, reel 1).

12. Dexter, *Historical Catalogue of Members,* 6, 8.

13. Savage, *Genealogical Dictionary of New England,* 1:184; 2:488; Dexter, *Historical Catalogue of Members,* 12, 14; *New Haven Town Records,* 1:120–121, 180, 196, 207, 254, 430, 484; 2:190–192, 207, 213, 267, 268, 276–277.

14. *New Haven Town Records,* 2:365, 394–395, 396–397. Watertown experienced similar discontent as early as 1659: *Watertown Records Comprising the First and Second Books of Town Proceedings, etc.* (Watertown) 59 (hereafter *Watertown Records*).

15. For similar divisions in the eighteenth century, see Edward M. Cook Jr., *The Fathers of the Towns: Leadership and Community Structure in Eighteenth-Century New England* (Baltimore, Md., 1976), 117–118. The prominent representatives with connections both to the towns and to the colonial governments generally were the "lesser gentry" whom Robert Emmet Wall Jr., so ably analyzes throughout *Massachusetts Bay: The Crucial Decade, 1640–1650* (New Haven, 1972). For the progression from deputy to assistant, see Jackson Turner Main, *Society and Economy in Colonial Connecticut* (Princeton, N.J., 1985), 322.

16. This study compiled birth order of sons only for those who lived to adulthood. Thus the second son in actual order of birth whose older brother had died as a child is listed as firstborn, and so on. Also the birth dates of all the listed sons had to be known. In some cases the first few sons' order of birth might be known but not later sons, because an apparent third or fourth son did not have a recorded birth date. Only the first few sons would have been included. Using these criteria, I found of all New England males whose birth order can be determined 49.3 percent were firstborn ($N = 946$), 27.7 percent second-born ($N = 531$), 13.7 percent third-born ($N = 263$), 5.7 percent fourth-born ($N = 110$), 2.8 percent fifth-born ($N = 54$), and .8 percent sixth-born ($N = 15$).

17. This paragraph and appendix C are based on probated wealth. Although the placement of a person's wealth at death quite likely was similar to his placement when holding office, it is possible that the relative positions had changed, as was true for Isaac Allerton. In those cases, the disparity between officeholders and the general population probably was even greater, for the wealthy in their later years had more to give as gifts (and therefore could plummet significantly) than did the less well-to-do.

18. Before 1660, 37.5 percent of selectmen, 42.7 percent of deputies, 50.0 percent of assistants, and 40.0 percent of governors were younger than forty when they began serving. After that date, 17.2 percent of selectmen, 19.6 percent of representatives, 23.1 percent of assistants, and no governors were younger than forty. Throughout the entire period no deputy governor was younger than forty

when entering office for the first time. Because the officeholders in this study had migrated to New England prior to 1650 or had been born there by that date, the data are biased toward these results. But even if the latter period is changed from 1660–1699 to 1660–1679, the pattern remains the same without exception. Also see, Cook, *Fathers of the Towns*, 115; and Robert deV. Brunkow, "Office-holding in Providence, Rhode Island, 1646 to 1686: A Quantitative Analysis," *William and Mary Quarterly*, 3d ser., 37 (April 1980): 242–243.

    19. A comparision of church members among the adult males of this study who were living in New England by 1650 finds: total population, 2,555 of 12,318 (20.7%); governors, 21 of 35 (60.0%); deputy governors, 16 of 33 (48.5%); assistants, 86 of 182 (47.3%); deputies, 468 of 991 (47.2%), selectmen, 192 of 298 (64.4%); town clerks, 52 of 107 (48.6%), and constables, 92 of 194 (47.4%). There can be little doubt that these figures, particularly for the general population, are too low and that they suggest a precision that doesn't exist. How low is impossible to know, for the number of people who don't appear in any record of the period (the poor, the transient, those whose records have disintegrated or disappeared; in short, the invisible) may nearly balance unlisted church members who are known by other types of records. We should also take into account that women typically comprised a higher percentage of church members than did men. Towns with even partial lists of church members may give a more accurate estimate of percentages of men and of deputies who were members, and at the very least they highlight the importance of church membership for holding office: Barnstable, 32 of 178 men (18.0%), deputies, 9 of 22 (40.9%); Braintree, 90 of 303 men (29.7%), deputies, 13 of 25 (52.0%); Charlestown, 243 of 738 men (32.9%), deputies, 47 of 69 (68.1%); Chelmsford, 32 of 70 men (45.7%), deputies, 4 of 6 (66.7%); Dorchester, 258 of 629 men (41.0%), deputies, 43 of 73 (58.9%); Farmington, 16 of 100 men (16.0%), deputies, 8 of 18 (44.4%); Middletown, 9 of 63 men (14.3 %), deputies, 3 of 10 (30.0%); Milford, 32 of 194 men (16.5%), deputies, 7 of 22 (31.8%); New Haven, 185 of 532 men (34.8%), deputies, 16 of 31 (51.6%); New London, 36 of 210 men (17.1%), deputies, 12 of 22 (54.5%); Reading, 21 of 94 men (22.3%), deputies, 3 of 11 (27.3%); Roxbury, 178 of 454 men (39.2%), deputies, 37 of 49 (75.5%); Salem, 235 of 1036 men (22.7%), deputies, 34 of 71 (47.9%); Wenham, 21 of 67 men (31.3%), deputies, 7 of 12 (58.3%); Windsor, 65 of 403 men (16.1%), deputies, 18 of 45 (40.0%). Although partial lists for Bristol, Danvers, Milton, and Topsfield are included for the overall population of this study, their numbers within the towns were insufficient to be meaningful. "Catalog of Admissions to Full Communion," in William I. Budington, *The History of the First Church, Charlestown* (Boston, 1845), 247–251; Samuel Danforth, "Rev. Samuel Danforth's Records of the First Church in Roxbury, Mass.," in *New England Historical and Genealogical Register,* 34 (April–October, 1880): 84–89, 162–166, 297–301, 359–363; Dexter, *Historical Catalogue of the Members of the First Church of Christ in New Haven;* H. G. Dunnel, ed., "List of Members of the Old Church, Topsfield," *New England Historical and Genealogical Register* 16 (July 1862), 212–215; John Eliot, "The Rev. John Eliot's Record of Church Members, Roxbury, Mass.," in *City of Boston Report of the Record Commissioners* (Boston, 1884), 6:73–103; Farmington (Conn.) Church Records, Connecticut State Library (microfilm); Fiske, *Notebook of The Reverend John Fiske;* John H. Gould, ed. "Early Records of the Church in Topsfield," *Essex Institute Historical Collections,* 24 (1887): 181–205; Middletown (Conn.) Church Records, Connecticut

State Library (microfilm); Milford (Conn.) Church Records, Connecticut State Library (microfilm); "Milton (Mass.) Church Records," *New England Historical and Genealogical Register* 22 (July 1868): 259–263; New London (Conn.) Church Records, Connecticut State Library (microfilm); Richard D. Pierce, ed., *The Records of the First Church in Salem Massachusetts, 1629–1736* (Salem, Mass., 1974); Reading (Mass.) Church Records, Reading Public Library (transcript); "Records of the First Church at Braintree, Mass.," *New England Historical and Genealogical Register* 59 (January 1905): 87–91; *Records of the First Church at Dorchester in New England, 1636–1734* (Boston, 1891); "Scituate [Mass.] and Barnstable [Mass.] Church Records," *New England Historical and Genealogical Register,* 9 (July 1855): 279–287 and 10 (January 1856): 40–43; "The First Record-Book of the First Church in Charlestown, Massachusetts," *New England Historical and Genealogical Register* 23 (April, July, and October 1869): 190–191, 279–284, and 435–442; Windsor (Conn.) Church Records, Connecticut State Library (microfilm); *List of Freemen of Massachusetts, 1630–1691,* comp. Lucius R. Paige (reprint, Baltimore, 1978). Edward M. Cook Jr., finds at least 70 percent of selectmen in "eight Massachusetts and Connecticut towns from 1650 to 1699 were members of the local church, *Fathers of the Towns,* 122–123. For a thorough analysis of the concepts for the "good ruler," see T. H. Breen, *The Character of the Good Ruler: Puritan Political Ideas in New England, 1630–1730* (New York, 1970).

20. Caution should be the byword here. Because of incomplete church records, it is possible that those I identify in this paragraph as non–church members may have been members. Clements, for example, may have joined a church, but in Haverhill where a majority of the men were not freemen and possibly not church members (some church members declined to become freemen, and the extant records do not allow us to know with certainty how many they were) it is plausible that he could have been elected as a non–church member. See Robert Emmet Wall Jr., "The Massachusetts Bay Colony Franchise in 1647," *William and Mary Quarterly,* 3d ser., 27 (January 1970): 137–140; and Foster, *Their Solitary Way,* 174–176.

21. See B. Katherine Brown, "Freemanship in Puritan Massachusetts," *American Historical Review* 59 (July 1954): 865–883, and "Puritan Democracy in Dedham, Massachusetts: Another Case Study," *William and Mary Quarterly,* 3d ser., 24 (July 1967): 378–396; Foster, *Their Solitary Way,* 173–179, and "The Massachusetts Franchise in the Seventeenth Century," *William and Mary Quarterly,* 3d ser., 24 (October 1967): 613–623; David H. Fowler, "Connecticut's Freemen: The First Forty Years," *William and Mary Quarterly,* 3d ser., 15 (July 1958): 312–333; George D. Langdon Jr., "The Franchise and Political Democracy in Plymouth Colony," *William and Mary Quarterly,* 3d ser., 20 (October 1963): 513–526; Richard C. Simmons, "Godliness, Property and the Franchise in Puritan Massachusetts: an Interpretation," *Journal of American History* 55 (December 1968): 495–511; and Wall, "Massachusetts Bay Colony Franchise," 136–144.

22. Wall, "Massachusetts Bay Colony Franchise," 143.

23. Winthrop, "A Modell of Christian Charity," in *Winthrop Papers,* 2:282.

24. Although David D. Hall argues that "the mass of people in New England seem to have been relatively homogeneous in their social rank and practices," most other historians have uncovered various degrees of stratification. See Hall, *Worlds of Wonder,* 14; John Demos, *A Little Commonwealth: Family Life in*

Plymouth Colony (New York, 1970), 37; Flaherty, *Privacy in Colonial New England,* 96; Foster, *Their Solitary Way,* 32; Richard P. Gildrie, *Salem, Massachusetts, 1626–1683: A Covenant Community* (Charlottesville, Va., 1975), 65; Lockridge, *A New England Town,* 11; Main, *Society and Economy in Colonial Connecticut,* 31, 88; Edmund S. Morgan, *The Puritan Family, Religion and Domestic Relations in Seventeenth-Century New England* (New York, rev. ed., 1966), 19; Wall, *Massachusetts Bay,* 21. For England, see Barry Reay, "Introduction: Popular Culture in Early Modern England," in Barry Reay, ed., *Popular Culture in Seventeenth-Century England* (New York, 1985), 18; David Underdown, *Revel, Riot, and Rebellion: Popular Politics and Culture in England, 1603–1660* (Oxford, 1985), 40; and Keith Wrightson, *English Society, 1580–1680* (New Brunswick, N.J., 1982), 140–141.

25. *Town Records of Salem* (1634–1691), 3 vols. (Salem, Mass., 1868, 1913, 1934), 1:55; *Watertown Records,* 62; Winthrop, *Journal,* 1:279; Main, *Society and Economy in Colonial Connecticut,* 325, 358.

5. Life Cycle, Gender, and Family (pp. 73–97)

1. John Russell Bartlett, ed., *Records of the Colony of Rhode Island, and Providence Plantations in New England* (Providence, R.I., 1856–1858), 2:101 (hereafter *Rhode Island Records*); G. Andrews Moriarty, "Herodias (Long) Hicks-Gardiner-Porter: A Tale of Old Newport," in *Genealogies of Rhode Island Families from Rhode Island Periodicals* (Baltimore, Md., 1983), 599.

2. Peter Laslett analyzing the age at first marriage of 1,007 women in Canterbury between 1619 and 1660 found only one girl who married as young as thirteen and only seventeen of that group who married before the age of seventeen: *The World We Have Lost Further Explored* (New York, rev. ed., 1984), 82–83. For other studies of ages at first marriage in seventeenth-century England, see Wrightson, *English Society,* 68; and E. A. Wrigley and R. S. Schofield, *The Population History of England, 1541–1871: A Reconstruction* (Cambridge, Mass., 1981), 255. For Herodias's assessment that she was "taken," see *Rhode Island Records,* 2:101.

3. Moriarty, "Herodias (Long)," 599, 605; Savage, *Genealogical Dictionary of New England,* 2:410.

4. *Rhode Island Records,* 2:101; John Hicks to John Coggeshall, 12 December 1645, quoted in Moriarty, "Herodias (Long)," 600; the usually reliable Clarence Almon Torrey states that they divorced on 3 December 1644, which, if true, would have made Hicks's New York divorce unnecessary, *New England Marriages Prior to 1700* (Baltimore, Md., 1985), 368 ; the New York divorce decree in the original Dutch and with an English translation is in Moriarty, "Herodias (Long)," 600–601.

5. John Osborne Austin, *The Genealogical Dictionary of Rhode Island* (Albany, N.Y., 1887; reprint, Baltimore, 1982), 81; *Rhode Island Records,* 2:99–100 for Stanton's account, and for the procedure for becoming married see 1:187; Moriarty, "Herodias (Long)," 605–606. Mary Beth Norton finds a large number of colonists who followed the "traditional English practice" of informal marriages: *Founding Mothers & Fathers: Gendered Power and the Forming of American Society* (New York, 1996), 66–67. That may have been the case in the Long-Gardiner union; but considering that Herodias Long became a Quaker and

that they were married in the home of Quakers, it seems more likely that they had a Quaker ceremony and a Quaker marriage.

6. Moriarty, "Herodias (Long)," 601; for descriptions and analyses of New England Quakers and martyrdom, see Chu, *Neighbors, Friends, or Madmen,* 40–50; Kai T. Erikson, *Wayward Puritans: A Study in the Sociology of Deviance* (New York, 1966), 107–136; Gura, *A Glimpse of Sion's Glory,* 144, 147, 148, 211; Hall, *Worlds of Wonder,* 186–189; and Pestana, *Quakers and Baptists in Colonial Massachusetts,* 25, 32–35.

7. *Rhode Island Records,* 2:101–102; Martin, *Profits in the Wilderness,* 77–78.

8. *Rhode Island Records,* 2:102–103.

9. Moriarty, "Herodias (Long)," 604; Savage, *Genealogical Dictionary of New England,* 3:461; Martin, *Profits in the Wilderness,* 73–74.

10. Moriarty, "Herodias (Long)," 605–606.

11. This is based on records of 22,212 people who either migrated to New England before 1650 or were born there between 1620 and 1649. The data come from Savage's *Genealogical Dictionary of New England,* supplemented, modified, and corrected by genealogies, passenger lists, town, county, and colony records, church records, town and church histories, and firsthand accounts. 1,007 women who married in New England and whose age at marriage is known form the population on which this paragraph is based. Also see, Archer, "New England Mosaic," 489–492; Demos, *A Little Commonwealth,* 151, 193; Greven, *Four Generations,* 33–37; Douglas Lamar Jones, *Village and Seaport: Migration and Society in Eighteenth-Century Massachusetts* (Hanover, N.H., 1981), 70–72; Kenneth Lockridge, "The Population of Dedham, Massachusetts, 1636–1736," *Economic History Review,* 2d ser., 19 (1966): 330; Daniel Scott Smith, "The Demographic History of Colonial New England," *Journal of Economic History* 32 (March 1972): 176. For England see Laslett, *World We Have Lost,* 82–83; Wrightson, *English Society,* 68, and Wrigley and Schofield, *Population History of England,* 255. For France see Pierre Goubert, "Recent Theories and Research in French Population between 1500 and 1700," in D. V. Glass and D. E. C. Eversley, eds., *Population in History: Essays in Historical Demography* (Chicago, 1965), 468.

12. All citations from the previous footnote apply here as well.

13. Archer, "New England Mosaic," 481, 487; Cressy, *Coming Over,* 52; Jones, *Seaport and Village,* 70–71; Anthony Salerno, "The Social Background of Seventeenth-Century Emigration to America," *Journal of British Studies,* 19 (1979): 32–33; Smith, "Demographic History of Colonial New England," 176; Roger Thompson, *Mobility and Migration: East Anglian Founders of New England, 1629–1640* (Amherst, Mass., 1994), 122, 225. Otherwise valuable studies that focus primarily on emigrants from East Anglia and Kent find family migration, few single and unattached men, and a nearly even sex ratio: see Anderson, "Migrants and Motives," 348–349, 357, and *New England's Generation,* 20–21; and Breen and Foster, "Moving to the New World," 196.

14. Archer, "New England Mosaic," 491. For a review of early marriages and the age at menarche see Laslett, *World We Have Lost,* 82–85.

15. This paragraph is based on populations of 11 fourteen year olds, 30 thirty fifteen year olds, and 71 sixteen year olds. For order of birth and family size, the numbers are 11 fourteen year olds, 29 fifteen year olds, and 65 sixteen year olds. For residence at marriage, the numbers are 11 fourteen year olds, 28 fifteen year

olds, and 54 sixteen year olds. For the Hough material, see Savage, *Genealogical Dictionary of New England*, 2:469.

16. For Elizabeth Tilley see Bradford, *Of Plymouth Plantation*, 442, 446, and Savage, *Genealogical Dictionary of New England*, 4:303; and 2:479–480. For Elizabeth Sheaffe, see Savage, *Geneaological Dictionary of New England*, 4:66; and 2:247, and *Suffolk County Wills: Abstracts of the Earliest Wills Upon Record in the County of Suffolk, Massachusetts* (Baltimore, Md., 1984), 169–170. For Esther Warham, see Savage, *Genealogical Dictionary of New England*, 4:417–418; and 3:172. For marriages between merchant families, see Bernard Bailyn, *The New England Merchants in the Seventeenth Century* (Cambridge, Mass., 1955), 135–137.

17. Archer, "New England Mosaic," 494–496. For Hannah Hollard, see Savage, *Genealogical Dictionary of New England*, 2:447; and 1:107–108.

18. *Plymouth Colony Records*, 2:82–83, 112–113, and 5:10–11; *The Early Records of the Town of Warwick* (Providence, R.I., 1926; hereafter *Warwick Town Records*), 235–236, 267, 317–318, 333–334; *Fourth Report of the Record Commisioners of the City of Boston, Dorchester Town Records* (Boston, 2d ed., 1883; hereafter *Dorchester Town Records*), 150; *Watertown Records*, 104, 105.

19. *Dorchester Town Records*, 236; *Report of the Record Commissioners of the City of Boston, Containing the Boston Records from 1660 to 1701* (Boston, 1881; hereafter *Boston Town Records, 1660–1701*), 7:67. Francis Bale, most likely, was the person Savage refers to as Francis Ball of Dorchester who was married to Abigail Salter, but the spelling also could be for a Francis Bailey, if such a person existed. See Savage, *Genealogical Dictionary of New England*, 1:106.

20. Bradford, *Of Plymouth Plantation*, 234, 442, 443, 446–447; Savage, *Genealogical Dictionary of New England*, 1:179; 2, 95.

21. *Plymouth Colony Records*, 1:36–37, 43; 2:12, 38, 58–59, 67–68; Demos, *A Little Commonwealth*, 113.

22. For restrictions on husking corn, see *New Haven Town Records*, 2:186. For markets and fairs, see Nathaniel B. Shurtleff, ed., *Records of the Governor and Company of the Massachusetts In New England* (Boston, 1853; hereafter *Records of the Governor and Company*), 1:112, 241; *Watertown Records*, 5; *Plymouth Colony Records*, 1:32; J. Hammond Trumbull, ed., *The Public Records of the Colony of Connecticut, Prior to the Union with New Haven Colony, May, 1665* (Hartford, 1850), 1:91, 125; and Edward Johnson, *Wonder-Working Providence of Sions Saviour in New England* (London, 1653) ed. J. Franklin Jameson (New York, 1910), 250. For restrictions on Harvard students, see Harvard College Records, 1636–1750, in *Publications of the Colonial Society of Massachusetts* 15 (Boston, 1915): 27. For regulations on young people during church services, see *Boston Town Records, 1660–1701*, 131; *New Haven Town Records*, 1:448–449; *Watertown Records*, 86; *Dorchester Town Records*, 146; *Town Records of Salem* 2:209–210 .

23. For the punishment of John Hubbell and Abigail Burt, see *Colonial Justice in Western Massachusetts, 1639–1702: The Pynchon Court Record*, ed. and intro. Joseph H. Smith (Cambridge, Mass., 1961; hereafter *Pynchon Court Record*), 209. Hugh Peter to John Winthrop, c. February 1641, in *Winthrop Papers*, 4:316; John Endecott to John Winthrop, 12 February 1641, in *Winthrop Papers*, 4:321.

24. Lucy Downing to John Winthrop Jr., 17 December 1648, in *Winthrop*

Papers, 5:290; Emmanuel Downing to John Winthrop, 5 January 1649, in ibid., 5:300–301; Emmanuel Downing to John Winthrop, 22 January 1649, in ibid., 5:304; John Norton to John Winthrop, 26 January 1649, in ibid., 5:305–306; Lucy Downing to John Winthrop, c. February 1649, in ibid., 5:309–310; Savage, *Genealogical Dictionary of New England*, 3:293–294.

25. John J. Waters, "Family, Inheritance, and Migration in Colonial New England: The Evidence from Guilford, Connecticut," *William and Mary Quarterly*, 3d ser., 39 (January 1982): 78; Morgan, *Puritan Family*, 55–58. Daniel Scott Smith demonstrates that the birth order of sons played a part in the choice of marriage partner, with an eldest son more likely than younger brothers to take a mate whose family was wealthier than his own while younger sons were more likely than their eldest brothers to marry a woman whose family was less wealthy than their own: "Parental Power and Marriage Patterns: An Analysis of Historical Trends in Hingham, Massachusetts," *Journal of Marriage and the Family* 35 (August 1973): 424.

26. Demos, *A Little Commonwealth*, 157, 159, 162–164; Morgan, *Puritan Family*, 29–34; *Rhode Island Records*, 1:187; Winthrop, *Journal*, 2:330; Bradford, *Of Plymouth Plantation*, 86; Lechford, *Plain Dealing*, 86–87; Sewall, *Diary*, 1:53.

27. Morgan, *Puritan Family*, 34; Edmund S. Morgan, "The Puritans and Sex," *New England Quarterly*, 15 (1942): 591–607; Demos, *A Little Commonwealth*, 95–96; Laurel Thatcher Ulrich, *Good Wives: Image and Reality in the Lives of Women in Northern New England, 1650–1750* (New York, 1982), 93–96; Flaherty, *Privacy in Colonial New England*, 76–84.

28. Morgan, *Puritan Family*, 41; Demos, *A Little Commonwealth*, 96; Ulrich, *Good Wives*, 94; Winthrop, *Journal*, 2:161–163.

29. Morgan, *Puritan Family*, 34–37; Demos, *A Little Commonwealth*, 96–97; Ulrich, *Good Wives*, 94; *Plymouth Colony Records*, 5:94, 99, 110–111, 127.

30. Morgan, *Puritan Family*, 130; Demos, *A Little Commonwealth*, 152–153; *Plymouth Colony Records*, 4:83; 5:27, 51, 221; *New Haven Town Records*, 1:497–499, 505–507.

31. Martin Ingram, "The Reform of Popular Culture? Sex and Marriage in Early Modern England," in Barry Reay, ed., *Popular Culture in Seventeenth-Century England* (New York, 1985), 146; Demos, *A Little Commonwealth*, 152–153; Demos, "Families in Colonial Bristol, Rhode Island: An Exercise in Historical Demography," *William and Mary Quarterly*, 3d ser., 25 (January 1968): 56; Greven, *Four Generations*, 112–116; Ulrich, *Good Wives*, 94–96. Boston was enough different from other towns and villages that in 1672, John Hull suspected a brothel was in their midst: *Diaries of John Hull*, 232.

32. Archer, "New England Mosaic," 492–493; Demos, *A Little Commonwealth*, 192, and "Families in Colonial Bristol, Rhode Island," 47; Greven, *Four Generations*, 30; Lockridge, "Population of Dedham," 330; Susan L. Norton, "Population Growth in Colonial America: A Study of Ipswich, Massachusetts," *Population Studies* 25 (November, 1971): 444; Stephanie Grauman Wolf, *Urban Village: Population, Community, and Family Structure in Germantown, Pennsylvania, 1683–1800* (Princeton, N.J., 1976), 268.

33. Archer, "New England Mosaic," 488–489; Lockridge, "Population of Dedham," 329; Norton, "Population Growth in Colonial America," 442–443; Greven, *Four Generations*, 189; Demos, *A Little Commonwealth*, 131–132;

Gerald F. Moran and Maris A. Vinovskis, "The Puritan Family and Religion: A Critical Reappraisal," *William and Mary Quarterly*, 3d ser., 39 (1982): 52; Laslett, *World We Have Lost*, 112; Wrigley and Schofield, *Population History of England*, 249; Lawrence Stone, *The Family, Sex and Marriage in England, 1500–1800* (New York, 1977), 68–69; Goubert, "French Population Between 1500 and 1700," 468.

34. Demos, *A Little Commonwealth*, 62, and "Demography and Psychology in the Historical Study of Family-Life: A Personal Report," in Peter Laslett and Richard Wall, eds., *Household and Family in Past Time* (Cambridge, 1972), 562; Greven, *Four Generations*, 214, 265; Laslett, *World We Have Lost*, 93; Waters, "Family, Inheritance, and Migration in Colonial New England," 70–71, and "The Traditional World of the New England Peasants: A View from Seventeenth-Century Barnstable," *New England Historic and Genealogical Register* 130 (January 1976): 8; Flaherty, *Privacy in Colonial New England*, 175–179.

35. Roger Thompson, *Mobility and Migration*, 203–204; Demos, *A Little Commonwealth*, 118, 124; Greven, *Four Generations*, 215, 221; Daniel Vickers, *Farmers & Fishermen: Two Centuries of Work in Essex County, Massachusetts, 1630–1850* (Chapel Hill, N.C., 1994), 232, 239.

36. For Winthrop's comments on Ann Hopkins, see his *Journal*, 2:225. For the controversy over women attending religious meetings in Rhode Island, see ibid., 1:286–287. For extensive commentary on misogyny and related attitudes of male superiority and female inferiority, see Carol F. Karlsen, *The Devil in the Shape of a Woman: Witchcraft in Colonial New England* (New York, 1987) and Koehler, *A Search for Power* (Urbana, Ill., 1980).

37. Ulrich, *Good Wives*, 35–50 and passim; Morgan, *Puritan Family*, 29–64; Demos, *A Little Commonwealth*, 82–99; Stephen Bachiler to John Winthrop, 3 May 1647, *Winthrop Papers*, 5:224.

38. Ulrich, *Good Wives*, 149–152; Savage, *Genealogical Dictionary of New England*, 2:493; 4:53, 55; genealogical appendix in Sewall, *Diary*, 2:1,076–1,077. Sewall indicated that Sarah was named for "Sarah's standing in the Scripture," and also for his mother who "had a sister Sarah; and none of my sisters of that name," *Diary*, 1:324. This section on naming practices has been informed by Daniel Scott Smith, "Continuity and Discontinuity in Puritan Naming: Massachusetts, 1771," *William and Mary Quarterly*, 3d ser., 51 (January 1994): 67–91.

39. Thomas Shepard, *God's Plot: Being the Autobiography & Journal of Thomas Shepard*, ed. and intro. Michael McGiffert (Amherst, Mass., 1972), 34; Sewall, *Diary*, 1:175; Hall, *Worlds of Wonder*, 10.

40. This is based on 6,412 male emigrants, 3,187 female emigrants, 3,824 males born in New England by 1650, and 3,430 females born in New England by 1650. One other type of name appears in the records: the hortatory or moral virtue appellation, such as Fearnot, Increase, Patience, Praisever, Restore, and Silence; these, however, were much less frequent and many of them were unique.

41. The numbers for birth order on which this study is based are: firstborn, 887; second-born, 500; third-born, 246, and fourth- and later-born, 165. There were also 2,037 sons whose order of birth is unknown. The percentage of core English names for the unknown sons was 39.4, which is quite close to the average for all New England–born sons. To determine the relative variety of names, ratios of different names divided by total names were created. 1.0 represents all names being different, and .001 represents only one name for a thousand people: the larger the number, the greater the diversity. Unknowns were 155/2037 (.076),

first-borns 110/877 (.125), second-borns 87/500 (.174), third-borns 56/246 (.228), and fourth- and later-borns 59/165 (.358). Although there probably was a number beyond which there would be diminishing diversity, these figures combined with the percentages of particular names suggest that younger sons in large families were more likely than their older brothers to receive names new to a particular family. Neither Herodias Long nor George Gardiner were Puritans, and they named their children Benoni, Henry, George, William, Nicholas, Dorcas, and possibly Rebecca; see Moriarty, "Herodias (Long)," 605.

42. Ross W. Beales Jr., "In Search of the Historical Child: Miniature Adulthood and Youth in Colonial New England," *American Quarterly* 27 (1975): 379–398; Karin Calvert, *Children in the House: The Material Culture of Early Childhood, 1600–1900* (Boston, 1992), 45; Demos, *A Little Commonwealth,* 100–106, 131–150; Morgan, *Puritan Family,* 65–75; Ulrich, *Good Wives,* 154–158; Zuckerman, *Peaceable Kingdoms,* 80; David E. Stannard, *The Puritan Way of Death: A Study in Religion, Culture and Social Change* (New York, 1977), 46; Foster, *Long Argument,* 181; Anderson, *New England's Generation,* 159.

43. Archer, "New England Mosaic," 494–497. For the Chesapeake, see Darrett B. Rutman and Anita H. Rutman, *A Place in Time: Middlesex County, Virginia, 1650–1750 and Explicatus* (New York, 1984), 52, and "'Now-Wives and Sons-in-Law': Parental Death in a Seventeenth-Century Virginia County," in Thad W. Tate, and David L. Ammerman, eds., *The Chesapeake in the Seventeenth Century: Essays on Anglo-American Society* (Chapel Hill, N.C., 1979), 172; David W. Jordan, "Political Stability and the Emergence of a Native Elite in Maryland," in Tate and Ammerman, *Chesapeake,* 247; and Lorena S. Walsh, "'Till Death Us Do Part': Marriage and Family in Seventeenth-Century Maryland," in Tate and Ammerman, *Chesapeake,* 128.

44. Savage, *Genealogical Dictionary of New England,* 1:316; Anderson, *New England Generation,* 13–14, 138. See Appendix D for distribution of wealth.

45. *Suffolk County Wills,* 130–131.

46. Ulrich, *Good Wives,* 7, 38; Demos, *A Little Commonwealth,* 85–86; Morgan, *Puritan Family,* 58–59; Marylynn Salmon, *Women and the Law of Property in Early America* (Chapel Hill, N.C., 1986), 183.

47. Demos, *A Little Commonwealth,* 164–170; Greven, *Four Generations,* passim; Waters, "Traditional World of New England Peasants," 6–7; Savage, *Genealogical Dictionary of New England,* 1:316.

48. *Records of the Court of Assistants of the Colony of the Massachusetts Bay, 1630–1692,* 3 vols. (Boston, 1901–1928), 3:126–127.

49. Savage, *Genealogical Dictionary of New England,* 3:284; Anderson, *New England's Generation,* 13–14, 118, 126–127; *Plymouth Colony Records,* 4: passim; *Records of the Court of Assistants,* 3:122–124.

50. *Records of the Court of Assistants,* 3:121–129.

6. Lusty Young Men and Wicked Women (pp. 98–110)

1. *New Haven Town Records,* 1:238.
2. Ibid., 1:238–239.
3. Ibid., 1:239.
4. Ibid., 1:239–240.

5. Ibid., 2:109–111.

6. Ibid., 2:112–113.

7. Ibid., 2:115–117, 125–127, 179–180.

8. Savage, *Genealogical Dictionary of New England*, 2:183; 4:462.

9. Bradford, *Of Plymouth Plantation*, 92; Johnson, *Wonder-Working Providence*, 44–45; Nathaniel Ward to John Winthrop Jr., 24 December 1636, *Winthrop Papers*, 3:216.

10. Daniel Vickers, "Work and Life on the Fishing Periphery of Essex County, 1630–1675," in David D. Hall and David Grayson Allen, eds., *Seventeenth-Century New England* (Boston, 1984), 100; *Mourt's Relation*, 201.

11. Bradford, *Of Plymouth Plantation*, 299–301.

12. N. E. H. Hull, *Female Felons: Women and Serious Crime in Colonial Massachusetts* (Urbana, Ill., 1987), 46, 48, 55, 61; *Records of the Court of Assistants, Mass. Bay*, 1:29–30, 115, 125, 228 and 2:78; *Plymouth Colony Records*, 2:132–134; *New Hampshire Court Records*, 293–294; Winthrop, *Journal*, 1:282–283; *Winthrop Papers*, 5:151–152; Sewall, *Diary*, 1:153, 282, 310, 397, 399, 400; Cotton Mather, *Diary*, 164–165.

13. For fornication, see chapter 5; for Massachusetts Bay reaction to fornication between two servants, see Winthrop, *Journal*, 2:38; for Stephen Hopkins and Dorothy Temple, see *Plymouth Colony Records*, 1:113. For examples of sexual crimes, see the following: adultery, see chapter 5; rape and attempted rape, see *Records of the Court of Assistants, Mass. Bay*, 1:50, and 2:64, 65; masturbation, see *Pynchon Court Record*, 224; bestiality, see *Plymouth Colony Records*, 2:44; sodomy, see *Plymouth Colony Records*, 2:35–36. For the affair between Sarah Norman and Mary Hammon, see *Plymouth Colony Records*, 2:163. Also see Richard Godbeer, "The Cry of Sodom": Discourse, Intercourse, and Desire in Colonial New England," *William and Mary Quarterly*, 3d ser., 52 (April 1995): 259–286.

14. *The Book of the General Lawes and Libertyes Concerning the Inhabitants of the Massachusets* (Cambridge, 1648), ed. and intro. Thomas G. Barnes (San Marino, Calif., 1975), 29–31; *Plymouth Colony Records*, 1:38; *Rhode Island Records*, 1:185; *New Hampshire Court Records*, 133–134.

15. *Plymouth Colony Records*, 1:68; *New Hampshire Court Records*, 139–140; *Dorchester Town Records*, 121. For the subversive possibilities of ordinaries, see David W. Conroy, *In Public Houses: Drink & the Revolution of Authority in Colonial Massachusetts* (Chapel Hill, N.C., 1995), 2 and passim.

16. *New Haven Town Records*, 1:55–56, 125–126. For other homes where young people "mispent their time," see ibid., 1:487–488.

17. Roger Williams to John Winthrop, September 1636, *Winthrop Papers*, 3:296–298; Winthrop, *Journal*, 2:323–324.

18. Bradford, *Of Plymouth Plantation*, 75. Samuel Eliot Morison constructed a list of the passengers of the *Mayflower* with designations for the signers of the compact in ibid., 441–443. Also see Salisbury, *Manitou and Providence*, 142.

19. *Lawes and Libertyes*, 25–26; *Records of the Town of Plymouth, 1635 to 1705* (Plymouth, Mass., 1889), 138–139.

20. *Rhode Island Records*, 1:279–280; Bradford, *Of Plymouth Plantation*, 120–121; Salisbury, *Manitou and Providence*, 143; Flaherty, *Privacy in Colonial New England*, 175, 178–179; Edgar J. McManus, *Law and Liberty in Early New England: Criminal Justice and Due Process, 1620–1692* (Amherst, Mass., 1993), 39; *Plymouth Colony Records*, 3:201; *Dorchester Town Records*, 158–159; *New Haven Town Records*, 3:36.

21. *Plymouth Colony Records,* 1:21, 87; *Watertown Records,* 49, 52, 60.

22. *Boston Town Records, 1660–1701,* 21, 156–157.

23. *Rhode Island Records,* 1:332; *Lawes and Libertyes,* 11. Lawrence Stone discusses servitude as a form of social and political control in early modern England: *The Family, Sex and Marriage in England,* 22.

24. *Boston Town Records, 1660–1701,* 8–9; *New Haven Town Records,* 1:35; Thompson, *Sex in Middlesex,* 104.

25. *Rhode Island Records,* 1:53; Nathaniel Ward to John Winthrop Jr., 24 December 1635, *Winthrop Papers,* 3:216.

26. Lechford, *Plain Dealing,* 69; also see William Hammond to Sir Simonds D'Ewes, 26 September 1633, in Emerson, *Letters from New England,* 111.

27. Flaherty, *Privacy in Colonial New England,* 177.

28. Archer, "New England Mosaic," table I, 479, 480, 481, 492, 497; Foster, *Long Argument,* 182.

29. Foster, *Long Argument,* 109, 114. See John Winthrop's "A Modell of Christian Charity," *Winthrop Papers,* 2:282–295, for an example of the Puritan leadership's commitment to a national covenant. In the famous "Citty upon a Hill" passage was Winthrop's warning of what would happen should they violate the covenant: "if wee shall deale falsely with our god in this worke wee have undertaken and soe cause him to withdrawe his present help from us."

30. Men too were accused of witchcraft, but in general witchcraft was a female crime. For analyses of the characteristics of those charged, tried, and convicted of being witches, see John Putnam Demos, *Entertaining Satan: Witchcraft and the Culture of Early New England* (New York, 1982), particularly 57–94, and Karlsen, *Devil in the Shape of a Woman.* Also useful are: Paul Boyer and Stephen Nissenbaum, *Salem Possessed: The Social Origins of Witchcraft* (Cambridge, Mass., 1974); George Lincoln Burr, ed., *Narratives of the Witchcraft Cases, 1648–1706* (New York, 1914); Richard Godbeer, *The Devil's Dominion: Magic and Religion in Early New England* (New York, 1992); David D. Hall, "Witchcraft and the Limits of Interpretation," *New England Quarterly* 58 (1985): 253–281; Chadwick Hansen, *Witchcraft at Salem* (New York, 1969); Peter Charles Hoffer, *The Devil's Disciples: Makers of the Salem Witchcraft Trials* (Baltimore, Md., 1996); Alan Macfarlane, *Witchcraft in Tudor and Stuart England* (London, 1970); Bernard Rosenthal, *Salem Story: Reading the Witch Trials of 1692* (New York, 1993); and Richard Weisman, *Witchcraft, Magic, and Religion in 17th Century Massachusetts* (Amherst, Mass., 1984).

31. See Hull, *Female Felons,* 141. Cornelia Hughes Dayton's comparison of the legal treatment of Connecticut women in the seventeenth century with later in the eighteenth century also is helpful: *Women before the Bar: Gender, Law, & Society in Connecticut, 1639–1789* (Chapel Hill, N.C., 1995).

7. Economic Behavior and Beliefs (pp. 111–133)

1. Two works by Bernard Bailyn particularly informed this chapter's biographical treatment of Robert Keayne: "The *Apologia* of Robert Keayne," *William and Mary Quarterly,* 3d ser., 7 (October 1950): 568–587, and his introduction to Robert Keayne, *The Apologia of Robert Keayne: The Self-Portrait of a Puritan Merchant,* ed. and intro. Bernard Bailyn (reprint, Gloucester, Mass., 1970), vii–xii.

2. Bailyn, "The *Apologia* of Robert Keayne," 570–571, 581–582; Keayne, *Apologia*, 1–2.

3. Bernard Bailyn, *The New England Merchants in the Seventeenth Century* (Cambridge, Mass., 1955), 26–41; Darrett B. Rutman, *Winthrop's Boston: A Portrait of a Puritan Town, 1630–1649* (Chapel Hill, N.C., 1965), 178–183.

4. Bailyn, "The *Apologia* of Robert Keayne," 569, 572, 576; *Records of the Governor and Company*, 1:211. Among his wishes was to be buried "as a soldier in a military way": Keayne, *Apologia*, 3. For comments on the social and economic benefits of the Artillery Company, particularly for merchants, see Louise A. Breen, "Religious Radicalism in the Puritan Officer Corps: Heterodoxy, the Artillery Company, and Cultural Integration in Seventeenth-Century Boston," *New England Quarterly* 68 (March 1995): 7–8.

5. Keayne, *Apologia*, 20, 75, 82.

6. Ibid., 17–18, 46, 48.

7. Battis, *Saints and Sectaries*, 103, 264; Bailyn, *New England Merchants*, 40–41; *Records of the Governor and Company*, 1:281; Winthrop, *Journal*, 1:315–318.

8. Bailyn, "*Apologia* of Robert Keayne," 568, 572–577.

9. Bailyn, introduction to Keayne, *Apologia*, ix.

10. Keayne, *Apologia*, 5, 9, 29, 30, 78–79.

11. Ibid., 5, 9, 28–29, 32.

12. Ibid., 5, 6–14, 18, 22–24, 25–26, 32, 38–43, 87–88, 91, 92.

13. Ibid., 24–25.

14. Ibid., 43–45.

15. Ibid., 65–67.

16. Ibid., 13–14.

17. Ibid., 38–41, 88.

18. Ibid., 67, 86.

19. Ibid., 78.

20. For examples of his beleaguered attitude, see ibid., 5, 17, 18, 42, 46, 48, 62, 63, 64, 74, 83, 85. For his defense of town gifts, delay of giving them, his substantial estate, his attempts to reduce taxes, and his choice of executor, see ibid., 15–17; 26–28; 81–83; 83–85; 92. As it later was inventoried, his estate was £2,569, substantially lower than the £4,000 he projected: ibid., 78 n., and *Suffolk County Wills*, 75.

21. Winthrop, *Journal*, 1:315–316; Keayne, *Apologia*, 52–53.

22. Keayne, *Apologia*, 52–54. Bernard Bailyn speculates that Keayne's antagonist was Richard Bellingham, which seems unlikely considering Keayne left a bequest of forty shillings for Bellingham: Bailyn, "*Apologia* of Robert Keayne," 574 n.; Keayne, *Apologia*, 87.

23. Winthrop, *Journal*, 1:315; Keayne, *Apologia*, 58, 62.

24. Winthrop, *Journal*, 1:112, 152, 316; 2:24; *Records of the Court of Assistants, Massachusetts Bay*, 2:31, 39; Bailyn, *New England Merchants*, 32–33; Daniel Vickers, *Farmers & Fishermen: Two Centuries of Work in Essex County, Massachusetts, 1630–1850* (Chapel Hill, N.C., 1994), 26–27.

25. Winthrop, *Journal*, 1:316–317.

26. Ibid., 317–318. For a discussion of just price, see Stephen Innes, *Creating the Commonwealth: The Economic Culture of Puritan New England* (New York, 1995), 162–171.

27. Ibid., 318; Bailyn, "*Apologia* of Robert Keayne," 573; *Records of the Governor and Company,* 1: 290.

28. Keayne, *Apologia,* 55–57.

29. Ibid., 46, 48, 52.

30. Bailyn, "*Apologia* of Robert Keayne," 577–579; Keayne, *Apologia,* 5, 6, 9, 12, 14, 16, 18, 19, 21, 24, 25, 29, 30, 33, 34, 35, 38, 43, 45, 62, 73, 78, 80, 84.

31. Bailyn, *New England Merchants,* passim; Winthrop, *Journal,* 2:227.

32. Bailyn, *New England Merchants,* passim.

33. Letters from John Winter to Robert Trelawny, in *The Trelawny Papers* ed. James Phinney Baxter (Portland, Maine, 1884): 7 July 1634, 44; 15 August 1636, 92–94; 8 July 1637, 108–109; 30 July 1638, 136–137; 29 July 1641, 282, 285.

34. John Winter to Robert Trelawny, 15 August 1636, in ibid., 92–93; Narias Hawkins to Robert Trelawny, 29 June 1636, in ibid., 97; Richard Gibson to Robert Trelawny, July 1639, in ibid., 160; John Winter to Robert Trelawny, 10 July 1639, in ibid., 170.

35. Letters from John Winter to Robert Trelawny, in ibid.: 18 June 1634, 28; 7 July 1634, 46; 10 August 1634, 47; 8 July 1637, 110; 10 July 1637, 114; 29 July 1637, 118; 30 July 1638, 141; 12 December 1639, 202–203. Narias Hawkins to Robert Trelawny, 28 June 1636, in ibid., 96.

36. Keayne, *Apologia,* 80; Martin, *Profits in the Wilderness,* 9–216.

37. Keayne, *Apologia,* 48; *Records of the Court of Assistants, Massachusetts Bay,* 2:31, 39; Winthrop, *Journal,* 1:112, 152; 2:24; *Plymouth Colony Records,* 1:36; *Records of Governor and Company,* 1:223; Wood, *New England's Prospect,* 67–68.

38. Bailyn, *New England Merchants,* 46–47; Winthrop, *Journal,* 2:31.

39. Archer, "New England Mosaic," 486–487; Cressy, *Coming Over,* 52–63. For examples of gifts and a business partnership, see Keayne, *Apologia,* 42–43, 91. For servant abuse in the brief span of 1655 to 1658 in one small colony, see *Plymouth Colony Records,* 3:71–73, 82, 83, 88, 119, 132, 134. For restrictions on servant behavior, see George Cese's indenture in *Warwick Town Records,* 289–290.

40. Vickers, *Farmers & Fishermen,* 32, 60.

41. Ibid., 64, 77; Stephen Innes, *Labor in a New Land: Economy and Society in Seventeenth-Century Springfield* (Princeton, N.J., 1983), 72–82, 106–117; Ann Kussmaul, *Servants in husbandry in early modern England* (Cambridge, 1981), 80.

42. John Winthrop to William Bradford, 28 July 1637, *Winthrop Papers,* 3:457; Israel Stoughton to John Winthrop, 28 June 1637, ibid., 3:435; Hugh Peter to John Winthrop, 15 July 1637, ibid., 2:450; Roger Williams to John Winthrop, 10 November 1637, ibid., 3:509.

43. John Josselyn, *An Account of Two Voyages to New-England,* ed. Paul J. Lindholdt (London, 1674; reprint, Hanover, N.H., 1988), 24; Emmanuel Downing to John Winthrop, c. August 1645, *Winthrop Papers,* 5:39–40.

44. *Rhode Island Records,* 1:243; *Boston Town Records, 1660–1701,* 5.

45. Vickers, *Farmers & Fishermen,* 59, 230. The two major works that discuss slavery in seventeenth-century New England—Lorenzo J. Greene, *The Negro in Colonial New England, 1620–1776* (New York, 1942); William D. Piersen, *Black Yankees: The Development of an Afro-American Subculture in Eighteenth-Century New England* (Amherst, Mass., 1988)—focus almost entirely on the eighteenth century. The study of slavery, both Indian and African, in seventeenth-century New England deserves a full-length treatment.

46. Vickers, *Farmers & Fishermen,* 100-167.

47. Ibid., 77-82; Innes, *Labor in a New Land,* 44-71.

48. Darrett B. Rutman, *Husbandmen of Plymouth: Farms and Villages in the Old Colony, 1620-1692* (Boston, 1967), 24-25; Innes, *Labor in a New Land,* 48, 82-106.

49. Vickers, *Farmers & Fishermen,* 15; John J. McCusker, and Russell R. Menard, *The Economy of British America, 1607-1789* (Chapel Hill, N.C., 1985), 10; James A. Henretta, "Families and Farms: *Mentalité* in Pre-Industrial America," *William and Mary Quarterly,* 3d ser., 35 (January 1978): 3-32. There has been a spirited debate among historians during the last twenty years over the advent of capitalism in rural America. Although the focus of most of the studies is on the period from 1750 to 1860, there are implicit if not explicit comments on the nature of the seventeenth-century economy. In addition to Vickers, Allan Kulikoff offers alternatives between the "social historians" and the "market historians" (Kulikoff's terms), "The Transition to Capitalism in Rural America," *William and Mary Quarterly,* 3d ser., 46 (January 1989): 120-144, and *The Agrarian Origins of American Capitalism* (Charlottesville, Va., 1992). See also James A. Henretta, *The Origins of American Capitalism: Collected Essays* (Boston, 1992); Christopher Clark, *The Roots of Rural Capitalism: Western Massachusetts, 1780-1860* (Ithaca, N.Y., 1990); Michael Merrill, "Cash Is Good to Eat: Self-Sufficiency and Exchange in the Rural Economy of the United States," *Radical History Review,* no. 3 (1977): 42-71, and "Putting 'Capitalism' in Its Place: A Review of Recent Literature," *William and Mary Quarterly,* 3d ser., 52 (April 1995): 315-326; James T. Lemon, "Early Americans and Their Social Environment," *Journal of Historical Geography* 6 (1980): 115-131; and Winifred Barr Rothenberg, *From Market-Places to a Market Economy: The Transformation of Rural Massachusetts, 1750-1850* (Chicago, 1992). For a valuable analysis of seventeenth-century New England economic values and practices, see Innes, *Creating the Commonwealth,* passim.

50. The discussion of competence in this and following paragraphs, though not in full agreement, is informed by the work of Daniel Vickers: *Farmers & Fishermen,* 13-39; "Competency and Competition: Economic Culture in Early America," *William and Mary Quarterly,* 3d ser., 47 (January 1990): 3-29. For Keayne's use of "comfort," see his *Apologia,* 5, 8, 14, 20, 23, 25, 26, 27, 28, 30, 32, 33, 37, 40, 41, 45, 46, 50, 62, 64, 68, 75, 76, 77, 78, 80.

51. *Records of the Governor and Company,* 1:112, 241; *Watertown Records,* 5; *Plymouth Colony Records,* 1:32; *Connecticut Records,* 1:91, 125; Josselyn, *Two Voyages to New-England,* 114; David Grayson Allen, "'Both Englands,'" in David D. Hall and David Grayson Allen, eds., *Seventeenth-Century New England* (Boston, 1984), 75.

52. Johnson, *Wonder-Working Providence,* passim.

53. Innes, *Labor in a New Land,* 44-71; John Fessenden Confession in *Shepard's Confessions,* 176; Martin, *Profits in the Wilderness,* 127-128; Henretta, "Families and Farms," 3-32; Vickers, *Farmers & Fishermen,* 13-29, 64-77.

54. Vickers, *Farmers & Fishermen,* 15-19.

55. Ulrich, *Good Wives,* 35-50 (the quotation is 37-38); Daniel Vickers, "Working the Fields in a Developing Economy: Essex County, Massachusetts, 1630-1675," in Stephen Innes, ed., *Work and Labor in Early America* (Chapel Hill, N.C., 1988), 50; Innes, *Labor in a New Land,* 117-121; *Plymouth Colony Records,* 4:54; *Boston Town Records, 1660-1701,* 60.

56. Ulrich, *Good Wives*, 51–67; *Plymouth Colony Records*, 2:132.

57. Vickers, *Farmers & Fishermen*, 14; *Boston Town Records, 1660–1701*, 87.

58. Alan Macfarlane, *The Origins of English Individualism: The Family, Property and Social Transition* (London, 1978), 163, 195–196; Wrightson, *English Society*, 223; and Innes, *Creating the Commonwealth*, passim.

8. Scattered Like Swedes: New England Towns (pp. 134–151)

1. *Rhode Island Records*, 2:250–251; John Mason to John Allyn and others, 3 August 1670, in ibid., 349.

2. For a clear presentation of these complex events and their subsequent repercussions, see Sydney V. James, *Colonial Rhode Island: A History* (New York, 1975), 81–113; also see Richard S. Dunn, *Puritans and Yankees: The Winthrop Dynasty of New England, 1630–1717* (Princeton, N.J., 1962) and Robert C. Black III, *The Younger John Winthrop* (New York, 1966).

3. *Rhode Island Records*, 1:455–456; James, *Colonial Rhode Island*, 85.

4. *Rhode Island Records*, 457; Extract of letter from Roger Williams to John Mason, in ibid., 459.

5. Dunn, *Puritans and Yankees*, 117–142; Black, *Younger John Winthrop*, 206–243; "Agreement between the agents of Connecticut and Rhode Island, about the limitts of the two collonies," 7 April 1663, in *Rhode Island Records*, 1:518.

6. Dunn, *Puritans and Yankees*, 142; *Rhode Island Records*, 2:32–33, 51; Benedict Arnold and William Brenton to John Winthrop Jr., 10 March 1664, in *Rhode Island Records*, 2:34–36; Richard Smith to Edward Hutchinson, May 14, 1664, in *Rhode Island Records*, 2:47–48.

7. Dunn, *Puritans and Yankees*, 158–160; Black, *Younger John Winthrop*, 285–287; *Rhode Island Records*, 2:59–60, 93–95.

8. *Rhode Island Records*, 2:140, 227–231; John Allyn to William Brenton and others, 17 October 1667, in ibid., 2:226.

9. Ibid., 2:250–251; General Assembly of Rhode Island to General Assembly of Connecticut, 14 May 1669, in ibid., 2:247–249.

10. Ibid., 2:312–318.

11. Ibid., 2:318–320, 325–326.

12. Ibid., 2:332–335, 367–370, 375, 387–390; General Assembly of Rhode Island to General Assembly of Connecticut, 6 May 1671, in ibid., 2:376–378; John Allyn to Benedict Arnold and others, 11 May 1671, in ibid., 2:378–380.

13. Bruce C. Daniels, *The Connecticut Town: Growth and Development, 1635–1790* (Middletown, Conn., 1979), 14, 181–182, and *Dissent and Conformity on Narragansett Bay: The Colonial Rhode Island Town* (Middletown, Conn., 1983), 16; Nathaniel Ward to John Winthrop, April 1640, in *Winthrop Papers*, 4:222.

14. Examples of all the reasons for imprecise boundaries abound in colonial records, and all can be seen in the Westerly episode. A good example of the confusion that could arise when English and Indian concepts of land were combined so as to determine boundaries can be seen in *Plymouth Colony Records*, 4:93: "Awanno the Indian and Awampocke theire land is bounded on the easterly corner with a Rid oake tree and soe Runing Southerly one hundred Rod to a great

pond; and from thence westerly to a little pond which is fifty rod distance and soe bounded on the north corner with a bush."

15. Ezekiel Rogers to John Winthrop, 31 August 1640, in *Winthrop Papers*, 4:282.

16. James A. Henretta, "The Morphology of New England Society in the Colonial Period, *Journal of Interdisciplinary History* 2 (fall 1971): 381; Rutman, *Winthrop's Boston*, 25–29; Thomas Dudley to the Countess of Lincoln, 12–28 March 1631, in Young, ed., *Chronicles of the First Planters of the Colony of Massachusetts Bay*, 314; Martin, *Profits in the Wilderness*, 28; David Grayson Allen, "'Both Englands,'" in Hall and Allen, eds., *Seventeenth-Century New England*, 73–74; Daniels, *Connecticut Town*, 9–10; John Winthrop to Sir Simonds D'Ewes, 20 July 1635, in Emerson, *Letters from New England*, 154.

17. David Grayson Allen, *In English Ways: The Movement of Societies and the Transferal of English Local Law and Custom to Massachusetts Bay in the Seventeenth Century* (Chapel Hill, N.C., 1981), 19–54 and passim; Greven, *Four Generations*, 42–43; Lockridge, *A New England Town*, 12–13.

18. Allen, *In English Ways*, 117–160; Joseph S. Wood, "Village and Community in Early Colonial New England," in Robert Blair St. George, ed., *Material Life in America, 1600–1860* (Boston, 1988), 165; David Thomas Konig, *Law and Society in Puritan Massachusetts: Essex County, 1629–1692* (Chapel Hill, N.C., 1979), 30.

19. Rutman, *Husbandmen of Plymouth*, 23; Charles E. Clark, *The Eastern Frontier: The Settlement of Northern New England, 1610–1763* (New York, 1970), 198.

20. Henretta, "Morphology of New England Society," 381; Greven, *Four Generations*, 52, 56–57; Lockridge, *A New England Town*, 12–13, 82; Konig, *Law and Society*, 117.

21. Bushman, *From Puritan to Yankee*, 60; Anne Bush Maclear, *Early New England Towns: A Comparative Study of Their Development* (New York, 1908), 31; Richard P. Gildrie, *Salem, Massachusetts, 1626–1683: A Covenant Community* (Charlottesville, Va., 1975), 69; Lockridge, *A New England Town*, 14, 59.

22. Martin, *Profits in the Wilderness*, 5, 138, 248–249, passim; Rutman, *Winthrop's Boston*, 58, 249; Daniels, *Connecticut Town*, passim, and *Dissent and Conformity on Narragansett Bay*, passim.

23. Main, "The Distribution of Property in Colonial Connecticut," in James Kirby Martin, ed., *The Human Dimensions of Nation Making: Essays on Colonial and Revolutionary America* (Madison, Wis., 1976), 75, 77; Innes, *Labor in a New Land*, xvi; Cook, *The Fathers of the Towns: Leadership and Community Structure in Eighteenth-Century New England* (Baltimore, Md., 1976), 172–181.

24. Rutman, *Winthrop's Boston*, vii, 152, 158, 200, passim. This book was nearly drowned in the marvelous tidal wave of town studies in 1970, and it continues too often to be overlooked. It is essential for understanding New England towns.

25. Gildrie, *Salem*, 105, 122, 169, passim; Boyer and Nissenbaum, *Salem Possessed*, passim.

26. *Watertown Records*, 113; *New Haven Town Records*, 1:266, 380; 2:308; *Boston Town Records 1660–1701*, 106, 114–115, 147, 151; 7:18, 40, 56, 58, 62, 105–106, 125, 132, 216; *Salem Town Records*, 1:127; 2:32, 243, 303–305; *Diary of Samuel Sewall*, 1:28; *Diaries of John Hull*, 242–243.

27. Absolute equality in the distribution of wealth is all but impossible in societies with individual possessions. There is a life cycle of wealth. During the

seventeenth century, a person was most poor (or least affluent) in early adulthood, most prosperous during late middle age, and in a declining economic state (typically because of gifts to adult sons and daughters) during old age. See Henretta, "Families and Farms," 7; Alice Hanson Jones, "Wealth Estimates for the New England Colonies about 1770," *Journal of Economic History* 32 (March 1972): 120; Gloria L. Main, "Inequality in Early America: The Evidence from Probate Records of Massachusetts and Maryland," *Journal of Interdisciplinary History* 7 (spring 1977): 580; and Jackson Turner Main, "Distribution of Property in Connecticut," 61, 63. For comparisons of distribution of wealth with other American regions and other times, see G. L. Main, "Inequality in Early America," 560–561; J. T. Main, "Distribution of Property in Connecticut," 60; and G. B. Warden, "Inequality and Instability in Eighteenth-Century Boston: A Reappraisal," *Journal of Interdisciplinary History* 6 (spring 1976): 602. For an analysis of the increasing economic polarization of Salem during this period, see Donald Warner Koch, "Income Distribution and Political Structure in Seventeenth-Century Salem, Massachusetts," *Essex Institute Historical Collections* 105 (1969): 56–58, 61.

28. Innes, *Labor in a New Land*, xvi–xxi, passim (like Rutman's *Winthrop's Boston*, Innes's book is an important antidote to any sweeping characterization of the New England town); Bailyn, *New England Merchants*, 55, 96; Allen, *In English Ways*, 82–116, 180–184; Johnson, *Wonder-Working Providence*, 68–69, 96, 73, 99.

29. In addition to appendix F, see Innes, *Labor in a New Land*, 45–47.

30. Ibid., xvi; Johnson, *Wonder-Working Providence*, 69–70, 71–72, 90.

31. Christine Leigh Heyrman, *Commerce and Culture: The Maritime Communities of Colonial Massachusetts, 1690–1750* (New York, 1984); and Daniel Vickers, "Work and Life on the Fishing Periphery of Essex County, 1630–1675," in Hall and Allen, *Seventeenth-Century New England*, 83–117, and *Farmers & Fishermen*.

32. Allen, *In English Ways*, 19–81, 165–180; Greven, *Four Generations*; Lockridge, *A New England Town*; Lucas, *Valley of Discord*; Sumner Chilton Powell, *Puritan Village: The Formation of a New England Town* (New York, 1965); John J. Waters, "Hingham, Massachusetts, 1631–1661: An East Anglian Oligarchy in the New World," *Journal of Social History* 1 (summer 1968): 351–370, and "The Traditional World of the New England Peasants: A View from Seventeenth-Century Barnstable," *New England Historical and Genealogical Register* 130 (January 1976): 3–21; and Johnson, *Wonder-Working Providence*, 116, 183.

33. Lockridge, *A New England Town*, 16. Although I am skeptical about Lockridge's characterization of Dedham, I continue to have the highest regard for his pathbreaking study.

34. Martin, *Profits in the Wilderness*, 205, 239–240, 301–302; Melvoin, *New England Outpost*.

35. Martin, *Profits in the Wilderness*; Allen, *In English Ways*, 216; *Watertown Records*, 2; *Dorchester Town Records*, 14.

36. Martin, *Profits in the Wilderness*, 171, 196, 222, 279, passim; Josiah Henry Benton, *Warning Out in New England, 1656–1817* (1911; reprint, Freeport, N.Y., 1970), 8–9, 11, 18–19; *Plymouth Colony Records*, 1:82; *Boston Town Records 1660–1701*, 103, 107, 119, 135, 152–153; 7:97; *Dorchester Town Records*, 130, 224, 227; *Salem Town Records*, 2:205.

37. Martin, *Profits in the Wilderness*, 229, 231, 233; The Governor and Assistants of Plymouth to the Governor and Assistants of Massachusetts, 6 February 1632, *Winthrop Papers*, 3:64–65; *Boston Town Records 1660–1701*, 90; *Dorchester Town Records*, 95; *Records of the Town of Plymouth, 1635 to 1705* (Plymouth, Mass., 1889), 169; *Braintree Town Records*, 5–6; *New Haven Town Records*, 1:20–22.

38. Martin, *Profits in the Wilderness*, 235; Rutman, *Winthrop's Boston*, 163; Allen, *In English Ways*, 216; Bushman, *From Puritan to Yankee*, 53; Daniels, *Connecticut Town*, 121; *Dorchester Town Records*, 99.

9. New England in the Seventeenth Century (pp. 152–157)

1. Alfred W. Crosby, *Ecological Imperialism: The Biological Expansion of Europe, 900–1900* (Cambridge, 1986), 6–7 and passim.

2. For a comparison of the economies of England, New England, and the Chesapeake, see Innes, *Creating the Commonwealth*, 278.

3. See Edmund S. Morgan, *American Slavery, American Freedom: The Ordeal of Colonial Virginia* (New York, 1975); and Kathleen M. Brown, *Good Wives, Nasty Wenches, and Anxious Patriarchs: Gender, Race, and Power in Colonial Virginia* (Chapel Hill, N.C., 1996).

4. Edgar J. McManus, *Law and Liberty in Early New England: Criminal Justice and Due Process, 1620–1692* (Amherst, Mass., 1993), 10 and passim; Dayton, *Women before the Bar*, 65 and passim.

BIBLIOGRAPHY

Primary Sources

"Abstracts of the Early Probate Records of New Haven, Book I, Part I, 1647–1687." *New England Historical and Genealogical Register* 81 (April 1927): 121–135.

Barnes, Thomas G., ed. *The Book of the General Lawes and Libertyes Concerning the Inhabitants of the Massachusets.* San Marino, Calif., 1975. (Originally published Cambridge, 1648.)

Bartlett, John Russell, ed. *Records of the Colony of Rhode Island, and Providence Plantations in New England.* Vol. 1, *1636–1663.* Vol. 2, *1664–1667.* Vol. 3, *1678–1706.* Providence, R.I., 1856–1858.

Batchellor, Albert Stillman, ed. *Probate Records of the Province of New Hampshire, 1635–1717.* Concord, N.H., 1907.

Bates, Samuel, ed. *Records of the Town of Braintree, 1640 to 1793.* Randolph, Mass., 1886.

Baxter, James Phinney, ed. *The Trelawny Papers.* Portland, Maine, 1884.

Bouton, Nathaniel, ed. *Documents and Records Relating to the Province of New-Hampshire, From the Earliest Period of its Settlement: 1623–1686.* Concord, N.H., 1867.

Bradford, William. *Of Plymouth Plantation, 1620–1647.* Edited by Samuel Eliot Morison. New York, 1952.

"Bradstreet's [Simon] Journal, 1664–1683." *New England Historical and Genealogical Register,* 9 (January 1855): 43–51.

Buddington, William I. "Catalog of Admissions to Full Communion." In *The History of the First Church, Charlestown.* Boston, 1845.

Burr, George Lincoln, ed. *Naratives of the Witchcraft Cases, 1648–1706.* New York, 1914.

Chamberlain, Richard. "Lithobolia, or the Stone-Throwing Devil" [1698]. In *Narratives of the Witchcraft Cases, 1648–1706,* edited by George Lincoln Burr, 58–77. New York, 1914.

Church, Benjamin. *Diary of King Philip's War, 1675–76.* Boston, 1716. Reprint, Chester, Conn., 1975.

Dane, John. "A Declaration of Remarkabell Prouedenses in the Corse of My Life." *New England Historical and Genealogical Register* 8 (April 1854): 149–156.

Danforth, Samuel, "Rev. Samuel Danforth's Records of the First Church in Roxbury, Mass." *New England Historical and Genealogical Register* 34 (April–October 1880): 84–89, 162–166, 297–301, 359–363.

"Danvers [Mass.] Church Records." *New England Historical and Genealogical Register* 11 (April–October 1857): 131–135 and 316–321.

Davenport, John. *Letters of John Davenport, Puritan Divine.* Edited by Isabel Macbeath Calder. New Haven, 1937.

Dexter, Franklin Bowditch. *Historical Catalogue of the Members of the First Church of Christ in New Haven, Connecticut, A.D. 1639–1914.* New Haven, Conn., 1914.

Dexter, Franklin Bowditch, and Zara Jones Powers, eds. *New Haven Town Records, 1649–1662, 1662–1684, and 1684–1769.* New Haven, Conn., 1917, 1919, & 1962.

Dow, George F., ed. *Probate Records of Essex County, Massachusetts, 1635–1681.* 3 vols. Salem, Mass., 1916–1920.

Dunnel, H. G., ed. "List of Members of the Old Church, Topsfield." *New England Historical and Genealogical Register* 16 (July 1862): 212–215.

Early Records of the Town of Warwick. Providence, R.I., 1926.

Easton, John. "A Relacion of the Indyan Warre" [5 February 1676]. In *Narratives of the Indian Wars, 1675–1699,* edited by Charles H. Lincoln. New York, 1913. Reprint, 1952.

Eliot, John. "The Rev. John Eliot's Record of Church Members, Roxbury, Mass." In *City of Boston Report of the Record Commissioners,* 6:73–103. Boston, 1884.

Emerson, Everett, ed. *Letters from New England: The Massachusetts Bay Colony, 1629–1638.* Amherst, Mass., 1976.

Farmington (Conn.) Church Records. Connecticut State Library. Microfilm.

"The First Record-Book of the First Church in Charlestown, Massachusetts." *New England Historical and Genealogical Register* 23 (April, July, and October 1869): 190–191, 279–284, 435–442.

Fiske, John. *The Notebook of The Reverend John Fiske, 1644–1675.* Edited and with an introduction by Robert G. Pope. Salem, Mass., 1974.

Fourth Report of the Record Commisioners of the City of Boston, Dorchester Town Records. 2d ed. Boston, 1883.

Gould, John H., ed. "Early Records of the Church in Topsfield." *Essex Institute Historical Collections* 24 (1887): 181–205.

Hall, David D., ed. *The Antinomian Controversy, 1636–1638: A Documentary History.* 2d ed. Durham, N.C., 1990.

Hammond, Otis G., ed. *New Hampshire Court Records, 1640–1692.* New Hampshire, 1943.

Harvard College Records, 1636–1750. In *Publications of the Colonial Society of Massachusetts* vol. 15. Boston, 1915.

Hoadley, Charles J., ed. *Records of the Colony and Plantation of New Haven, from 1638 to 1649.* Hartford, Conn., 1857.

———, ed. *Records of the Colony or Jurisdiction of New Haven, from May, 1653, to the Union.* Hartford, Conn., 1858.

Hotten, John Camden, ed. *The Original Lists of Persons of Quality, Emigrants, ... and Others Who Went from Great Britain to the American Plantations, 1600–1700.* London, 1874.

Hubbard, William. *The History of the Indian Wars in New England* [1677]. Edited by Samuel G. Drake. Roxbury, Mass., 1865. Reprint, New York, 1969.

Hull, John. *Diaries of John Hull, Mint-master and Treasurer of the Colony of Massachusetts Bay.* Boston, 1857. Reprinted in *A Library of American Puritan Writings, The Seventeenth Century.* Vol. 7, *Puritan Personal Writings: Diaries*, edited by Sacvan Bercovitch. New York, 1982.

James, Sydney V., ed. *Three Visitors to Early Plymouth: Letters about the Pilgrim Settlement in New England during Its First Seven Years.* Plymouth, Mass., 1963.

Johnson, Edward. *Wonder-Working Providence of Sions Saviour in New England* [London, 1653]. Edited by J. Franklin Jameson. New York, 1910.

Josselyn, John. *An Account of Two Voyages to New-England.* Edited by Paul J. Lindholdt. London, 1674. Reprint, Hanover, N.H., 1988.

Keayne, Robert. *The Apologia of Robert Keayne: The Self-Portrait of a Puritan Merchant.* Edited and with an introduction by Bernard Bailyn. Reprint, Gloucester, Mass., 1970.

Lechford, Thomas. *Plain Dealing: or, Newes from New-England.* London, 1642. Reprint, New York, 1969.

Lincoln, Charles H., ed. *Narratives of the Indian Wars, 1675–1699.* New York, 1913. Reprint, 1952.

"List of Baptisms from the Records of the Church of Christ at Bristol, R.I. (formerly Bristol, Mass.)." *New England Historical and Genealogical Register* 34 (April 1880): 132–135.

Manwaring, Charles William, comp. *A Digest of the Early Connecticut Probate Records.* Vol. 1. Hartford, Conn., 1902.

Mather, Cotton. *Diary of Cotton Mather, 1681–1709.* Edited by Worthington Chauncey Ford. 2 vols. New York, 1911.

———. *Magnalia Christi Americana; Or, The Ecclesiastical History of New England, From Its First Planting, in the Year 1620, Unto the Year of Our Lord 1698.* 2 vols. Hartford, Conn., 1853.

Middletown (Conn.) Church Records. Connecticut State Library. Microfilm.

Milford (Conn.) Church Records. Connecticut State Library. Microfilm.

Miller, Perry, and Thomas H. Johnson, eds. *The Puritans.* 2 vols. Revised ed. New York, 1963.

"Milton (Mass.) Church Records." *New England Historical and Genealogical Register* 22 (July 1868): 259–263.

Morton, Thomas. *New English Canaan or New Canaan* [Amsterdam, 1637]. With introductory matter and notes by Charles Francis Adams Jr. Boston, 1883. Reprint, New York, 1967.

New Haven (Conn.) Probate Record. Connecticut State Library, State Archives. Microfilm, reel 1.

New London (Conn.) Church Records. Connecticut State Library. Microfilm.

N.S. [possibly Nathaniel Saltonstall]. "The Present State of New-England with Respect to the Indian War" [1675]. In *Narratives of the Indian Wars, 1675–1699*, edited by Charles H. Lincoln, 24–50. New York, 1913. Reprint, 1952.

Paige, Lucius R., comp. *List of Freemen of Massachusetts, 1630–1691*. Boston, 1849. Reprint, Baltimore, Md., 1978.

Pierce, Richard D., ed. *The Records of the First Church in Salem Massachusetts 1629–1736*. Salem, Mass., 1974.

Pratt, Phineas. "A Decliration of the Afaires of the Einglish People [That First] Inhabited New England" [1662]. *Collections*, Massachusetts Historical Society, 4th ser., 4 (1858): 476–487.

Pulsifer, David, ed. *Records of the Colony of New Plymouth in New England, Laws, 1623–1682*. Boston, 1861.

Pynchon, John. *The Pynchon Papers, Letters of John Pynchon, 1654–1700*. Vol. 1. Edited by Carl Bridenbaugh. Boston, 1982.

Reading (Mass.) Church Records. Reading Public Library. Transcript.

Records of the Court of Assistants of the Colony of the Massachusetts Bay, 1630–1692. 3 vols. Boston, 1901–1928.

"Records of the First Church at Braintree, Mass." *New England Historical and Genealogical Register* 59 (January 1905): 87–91.

Records of the First Church at Dorchester in New England, 1636–1734. Boston, 1891.

Records of the Town of Plymouth, 1635 to 1705. Plymouth, Mass., 1889.

Report of the Record Commissioners of the City of Boston, Containing the Boston Records from 1660 to 1701. Boston, 1881.

Rowlandson, Mary. "Narrative of the Captivity of Mrs. Mary Rowlandson" [1682]. In *Narratives of the Indian Wars, 1675–1699*, ed. by Charles H. Lincoln, 112–167. New York, 1913. Reprint, 1952.

Sailors Narratives of Voyages along the New England Coast, 1524–1624. Boston, 1905. Reprint, New York, n.d.

"Scituate [Mass.] and Barnstable [Mass.] Church Records." *New England Historical and Genealogical Register* 9 (July 1855): 279–287 and 10 (January 1856): 40–43.

Second Report of the Record Commissioners of the City of Boston, Boston Town Records, 1634–1660. 3d ed. Boston, 1902.

Sewall, Samuel. *The Diary of Samuel Sewall, 1674–1729*. Edited by M. Halsey Thomas. 2 vols. New York, 1973.

Shepard, Thomas. *God's Plot: Being the Autobiography & Journal of Thomas Shepard*. Edited and with an introduction by Michael McGiffert. Amherst, Mass., 1972.

———. *Thomas Shepard's Confessions*. Edited and with an introduction by George Selement and Bruce C. Wooley. Boston, 1981.

Shurtleff, Nathaniel B., ed. *Records of the Colony of New Plymouth in New England*. 12 vols. Boston, 1855–1861.

———, ed. *Records of the Governor and Company of the Massachusetts In New England*. 5 vols. Boston, 1853–1854.

Smith, Joseph H., ed. *Colonial Justice in Western Massachusetts, 1639–1702: The Pynchon Court Record*. Cambridge, Mass., 1961.

Suffolk County Probate Records. 5. Microfilm.

Suffolk County Wills: Abstracts of the Earliest Wills Upon Record in the County of Suffolk, Massachusetts. Baltimore, Md., 1984.
Town Records of Salem, October 1, 1634 to November 7, 1659, 1659–1680, 1680–1691. 3 vols. Salem, Mass., 1868, 1913, and 1934.
Trumbull, J. Hammond, ed. *The Public Records of the Colony of Connecticut, Prior to the Union with New Haven Colony, May, 1665.* Hartford, Conn., 1850.
Watertown Records Comprising the First and Second Books of Town Proceedings, etc. Watertown, Mass., 1894.
Wigglesworth, Michael. *The Diary of Michael Wigglesworth, 1653–1657: The Conscience of a Puritan.* Edited and with an introduction by Edmund S. Morgan. Reprint, Gloucester, Mass., 1970.
Williams, Roger, *A Key into the Language of America* [London, 1643]. Edited by John J. Teunissen and Evelyn J. Hinz. Detroit, Mich., 1973.
Wills, Inventories, Etc., 1637 to 1685. County of Barnstable. Microfilm.
Windsor (Conn.) Church Records. Connecticut State Library. Microfilm.
Winthrop Papers. 5 vols. Boston, 1929–1947.
Winthrop, John. *Winthrop's Journal "History of New England," 1630–1649.* Edited by James Kendall Hosmer. 2 vols. New York, 1908.
Wood, William. *New England's Prospect* [1635]. Edited by Alden T. Vaughan. Amherst, Mass., 1977.
Young, Alexander, ed. *Chronicles of the First Planters of the Colony of Massachusetts Bay, From 1623 to 1636.* Boston, 1846. Reprint, Baltimore, Md., 1975.
Young, Alexander, ed. *Chronicles of the Pilgrim Fathers of the Colony of Plymouth, From 1602 to 1625.* Boston, 1844. Reprint, Baltimore, Md., 1974.

Secondary Sources

Adams, Charles Francis. *Three Episodes of Massachusetts History.* Boston, 1893.
Albro, John A. *The life of Thomas Shepard.* Boston, 1847.
Allen, David Grayson. "Both Englands." In *Seventeenth-Century New England,* edited by David D. Hall and David Grayson Allen, 55–82. Boston, 1984.
———. *In English Ways: The Movement of Societies and the Transferal of English Local Law and Custom to Massachusetts Bay in the Seventeenth Century.* Chapel Hill, N.C., 1981.
Anderson, Virginia DeJohn. "King Philip's Herds: Indians, Colonists, and the Problem of Livestock in Early New England." *William and Mary Quarterly,* 3d ser., 51 (October 1994): 601–624.
———. "Migrants and Motives: Religion and the Settlement of New England, 1630–1640." *New England Quarterly* 58 (September 1985): 339–383.
———. *New England's Generation: The Great Migration and the formation of society and culture in the seventeenth century.* New York, 1991.
Anderson, Virginia DeJohn, and David Grayson Allen. "Communications: On English Migration to Early New England." *New England Quarterly* 59 (September 1986): 408–424.

Archer, Richard. "New England Mosaic: A Demographic Analysis for the Seventeenth Century." *William and Mary Quarterly*, 3d ser., 47 (October 1990): 447–502.

Austin, John Osborne. *The Genealogical Dictionary of Rhode Island*. Albany, N.Y., 1887. Reprint, Baltimore, Md., 1982.

Axtell, James. *Beyond 1492: Encounters in Colonial North America*. New York, 1992.

———. *The Invasion Within: The Contest of Cultures in Colonial North America*. New York, 1985.

Bailyn, Bernard. "The *Apologia* of Robert Keayne." *William and Mary Quarterly*, 3d ser., 7 (October 1950): 568–587.

———. *Education in the Forming of American Society: Needs and Opportunities for Study*. Chapel Hill, N.C., 1960.

———. "New England and a Wider World: Notes on Some Central Themes of Modern Historiography." In *Seventeenth-Century New England*, edited by David D. Hall and David Grayson Allen, 323–328. Boston, 1984.

———. *The New England Merchants in the Seventeenth Century*. Cambridge, Mass., 1955.

———. *Voyagers to the West: A Passage in the Peopling of America on the Eve of the Revolution*. New York, 1986.

Banks, Charles Edward. *The Planters of the Commonwealth: A Study of the Emigrants and Emigration . . . 1620–1640*. Boston, 1930. Reprint, Baltimore, Md., 1979.

———. *Topographical Dictionary of 2885 English Emigrants to New England, 1620–1650*. Philadelphia, 1937. Reprint, Baltimore, Md., 1963.

Baritz, Loren. *City On A Hill: A History of Ideas and Myths in America*. New York, 1964.

Battis, Emery. *Saints and Sectaries: Anne Hutchinson and the Antinomian Controversy in the Massachusetts Bay Colony*. Chapel Hill, N.C., 1962.

Beales, Ross W., Jr. "In Search of the Historical Child: Miniature Adulthood and Youth in Colonial New England." *American Quarterly* 27 (1975): 379–398.

Benton, Josiah Henry. *Warning Out in New England, 1656–1817*. 1911. Reprint, Freeport, N.Y., 1970.

Bercovitch, Sacvan *The Puritan Origins of the American Self*. New Haven, Conn., 1975.

Bissell, Linda Auwers. "From One Generation to Another: Mobility in Seventeenth-Century Windsor, Connecticut." *William and Mary Quarterly*, 3d ser., 31 (January 1974): 79–110.

Black, Robert C., III. *The Younger John Winthrop*. New York, 1966.

Blake, John B. *Public Health in the Town of Boston, 1630–1822*. Cambridge, Mass., 1959.

Bolton, Charles Knowles. *The Real Founders of New England: Stories of Their Life Along the Coast, 1602–1628*. Boston, 1929. Reprint, Baltimore, Md., 1974.

Bonomi, Patricia U. *A Factious People: Politics and Society in Colonial New York*. New York, 1971.

Bourne, Russell. *The Red King's Rebellion: Racial Politics in New England, 1675–1678*. New York, 1990.

Boyer, Paul, and Stephen Nissenbaum. *Salem Possessed: The Social Origins of Witchcraft*. Cambridge, Mass., 1974.

Bozeman, Theodore Dwight. "The Puritans' 'Errand into the Wilderness' Reconsidered." *New England Quarterly* 59 (June 1986): 231–251.

———. *To Live Ancient Lives: The Primitivist Dimension in Puritanism*. Chapel Hill, N.C., 1988.

Breen, Louise A. "Religious Radicalism in the Puritan Officer Corps: Heterodoxy, the Artillery Company, and Cultural Integration in Seventeenth-Century Boston." *New England Quarterly* 68 (March 1995): 3–43.

Breen, T. H. "Creative Adaptations: Peoples and Cultures." In *Colonial British America: Essays in the New History of the Early Modern Era*, edited by Jack P. Greene and J. R. Pole, 195–232. Baltimore, Md., 1984.

———. "Persistent Localism: English Social Change and the Shaping of New England Institutions." *William and Mary Quarterly*, 3d ser., 32 (1975): 3–28.

———. *Puritans and Adventurers: Change and Persistence in Early America*. New York, 1980.

———. *The Character of the Good Ruler: Puritan Political Ideas in New England, 1630–1730*. New York, 1970.

———. "Who Governs: The Town Franchise in Seventeenth-Century Massachusetts." *William and Mary Quarterly*, 3d ser., 27 (July 1970): 460–474.

Breen, T. H., and Stephen Foster. "Moving to the New World: The Character of Early Massachusetts Immigration." *William and Mary Quarterly*, 3d ser., 30 (April 1973): 187–222.

———. "The Puritans' Greatest Achievement: A Study of Social Cohesion in Seventeenth-Century Massachusetts." *Journal of American History* 60 (June 1973): 5–22.

Bridenbaugh, Carl. *Cities in the Wilderness: The First Century of Urban Life in America, 1625–1742*. New York 1938.

———. *Fat Mutton and Liberty of Conscience: Society in Rhode Island, 1636–1690*. Providence, R.I., 1974.

———. *Vexed and Troubled Englishmen, 1590–1642*. New York, 1968.

Brown, B. Katherine. "Freemanship in Puritan Massachusetts." *American Historical Review* 59 (July 1954): 865–883.

———. "Puritan Democracy in Dedham, Massachusetts: Another Case Study." *William and Mary Quarterly*, 3d ser., 24 (July 1967): 378–396.

Brown, Kathleen M. *Good Wives, Nasty Wenches, and Anxious Patriarchs: Gender, Race, and Power in Colonial Virginia*. Chapel Hill, N.C. 1996.

Brown, Richard D. "The Emergence of Urban Society in Rural Massachusetts, 1760–1820." *Journal of American History* 61 (June 1974): 29–51.

Brunkow, Robert deV. "Officeholding in Providence, Rhode Island, 1646 to 1686: A Quantitative Analysis." *William and Mary Quarterly*, 3d ser., 37 (April 1980): 242–260.

Burke, Peter. *Popular Culture in Early Modern Europe*. New York, 1978.

———. "Popular Culture in Seventeenth-Century London." In *Popular Culture in Seventeenth-Century England,* edited by Barry Reay, 31–58. New York, 1985.

Bush, Sargent, Jr. "'Revising what we have done amisse': John Cotton and John Wheelwright, 1640." *William and Mary Quarterly,* 3d ser., 45 (October 1988): 733–750.

Bushman, Richard L. *From Puritan to Yankee: Character and the Social Order in Connecticut, 1690–1765.* New York, 1967.

Butler, Jon. *Awash in a Sea of Faith: Christianizing the American People.* Cambridge, Mass., 1990.

Calder, Isabel MacBeath. *The New Haven Colony.* New Haven, Conn., 1934.

Caldwell, Patricia. *The Puritan Conversion Narrative: The Beginnings of American Expression.* Cambridge, 1983.

Calvert, Karin. *Children in the House: The Material Culture of Early Childhood, 1600–1900.* Boston, 1992.

Campbell, Mildred. *The English Yeoman Under Elizabeth and the Early Stuarts.* New Haven, Conn., 1942.

Canup, John *Out of the Wilderness: The Emergence of an American Identity in Colonial New England.* Middletown, Conn., 1990.

Carr, Lois Green, and Russell Menard. "Immigration and Opportunity: The Freedman in Early Colonial Maryland." In *The Chesapeake in the Seventeenth Century: Essays on Anglo-American Society,* edited by Thad W. Tate and David L. Ammerman, 207–242. Chapel Hill, N.C., 1979.

Carr, Lois Green, Russell Menard, and Lorena S. Walsh. *Robert Cole's World: Agriculture & Society in Early Maryland.* Chapel Hill, N.C., 1991.

Carr, Lois Green, Philip D. Morgan, and Jean B. Russo, eds. *Colonial Chesapeake Society.* Chapel Hill, N.C., 1988.

Cave, Alfred A. "The Pequot Invasion of Southern New England: A Reassessment of the Evidence." *New England Quarterly* 62 (March 1989): 27–44.

———. "Who Killed John Stone? A Note on the Origins of the Pequot War." *William and Mary Quarterly,* 3d ser., 49 (July 1992): 509–521.

Ceci, Lynn. "Native Wampum as a Peripheral Resource in the Seventeenth-Century World-System." In *The Pequots in Southern New England: The Fall and Rise of an American Indian Nation,* edited by Laurence M. Hauptman and James D. Wherry, 48–63. Norman, Okla., 1990.

Chu, Jonathan M. *Neighbors, Friends, or Madmen: The Puritan Adjustment to Quakerism in Seventeenth-Century Massachusetts Bay.* Westport, Conn., 1985.

Clark, Charles E. *The Eastern Frontier: The Settlement of Northern New England, 1610–1763.* New York, 1970.

Clark, Christopher. *The Roots of Rural Capitalism: Western Massachusetts, 1780–1860.* Ithaca, N.Y., 1990.

Clark, Peter. *English Provincial Society from the Reformation to the Revolution: Religion, Politics and Society in Kent, 1500–1640.* Sussex, Eng., 1977.

Clark, Peter, and Paul Slack, eds. *Crisis and Order in English Towns, 1500–1700: Essays in Urban History.* Toronto, 1972.

Cohen, Charles Lloyd. *God's Caress: The Psychology of Puritan Religious Experience.* New York, 1986.

Conroy, David W. *In Public Houses: Drink & the Revolution of Authority in Colonial Massachusetts.* Chapel Hill, N.C., 1995.

Cook, Edward M., Jr. "Local Leadership and the Typology of New England Towns, 1700–1785." *Political Science Quarterly* 86 (December 1971): 586–608.

———. "Social Behavior and Changing Values in Dedham, Massachusetts, 1700 to 1775" *William and Mary Quarterly,* 3d ser., 27 (October 1970): 546–580.

———. *The Fathers of the Towns: Leadership and Community Structure in Eighteenth-Century New England.* Baltimore, Md., 1976.

Coolidge, John. "Hingham Builds A Meetinghouse." *New England Quarterly* 34 (December 1961): 435–461.

Cooper, James F., Jr. "Anne Hutchinson and the 'Lay Rebellion' Against the Clergy." *New England Quarterly* 61 (September 1988): 381–397.

Crandall, Ralph J. "New England's Second Great Migration: The First Three Generations of Settlement, 1630–1700." *New England Historical and Genealogical Register* 129 (October 1975): 347–360.

Cressy, David. *Coming Over: Migration and Communication Between England and New England in the Seventeenth Century.* Cambridge, 1987.

Cronon, William. *Changes in the Land: Indians, Colonists, and the Ecology of New England.* New York, 1983.

Crosby, Alfred W. *Ecological Imperialism: The Biological Expansion of Europe, 900–1900.* Cambridge, 1986.

Cummings, Abbot Lowell. *The Framed Houses of Massachusetts Bay, 1625–1725.* Cambridge, Mass., 1979.

Daniell, Jere R. *Colonial New Hampshire: A History.* Millwood, N.Y., 1981.

Daniels, Bruce C. *The Connecticut Town: Growth and Development, 1635–1790.* Middletown, Conn., 1979.

———. *Dissent and Conformity on Narragansett Bay: The Colonial Rhode Island Town.* Middletown, Conn., 1983.

Davisson, William I. "Essex County Price Trends: Money and Markets in 17th Century Massachusetts." *Essex Institute Historical Collections* 103 (April 1967): 144–185.

———. "Essex County Wealth Trends: Wealth and Economic Growth in 17th Century Massachusetts." *Essex Institute Historical Collections* 103 (1967): 291–342.

Dayton, Cornelia Hughes. *Women before the Bar: Gender, Law, & Society in Connecticut, 1639–1789.* Chapel Hill, N.C., 1995.

Demos, John. "Demography and Psychology in the Historical Study of Family-Life: A Personal Report." In *Household and Family in Past Time,* edited by Peter Laslett and Richard Wall, 561–569. Cambridge, 1972.

———. *Entertaining Satan: Witchcraft and the Culture of Early New England.* New York, 1982.

———. "Families in Colonial Bristol, Rhode Island: An Exercise in Historical Demography." *William and Mary Quarterly,* 3d ser., 25 (January 1968): 40–57.

———. *A Little Commonwealth: Family Life in Plymouth Colony.* New York, 1970.

———. *The Unredeemed Captive: A Family Story from Early America.* New York, 1994.

Dinkin, Robert J. "Seating the Meetinghouse in Early Massachusetts." In *Mate-*

rial Life in America, 1600–1860, edited by Robert Blair St. George, 407–418. Boston, 1988.

Dollar, Charles M., and Richard J. Jensen. *Historian's Guide To Statistics: Quantitative Analysis and Historical Research.* New York, 1971.

Donnelly, Marian Card. *The New England Meeting Houses of the Seventeenth Century.* Middletown, Conn., 1968.

Dow, George Francis. *Every Day Life in the Massachusetts Bay Colony.* Boston, 1935.

Dunn, Richard S. *Puritans and Yankees: The Winthrop Dynasty of New England, 1630–1717.* Princeton, N.J., 1962.

———. *Sugar and Slaves: The Rise of the Planter Class in the English West Indies, 1624–1713.* Chapel Hill, N.C., 1972.

Erikson, Kai T. *Wayward Puritans: A Study in the Sociology of Deviance.* New York, 1966.

Everitt, Alan. "The Marketing of Agricultural Produce." In *The Agrarian History of England and Wales, 1500–1640,* edited by Joan Thirsk, 4:466–592. Cambridge, 1967.

Fischer, David Hackett. *Albion's Seed: Four British Folkways in America.* New York, 1989.

Flaherty, David H. *Privacy in Colonial New England.* Charlottesville, Va., 1972.

Foster, Stephen. "English Puritanism and the Progress of New England Institutions, 1630–1660." In *Saints & Revolutionaries: Essays on Early American History,* edited by David Hall, John M. Murrin, and Thad W. Tate, 3–37. New York, 1984.

———. "The Godly in Transit: English Popular Protestantism and the Creation of a Puritan Establishment in America." In *Seventeenth-Century New England,* edited by David D. Hall and David Grayson Allens, 185–238. Boston, 1984.

——— *The Long Argument: English Puritanism and the Shaping of New England Culture, 1570–1700.* Chapel Hill, N.C., 1991.

———. "The Massachusetts Franchise in the Seventeenth Century." *William and Mary Quarterly,* 3d ser., 24 (October 1967): 613–623.

———. "New England and the Challenge of Heresy, 1630 to 1660: The Puritan Crisis in Transatlantic Perspective." *William and Mary Quarterly,* 3d ser., 38 (October 1981): 624–660.

———. *Their Solitary Way: The Puritan Social Ethic in the First Century of Settlement in New England.* New Haven, Conn., 1971.

Fowler, David H. "Connecticut's Freemen: The First Forty Years." *William and Mary Quarterly,* 3d ser., 15 (July 1958): 312–333.

French, Allen. *Charles I and the Puritan Upheaval: A Study of the Causes of the Great Migration.* Boston, 1955.

Galenson, David W. *White Servitude in Colonial America: An Economic Analysis.* New York, 1981.

Garvan, Anthony N. B. *Architecture and Town Planning in Colonial Connecticut.* New Haven, Conn., 1951.

Geertz, Clifford. *The Interpretation of Cultures.* New York, 1973.

Genealogies of Rhode Island Families from Rhode Island Periodicals. Baltimore, Md., 1983.

George, Charles H., and Katherine George. *The Protestant Mind of the English Reformation, 1570–1640*. Princeton, N.J., 1961.

Gildrie, Richard P. *Salem, Massachusetts, 1626–1683: A Covenant Community.* Charlottesville, Va., 1975.

Glaab, Charles N., and A. Theodore Brown. *A History of Urban America.* New York, 1967.

Godbeer, Richard. "'The Cry of Sodom': Discourse, Intercourse, and Desire in Colonial New England." *William and Mary Quarterly,* 3d ser., 52 (April 1995): 259–286.

———. *The Devil's Dominion: Magic and Religion in Early New England.* New York, 1992.

Goubert, Pierre. "Recent Theories and Research in French Population Between 1500 and 1700." In *Population in History: Essays in Historical Demography,* edited by D.V. Glass and D. E. C. Eversley, 457–473. Chicago, 1965.

Grant, Charles S. *Democracy in the Connecticut Frontier Town of Kent.* New York, 1961.

Greene, Jack P. *Pursuits of Happiness: The Social Development of Early Modern British Colonies and the Formation of American Culture.* Chapel Hill, N.C., 1988.

Greene, Jack P., and J. R. Pole, eds. *Colonial British America: Essays in the New History of the Early Modern Era.* Baltimore, Md., 1984.

Greene, Lorenzo J. *The Negro in Colonial New England, 1620–1776.* New York, 1942.

Greven, Philip J., Jr. *Four Generations: Population, Land, and Family in Colonial Andover, Massachusetts.* Ithaca, N.Y., 1970.

———. *The Protestant Temperament: Patterns of Child-Rearing, Religious Experience, and the Self in Early America.* New York, 1977.

Gura, Philip F. "'The Contagion of Corrupt Opinions' in Puritan Massachusetts: The Case of William Pynchon." *William and Mary Quarterly,* 3d ser., 24 (July 1982): 469–491.

———. *A Glimpse of Sion's Glory. Puritan Radicalism in New England, 1620–1660.* Middletown, Conn., 1984.

Hall, David D. *The Faithful Shepherd: A History of the New England Ministry in the Seventeenth Century.* Chapel Hill, N.C., 1972.

———. "On Common Ground: The Coherence of American Puritan Studies." *William and Mary Quarterly,* 3d ser., 44 (April 1987): 193–229.

———. "Understanding the Puritans." In *The State of American History,* edited by Herbert J. Bass, 330–349. Chicago, 1970.

———. "Witchcraft and the Limits of Interpretation. *New England Quarterly* 58 (1985): 253–281.

———. "A World of Wonders: The Mentality of the Supernatural in Seventeenth-Century New England." In *Seventeenth-Century New England,* edited by David D. Hall and David Grayson Allen, 239–274. Boston, 1984.

———. *Worlds of Wonder, Days of Judgment: Popular Religious Belief in Early New England*. New York, 1989. Reprint, Cambridge, Mass., 1990.

Hall, David D., and David Grayson Allen, eds. *Seventeenth-Century New England*. Boston, 1984.

Hall, Michael G. *The Last American Puritan: The Life of Increase Mather, 1639–1723*. Middletown, Conn., 1988.

Haller, William, Jr. *The Puritan Frontier: Town-Planting in New England Colonial Development, 1630–1660*. New York, 1951.

Hambrick-Stowe, Charles E. *The Practice of Piety: Puritan Devotional Disciplines in Seventeenth-Century New England*. Chapel Hill, N.C., 1982.

Handlin, Lilian. "Dissent in a Small Community." *New England Quarterly* 58 (June 1985): 193–220.

Hansen, Chadwick. *Witchcraft at Salem*. New York, 1969.

Harris, Cole "European Beginnings in the Northwest Atlantic: A Comparative View." In *Seventeenth-Century New England,* edited by David D. Hall and David Grayson Allen, 119–152. Boston, 1984.

Haskins, George Lee. *Law and Authority in Early Massachusetts: A Study in Tradition and Design*. New York, 1960.

Hauptman, Laurence M., and James D. Wherry, eds. *The Pequots in Southern New England: The Fall and Rise of an American Indian Nation*. Norman, Okla., 1990.

Hemphill, C. Dallett. "Women in Court: Sex-Role Differentiation in Salem, Massachusetts, 1636 to 1863." *William and Mary Quarterly,* 3d ser., 39 (January 1982): 164–175.

Henretta, James A. "Economic Development and Social Structure in Colonial Boston." *William and Mary Quarterly,* 3d ser., 22 (1965): 75–92.

———. *The Evolution of American Society, 1700–1815: An Interdisciplinary Analysis*. Lexington, Mass., 1973.

———. "Families and Farms: *Mentalité* in Pre-Industrial America." *William and Mary Quarterly,* 3d ser., 35 (January 1978): 3–32.

———. "The Morphology of New England Society in the Colonial Period." *Journal of Interdisciplinary History* 2 (fall 1971): 379–398.

———. *The Origins of American Capitalism: Collected Essays*. Boston, 1992.

———. "Social History as Lived and Written." *American Historical Review,* 84 (December 1979): 1,293–1,322.

Heyrman, Christine Leigh. *Commerce and Culture: The Maritime Communities of Colonial Massachusetts, 1690–1750*. New York, 1984.

———. "Specters of Subversion, Societies of Friends: Dissent and the Devil in Provincial Essex County, Massachusetts." In *Saints & Revolutionaries: Essays on Early American History,* edited by David D. Hall, John M. Murrin, and Thad W. Tate, 38–74. New York, 1984.

Hirst, Derek. *Authority and Conflict: England, 1603–1658*. Cambridge, Mass., 1986.

Hoffer, Peter Charles. *The Devil's Disciples: Makers of the Salem Witchcraft Trials*. Baltimore, Md., 1996.

Hofstadter, Richard. *America at 1750, A Social Portrait*. New York, 1971.

Homans, George Caspar. *English Villagers of the Thirteenth Century.* Cambridge, Mass., 1942.

Horn, James. *Adapting to a New World: English Society in the Seventeenth-Century Chesapeake.* Chapel Hill, N.C., 1994.

———. "Servant Emigration to the Chesapeake in the Seventeenth Century." In *The Chesapeake in the Seventeenth Century: Essays on Anglo-American Society,* edited by Thad W. Tate and David L. Ammerman, 51–95. Chapel Hill, N.C., 1979.

Hughes, Jonathan R. T., *The Governmental Habit: Economic Controls from Colonial Times to the Present.* New York, 1977.

Hull, N. E. H. *Female Felons: Women and Serious Crime in Colonial Massachusetts.* Champaign, Ill., 1987.

Humins, John H. "Squanto and Massasoit: A Struggle for Power." *New England Quarterly,* 60 (March 1987): 54–70.

Ingram, Martin. "The Reform of Popular Culture? Sex and Marriage in Early Modern England." In *Popular Culture in Seventeenth-Century England,* edited by Barry Reay, 129–165. New York, 1985.

Innes, Stephen. *Creating the Commonwealth: The Economic Culture of Puritan New England.* New York, 1995.

———. *Labor in a New Land: Economy and Society in Seventeenth-Century Springfield.* Princeton, N.J., 1983.

———, ed. *Work and Labor in Early America.* Chapel Hill, N.C., 1988.

James, Sydney V. *Colonial Rhode Island: A History.* New York, 1975.

Jennings, Francis. *The Invasion of America: Indians, Colonialism, and the Cant of Conquest.* Chapel Hill, N.C., 1975.

Jones, Alice Hanson. "Wealth Estimates for the New England Colonies about 1770." *Journal of Economic History* 32 (March 1972): 98–127.

Jones, Douglas Lamar. *Village and Seaport: Migration and Society in Eighteenth-Century Massachusetts.* Hanover, N.H., 1981.

Jones, Manfred. "The Wills of the Early Settlers of Essex County, Massachusetts." *Essex Institute Historical Collections* 96 (July 1960): 228–235.

Jordan, David W. "Political Stability and the Emergence of a Native Elite in Maryland." In *The Chesapeake in the Seventeenth Century: Essays on Anglo-American Society,* edited by Thad W. Tate and David L. Ammerman, 243–273. Chapel Hill, N.C., 1979.

Kammen, Michael. *People of Paradox: An Inquiry Concerning the Origins of American Civilization.* New York, 1972.

Karlsen, Carol F. *The Devil in the Shape of a Woman: Witchcraft in Colonial New England.* New York, 1987.

Kishlansky, Mark A. "Community and Continuity: A Review of Selected Works on English Local History." *William and Mary Quarterly,* 3d ser., 37 (January 1980): 139–145.

Knight, Janice. *Orthodoxies in Massachusetts: Rereading American Puritanism.* Cambridge, Mass., 1994.

Koch, Donald Warner. "Income Distribution and Political Structure in Seventeenth-Century Salem, Massachusetts." *Essex Institute Historical Collections* 105 (January 1969): 50–71.

Koehler, Lyle. "The Case of the American Jezebels: Anne Hutchinson and Female Agitation during the Years of Antinomian Turmoil, 1636–1640." *William and Mary Quarterly*, 3d ser., 31 (1974): 55–78.

———. *A Search for Power: The "Weaker Sex" in Seventeenth-Century New England.* Champaign, Ill., 1980.

Konig, David Thomas. *Law and Society in Puritan Massachusetts: Essex County, 1629–1692.* Chapel Hill, N.C., 1979.

Kulikoff, Allan. *The Agrarian Origins of American Capitalism.* Charlottesville, Va., 1992.

———. "The Transition to Capitalism in Rural America." *William and Mary Quarterly*, 3d ser., 46 (January 1989): 120–144.

Kupperman, Karen Ordahl. "Climate and Mastery of the Wilderness in Seventeenth-Century New England." In *Seventeenth-Century New England*, edited by David D. Hall and David Grayson Allen, 3–37. Boston, 1984.

———. *Settling With the Indians: The Meeting of English and Indian Cultures in America, 1580–1640.* Totowa, N.J., 1980.

Kussmaul, Ann. *Servants in Husbandry in Early Modern England.* Cambridge, 1981.

Labaree, Benjamin W. *Colonial Massachusetts: A History.* Millwood, N.Y., 1979.

———. *Patriots and Partisans: The Merchants of Newburyport, 1764–1815.* Cambridge, Mass., 1962.

Langdon, George D., Jr. "The Franchise and Political Democracy in Plymouth Colony." *William and Mary Quarterly*, 3d ser., 20 (October 1963): 513–526.

———. *Pilgrim Colony: A History of New Plymouth, 1620–1691.* New Haven, Conn., 1966.

Laslett, Peter. "Mean Household Size in England since the Sixteenth Century." In *Household and Family in Past Time*, edited by Peter Laslett and Richard Wall, 129–158. Cambridge, 1972.

———. *The World We Have Lost Further Explored.* Revised ed. New York, 1984.

Laslett, Peter, and John Harrison. "Clayworth and Cogenhoe." In *Historical Essays, 1600–1750, Presented to David Ogg*, edited by H. E. Bell and R. L. Ollard, 157–184. London, 1963.

Leach, Douglas Edward. *Flintlock and Tomahawk: New England in King Philip's War.* New York, 1958.

Lemon, James T. *The Best Poor Man's Country: A Geographical Study of Early Southeastern Pennsylvania.* Baltimore, Md., 1972.

———. "Early Americans and Their Social Environment." *Journal of Historical Geography* 6 (1980): 115–131.

———. "Spatial Order: Households in Local Communities and Regions." In *Colonial British America: Essays in the New History of the Early Modern Era*, edited by Jack P. Greene and J. R. Pole, 86–122. Baltimore, Md., 1984.

Lepore, Jill. *The Name of War: King Philip's War and the Origins of American Identity.* New York, 1998.

Levy, Barry. *Quakers and the American Family: British Settlement in the Delaware Valley.* New York, 1988.

Lockridge, Kenneth A. *Literacy in Colonial New England: An Enquiry into the Social Context of Literacy in the Early Modern West.* New York, 1974.

———. *A New England Town: The First Hundred Years.* New York, 1970.

———. "The Population of Dedham, Massachusetts, 1636–1736." *Economic History Review,* 2d ser., 19 (1966): 319–344.

———. *Settlement and Unsettlement in Early America: The Crisis of Political Legitimacy Before the Revolution.* Cambridge, 1981.

Lucas, Paul R. *Valley of Discord: Church and Society Along the Connecticut River, 1636–1725.* Hanover, N.H., 1976.

Ludwig, Allan I. *Graven Images: New England Stonecarving and its Symbols, 1650–1815.* Middletown, Conn., 1966.

Macfarlane, Alan. *The Family Life of Ralph Josselin: A Seventeenth-Century Clergyman.* Cambridge, 1970.

———. *The Origins of English Individualism: The Family, Property and Social Transition.* London, 1978.

———. *Witchcraft in Tudor and Stuart England.* London, 1970.

Maclear, Anne Bush. *Early New England Towns: A Comparative Study of Their Development.* New York, 1908.

Main, Gloria L. "The Correction of Biases in Colonial American Probate Records." *Historical Methods Newsletter* 8 (December 1974): 10–28.

———. "Inequality in Early America: The Evidence from Probate Records of Massachusetts and Maryland." *Journal of Interdisciplinary History* 7 (spring 1977): 559–562.

———. "Probate Records as a Source for Early American History." *William and Mary Quarterly,* 3d ser., 32 (1975): 89–99.

Main, Jackson Turner. "The Distribution of Property in Colonial Connecticut." In *The Human Dimensions of Nation Making: Essays on Colonial and Revolutionary America,* edited by James Kirby Martin, 54–104. Madison, Wis., 1976.

———. *Society and Economy in Colonial Connecticut.* Princeton, N.J., 1985.

Marcus, Gail Sussman. "'Due Execution of the Generall Rules of Righteousnesse': Criminal Procedure in New Haven Town and Colony, 1638–1658." In *Saints & Revolutionaries: Essays on Early American History,* edited by David D. Hall, John M. Murrin, and Thad W. Tate, 99–137. New York, 1984.

Martin, John Frederick. *Profits in the Wilderness: Entrepreneurship and the Founding of New England Towns in the Seventeenth Century.* Chapel Hill, N.C., 1991.

McCarl, Mary Rhinelander. "Thomas Shepard's Record of Relations of Religious Experience, 1648–1649." *William and Mary Quarterly,* 3d ser., 48 (July 1991): 432–466.

McCusker, John J., and Russell R. Menard. *The Economy of British America, 1607–1789.* Chapel Hill, N.C., 1985.

McGiffert, Michael. "American Puritan Studies in the 1960s." *William and Mary Quarterly,* 3d ser., 27 (1970): 36–67.

————. "From Moses to Adam: The Making of the Covenant of Works." *The Sixteenth Century Journal* 19 (summer 1988): 131–155.

————. "Grace and Works: The Rise and Division of Covenant Divinity in Elizabethan Puritanism." *The Harvard Theological Review* 75 (1982): 463–502.

McManus, Edgar J., *Law and Liberty in Early New England: Criminal Justice and Due Process, 1620–1692.* Amherst, Mass., 1993.

Meinig, D. W., *The Shaping of America: A Geographical Perspective on 500 Years of History.* Vol. 1, *Atlantic America, 1492–1800.* New Haven, 1986.

Melvoin, Richard I. *New England Outpost: War and Society in Colonial Deerfield.* New York, 1989.

Menard, Russell R. "British Migration to the Chesapeake Colonies in the Seventeenth Century." In *Colonial Chesapeake Society,* edited by Lois Green Carr, Philip D. Morgan, and Jean B. Russo, 99–132. Chapel Hill, N.C., 1988.

————. *The Economy of British America, 1607–1789.* Chapel Hill, N.C., 1985.

Merchant, Carolyn. *Ecological Revolutions: Nature, Gender, and Science in New England.* Chapel Hill, N.C., 1989.

Merrill, Michael. "Cash Is Good to Eat: Self-Sufficiency and Exchange in the Rural Economy of the United States." *Radical History Review,* no. 3 (1977): 42–71.

————. "Putting 'Capitalism' in Its Place: A Review of Recent Literature." *William and Mary Quarterly,* 3d ser., 52 (April 1995): 315–326.

Middlekauff, Robert. *The Mathers: Three Generations of Puritan Intellectuals, 1596–1728.* New York, 1971.

Miller, Lillian B. "The Puritan Portrait: Its Function in Old and New England." In *Seventeenth-Century New England,* edited by David D. Hall and David Grayson Allen, 153–184. Boston, 1984.

Miller, Perry. *Errand Into the Wilderness.* New York, 1956.

————. *The New England Mind: From Colony to Province.* Boston, 1953.

————. *The New England Mind: The Seventeenth Century.* Boston, 1961. (Originally published 1939.)

————. *Orthodoxy In Massachusetts, 1630–1650.* Cambridge, Mass., 1933.

Moran, Gerald F. "'Sisters' in Christ: Women and the Church in Seventeenth-Century New England." In *Women in American Religion,* edited by Janet Wilson James, 47–65. Philadelphia, 1980.

Moran, Gerald F., and Maris A. Vinovskis. "The Puritan Family and Religion: A Critical Reappraisal." *William and Mary Quarterly,* 3d ser., 39 (January 1982): 29–63.

Morgan, Edmund S. *American Slavery, American Freedom: The Ordeal of Colonial Virginia.* New York, 1975.

————. *The Puritan Dilemma: The Story of John Winthrop.* Boston, 1958.

————. *The Puritan Family, Religion and Domestic Relations in Seventeenth-Century New England.* Revised ed. New York, 1966.

————. "The Puritans and Sex." *New England Quarterly* 15 (1942): 591–607.

————. *Visible Saints, The History of a Puritan Idea.* New York, 1963.

Moriarty, G. Andrews. "Herodias (Long) Hicks-Gardiner-Porter: A Tale of Old Newport." In *Genealogies of Rhode Island Families from Rhode Island Periodicals,* 599–606. Baltimore, Md., 1983.

Morison, Samuel Eliot. *Builders of the Bay Colony.* Boston, 1930.
———. *Harvard College in the Seventeenth Century.* 2 vols. Cambridge, Mass., 1936.
Morrison, Kenneth M. *The Embattled Northeast: The Elusive Ideal of Alliance in Abenaki-Euramerican Relations.* Berkeley and Los Angeles, Calif., 1984.
Murrin, John M. "Magistrates, Sinners, and a Precarious Liberty: Trial by Jury in Seventeenth-Century New England." In *Saints & Revolutionaries: Essays on Early American History,* edited by David D. Hall, John M. Murrin, and Thad W. Tate, 152–206. New York, 1984.
Nash, Gary B. *Quakers and Politics: Pennsylvania, 1681–1726.* Princeton, N.J., 1968.
———. "Urban Wealth and Poverty in Pre-Revolutionary America." *Journal of Interdisciplinary History* 6 (spring, 1976): 545–584.
New England Begins: The Seventeenth Century. 3 vols. Boston, 1982.
New, John F. H. *Anglican and Puritan: The Basis of Their Opposition, 1558–1640.* Stanford, Calif., 1964.
Norton, Mary Beth. *Founding Mothers & Fathers: Gendered Power and the Forming of American Society.* New York, 1996.
Norton, Susan L. "Population Growth in Colonial America: A Study of Ipswich, Massachusetts." *Population Studies* 25 (November 1971): 433–452.
Pestana, Carla Gardina. *Quakers and Baptists in Colonial Massachusetts.* Cambridge, 1991.
Piersen, William D. *Black Yankees: The Development of an Afro-American Subculture in Eighteenth-Century New England.* Amherst, Mass., 1988.
Pope, Robert G. *The Half-Way Covenant: Church Membership in Puritan New England.* Princeton, N.J., 1969.
Potter, Jim. "Demographic Development and Family Structure." In *Colonial British America: Essays in the New History of the Early Modern Era,* edited by Jack P. Greene and J. R. Pole, 123–156. Baltimore, Md., 1984.
Powell, Sumner Chilton. *Puritan Village: The Formation of a New England Town.* New York, 1965.
Prest, W. R. "Stability and Change in Old and New England: Clayworth and Dedham." *Journal of Interdisciplinary History* 6 (winter 1976): 359–374.
Quinn, David B. *North America Earliest Discovery To First Settlements, The Norse Voyages to 1612.* New York, 1977.
Reay, Barry, ed. *Popular Culture in Seventeenth-Century England.* New York, 1985.
Reis, Elizabeth. "The Devil, the Body, and the Feminine Soul in Puritan New England." *Journal of American History* 82 (June 1995): 15–36.
Reps, John W. *Town Planning in Frontier America.* Princeton, N.J., 1969.
Richter, Daniel K. *The Ordeal of the Longhouse: The Peoples of the Iroquois League in the Era of European Colonization.* Chapel Hill, N.C., 1992.
Roberts, Gary Boyd. *English Origins of New England Families: From the New England Historical and Genealogical Register, first series.* Baltimore, Md. 1984.
———. *English Origins of New England Families: From the New England Historical and Genealogical Register, second series.* Baltimore, Md., 1985.

Rosenthal, Bernard. *Salem Story: Reading the Witch Trials of 1692.* New York, 1993.

Rothenberg, Winifred Barr. *From Market-Places to a Market Economy: The Transformation of Rural Massachusetts, 1750–1850.* Chicago, 1992.

———. "The Market and Massachusetts Farmers, 1750–1855." *Journal of Economic History* 41 (June 1981): 283–314.

Rutman, Darrett B. *American Puritanism, Faith and Practice.* Philadelphia, 1970.

———. *Husbandmen of Plymouth: Farms and Villages in the Old Colony, 1620–1692.* Boston, 1967.

———. *Winthrop's Boston: A Portrait of a Puritan Town, 1630–1649.* Chapel Hill, N.C., 1965.

Rutman, Darrett B., and Anita H. Rutman, "'Non-Wives and Sons-in-Law': Parental Death in a Seventeenth-Century Virginia County." In *The Chesapeake in the Seventeenth Century: Essays on Anglo-American Society,* edited by Thad W. Tate and David L. Ammerman, 153–182. Chapel Hill, N.C., 1979.

———. *A Place in Time: Middlesex County, Virginia, 1650–1750 and Explicatus.* New York, 1984.

Sachse, William L. "The Migration of New Englanders to England, 1640–1660." *American Historical Review* 53 (January 1948): 251–278.

Salerno, Anthony. "The Social Background of Seventeenth Century Emigration to America." *Journal of British Studies* 19 (1979): 31–52.

Salisbury, Neal. "Indians and Colonists in Southern New England after the Pequot War: An Uneasy Balance." In *The Pequots in Southern New England: The Fall and Rise of an American Indian Nation,* edited by Laurence M. Hauptman and James D. Wherry, 81–95. Norman, Okla., 1990.

———. *Manitou and Providence: Indians, Europeans, and the Making of New England, 1500–1643.* New York, 1982.

———. "Red Puritans: The 'Praying Indians' of Massachusetts Bay and John Eliot." *William and Mary Quarterly,* 3d ser., 31 (1974): 27–54.

Salmon, Marylynn. *Women and the Law of Property in Early America.* Chapel Hill, N.C., 1986.

Savage, James. *A Genealogical Dictionary of the First Settlers of New England, . . . Who Came Before May, 1692. . . .* 4 vols. Boston, 1860–1862. Reprint, Baltimore, Md., 1965.

Seelye, John. *Prophetic Waters: The River in Early American Life and Literature.* New York, 1977.

Selement, George. *Keepers of the Vineyard: The Puritan Ministry and Collective Culture in Colonial New England.* Lanham, Md., 1984.

Silverman, Kenneth. *The Life and Times of Cotton Mather.* New York, 1984.

Simmons, Richard C. "Godliness, Property and the Franchise in Puritan Massachusetts: An Interpretation." *Journal of American History* 55 (December 1968): 495–511.

Simmons, William S. "Cultural Bias in the New England Puritans' Perception of Indians." *William and Mary Quarterly,* 3d ser., 38 (January 1981): 56–72.

———. *Spirit of the New England Tribes: Indian History and Folklore, 1620–1984.* Hanover, N.H., 1986.

Simpson, Alan. *Puritanism in Old and New England*. Chicago, 1955.

Slater, Peter Gregg. *Children in the New England Mind, in Death and in Life*. Hamden, Conn., 1977.

Sly, John Fairfield. *Town Government in Massachusetts, 1620–1930*. Cambridge, Mass., 1930.

Smith, Daniel Scott. "Continuity and Discontinuity in Puritan Naming: Massachusetts, 1771." *William and Mary Quarterly*, 3d ser., 51 (January 1994): 67–91.

———. "The Demographic History of Colonial New England." *Journal of Economic History* 32 (March 1972): 165–183.

———. "Parental Power and Marriage Patterns: An Analysis of Historical Trends in Hingham, Massachusetts." *Journal of Marriage and the Family* 35 (August 1973): 419–428.

———. "A Perspective on Demographic Methods and Effects in Social History." *William and Mary Quarterly*, 3d ser., 39 (July 1982): 442–468.

———. "Underregistration and Bias in Probate Records: An Analysis of Data from Eighteenth-Century Hingham, Massachusetts." *William and Mary Quarterly*, 3d ser., 32 (1975): 100–110.

Smith, Page. *As A City Upon A Hill, The Town in American History*. New York, 1966.

Spufford, Margaret. *Contrasting Communities: English Villagers in the Sixteenth and Seventeenth Centuries*. Cambridge, 1974.

———. "Peasant Inheritance Customs and Land Distribution in Cambridgeshire from the Sixteenth to the Eighteenth Centuries." In *Family and Inheritance: Rural Society in Western Europe, 1200–1800*, edited by Jack Goody, Joan Thirsk, and E. P. Thompson, 156–176. Cambridge, 1976.

St. George, Robert. "'Heated' Speech and Literacy in Seventeenth-Century New England." In *Seventeenth-Century New England*, edited by David D. Hall and David Grayson Allen, 275–322. Boston, 1984.

Stannard, David E. "Death and Dying in Puritan New England." *American Historical Review* 78 (December 1973): 1,305–1,330.

———. *The Puritan Way of Death: A Study in Religion, Culture and Social Change*. New York, 1977.

Starna, William. "The Pequots in the Early Seventeenth Century." In *The Pequots in Southern New England: The Fall and Rise of an American Indian Nation*, edited by Laurence M. Hauptman and James D. Wherry, 33–47. Norman, Okla., 1990.

Stoever, William K. B. *"A Faire and Easie Way to Heaven": Covenant Theology and Antinomianism in Early Massachusetts*. Middletown, Conn., 1978.

Stone, Lawrence. *The Family, Sex and Marriage in England, 1500–1800*. New York, 1977.

Stout, Harry S. *The New England Soul: Preaching and Religious Culture in Colonial New England*. New York, 1986.

Tate, Thad W., and David L. Ammerman, eds. *The Chesapeake in the Seventeenth Century: Essays on Anglo-American Society*. Chapel Hill, N.C., 1979.

Taylor, Robert J. *Colonial Connecticut: A History*. Millwood, N.Y., 1979.

Thirsk, Joan. "Patterns of Agriculture in Seventeenth-Century England." In
   Seventeenth-Century New England, edited by David D. Hall and David Gray-
   son Allen, 39–54. Boston, 1984.
Thomas, Keith. *Religion and the Decline of Magic.* New York, 1971.
Thompson, Roger. *Mobility and Migration: East Anglian Founders of New En-
   gland, 1629–1640.* Amherst, Mass., 1994.
———. *Sex in Middlesex: Popular Mores in a Massachusetts County, 1649–1699.*
   Amherst, Mass., 1986.
Torrey, Clarence Almon. *New England Marriage Prior to 1700.* Baltimore, Md.,
   1985.
Trevor-Roper, H. R. *Archbishop Laud, 1573–1645.* London, 1962.
Trigger, Bruce G., ed. *Handbook of North American Indians: Northeast.* Vol. 15.
   Washington, D.C., 1978.
Ulrich, Laurel Thatcher. *Good Wives: Image and Reality in the Lives of Women
   in Northern New England, 1650–1750.* New York, 1982.
Underdown, David. *Revel, Riot, and Rebellion: Popular Politics and Culture in
   England, 1603–1660.* Oxford, 1985.
Vaughan, Alden T. *New England Frontier: Puritans and Indians, 1620–1675.*
   Boston, 1965.
Vickers, Daniel. "Competency and Competition: Economic Culture in Early
   America." *William and Mary Quarterly,* 3d ser., 47 (January 1990): 3–29.
———. *Farmers & Fishermen: Two Centuries of Work in Essex County, Massa-
   chusetts, 1630–1850.* Chapel Hill, N.C., 1994.
———. "Work and Life on the Fishing Periphery of Essex County, 1630–1675."
   In *Seventeenth-Century New England,* edited by David D. Hall and David
   Grayson Allen, 83–117. Boston, 1984.
———. "Working the Fields in a Developing Economy: Essex County, Massachu-
   setts, 1630–1675." In *Work and Labor in Early America,* edited by Stephen
   Innes, 49–69. Chapel Hill, N.C., 1988.
Vinovskis, Maris A. "Mortality Rates and Trends in Massachusetts Before
   1860." *Journal of Economic History* 32 (March 1972): 184–213.
Wall, Robert Emmet, Jr. "The Massachusetts Bay Colony Franchise in 1647."
   William and Mary Quarterly, 3d ser., 27 (January 1970): 136–144.
———. *Massachusetts Bay: The Crucial Decade, 1640–1650.* New Haven,
   Conn., 1972.
Walsh, Lorena S. "'Till Death Us do Part': Marriage and Family in Seventeenth-
   Century Maryland." In *The Chesapeake in the Seventeenth Century: Essays
   on Anglo-American Society,* edited by Thad W. Tate and David L. Ammerman,
   126–152. Chapel Hill, N.C., 1979.
Walzer, Michael. "Puritanism as a Revolutionary Ideology." *Past and Present,* 3
   (1964): 59–90.
———. *The Revolution of the Saints: A Study in the Origins of Radical Politics.*
   Cambridge, Mass., 1965.
Warden, G. B. "Inequality and Instability in Eighteenth-Century Boston: A Reap-
   praisal." *Journal of Interdisciplinary History* 6 (spring 1976): 585–620.

Warner, Sam Bass, Jr. *The Private City: Philadelphia in Three Periods of Its Growth*. Philadelphia, 1968.

———. *The Urban Wilderness: A History of the American City*. New York, 1972.

Waters, John J. "Family, Inheritance, and Migration in Colonial New England: The Evidence from Guilford, Connecticut." *William and Mary Quarterly*, 3d ser., 39 (January 1982): 64–86.

———. "From Democracy to Demography: Recent Historiography on the New England Town." In *Perspectives on Early American History: Essays in Honor of Richard B. Morris,* edited by Alden T. Vaughan and George Athan Billias, 222–249. New York, 1973.

———. "Hingham, Massachusetts, 1631–1661: An East Anglian Oligarchy in the New World." *Journal of Social History* 1 (summer 1968): 351–370.

———. *The Otis Family in Provincial and Revolutionary Massachusetts*. Chapel Hill, N.C., 1968.

———. "The Traditional World of the New England Peasants: A View from Seventeenth-Century Barnstable." *New England Historical and Genealogical Register* 130 (January 1976): 3–21.

Webb, Stephen Saunders. *1676: The End of American Independence*. New York, 1984.

Weisman, Richard. *Witchcraft, Magic, and Religion in 17th-Century Massachusetts*. Amherst, Mass., 1984.

White, Richard. *The Middle Ground: Indians, Empires, and Republics in the Great Lakes Region, 1650–1815*. New York, 1991.

Winslow, Ola Elizabeth. *Meetinghouse Hill, 1630–1783*. New York, 1952.

Wolf, Stephanie Grauman. *Urban Village: Population, Community, and Family Structure in Germantown, Pennsylvania, 1683–1800*. Princeton, N.J., 1976.

Wood, Joseph S. "Village and Community in Early Colonial New England." In *Material Life in America, 1600–1860,* edited by Robert Blair St. George, 159–169. Boston, 1988.

Wrightson, Keith. *English Society 1580–1680*. New Brunswick, N.J., 1982.

Wrigley, E. A., and R. S. Schofield. *The Population History of England, 1541–1871: A Reconstruction*. Cambridge, Mass., 1981.

Ziff, Larzer. *The Career of John Cotton: Puritanism and the American Experience*. Princeton, N.J., 1962.

Zuckerman, Michael. *Peaceable Kingdoms: New England Towns in the Eighteenth Century*. New York, 1970.

———. "The Social Context of Democracy in Massachusetts." *William and Mary Quarterly,* 3d ser., 25 (October 1968): 523–544.

INDEX

Abenaki (Indians), 8, 25
Adey, Web, 106
Adkinson, Mary, 87
Agawam (Indian village), 10
age at first child, women, 78
age at marriage, 155; comparison with
    England, 77–78; comparison with
    France, 78; in England, 73; men, 78;
    reasons for girls', 78–80; women,
    77–78. *See also* towns
age structure: compared to England, 6,
    94, 109; compared to Chesapeake,
    154; and political office, 69; result of
    young people, 109; sex ratio, 78
agents, 122
Alden, John, 105
Allen, George, 69–70
Allerton, Isaac, 63, 64
Alling, John, 100
Almy, Job, 80
Almy, Mary, 80
Ancient and Honorable Artillery Com-
    pany, 112, 114, 116
Andover (Mass.), 141, 143
Andrews, Deborah Abbot, 61
Andrews, Elizabeth Peck, 61
Andrews, Nathan, 61, 62
Andrews, Samuel, 61, 62
Andrews, William, 59, 61
Anglicans, 52
antinomian episode, 113
antinomianism, 49
apprenticing of children, 80–82
Arminianism, 31
Arnold, Benedict, 90, 135
artisans, 129, 130; and capitalist *mental-
    ité,* 125, 133; economic behavior and
    location, 125
Aspinet, 18
Aspinwall, William, 44, 45

assistants, 66, 67, 68
Atherton Company, 135, 136, 137, 138
Atherton, Humphrey, 135
Auger, Nicholas, 61, 62
Ayers, Thomas, 84

Bachiler, Stephen, 91
Badcock, James, 136, 138, 139
Bailyn Bernard, 121
Baker, John, 80
Baker, Mary, 80
Baker, William (with Indians), 24
Baker, William (father), 80
Baker, William (son), 80
Bale, Francis, 81
Ball, Allen, 64
Ball, Dorothy, 64
Ballentine, Hannah Hollard, 80
Ballentine, William, 80
Ballou, Lydia, 77
Balston, William, 49
Baptists, 51
Barnes, Mary, 64
Barnes, Thomas, 64
Bassum, Joshua, 106–107
Bellingham, Richard, 67, 68
Benham, John, 63, 64
Benjamin, Samuel, 106–107
Bermuda, 127
Beverly (Mass.), 144
Billerica (Mass.), 129
Billington, Christian Penn, 81–82
Billington, Elizabeth, 82
Billington, Ellen, 81
Billington, Francis, 81–82
Billington, John, 81
Billington, Joseph, 82
Bishop, Alice, 132
Bishop, James, 65, 66
Bishop, Thomas, 70